JET BOSS

a female pilot on taking risks and flying high

a flying memoir by
Captain Laura Savino

Jet Boss: a female pilot on taking risks and flying high

by Laura Savino

Published by Freedom Forge Press, LLC

www.FreedomForgePress.com

ISBN: 9-781940-553115

For my sons, Nicholas and Robert –
the purpose of everything in my life.

Thank you to my parents for always being on my side,
and for giving me the freedom to find my own way.

A deep appreciation for my friends and colleagues,
whose shared experiences I wouldn't trade for
anything in the world.

Contents

Part 3: Arrival

End Matter

AUTHOR'S NOTE

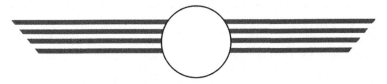

The world of aviation includes a diverse swath of skilled professionals. This story is told from my little corner of this world, offering my perspective, opinion, and feelings. Though this story is told through my eyes, I wish to be respectful of all views. I encourage any dissenting readers to write their own memoir, but please change my name and make me a bit taller.

I recount events accurately to the absolute best of my ability – referring to my logbooks, notes, photographs, saved scrapbook items, consultations with friends, family and colleagues, and the internet when applicable. Some names, locations, and flight numbers have been changed to protect privacy, while other names remain true to offer appreciation and credit. Quotations don't necessarily represent verbatim dialogue, but rather represent the spirit of the conversation.

The views expressed are mine alone. At no time am I speaking on the behalf of United Airlines, or any other entity.

"Nicholas, what do you want to be when you grow up?" my four-year-old son's pre-school teacher asked him. "Do you want to be a pilot?" she offered.

"Ewww," he exclaimed in disgust, "that's a girl's job!"

Perspective is everything.

Laura Savino

PART

TAKEOFF

Laura Savino

INSIDE THE CUCKOO'S NEST

Matchbox cars crawled below me as I streamed down from the sky pointing my Boeing 737 directly at a tiny strip of pavement at the Los Angeles International Airport, LAX. I cinched my five-point harness; my cue to shut out the stunning view filling my windshield and focus only on that runway, my instruments and anything between those two.

"United 322, descend and maintain 10,000," scratched over our radio from an air traffic controller, a guy hunched over a screen in a windowless room, playing an endless video game with us as spaceship invader number 322.

Dean, the captain on this aircraft, dialed the new clearance in as I eased the throttles back to step down our altitude from the first officer's seat beside him.

I slid my seat forward until I found the sweet spot where the control yoke comfortably rested in my palm and my toes tapped on the rudder pedals at just the right angle to land the plane. This flight and everything about it drummed along with the comfort of soothing routine.

Without warning, something black shot out from between my ankles and smacked into my face, brushing my lips with a soiled taste. I slammed backwards into my seat as the creature rebounded off my teeth and pivoted upwards until it whacked the systems control panel above my head. This thing darted in every direction, like an out-of-control pin ball.

"What the hell!" Dean yelped my thoughts. "What is that?"

Was it a bat? A bird? Some flying desert reptile we had picked up on the ground in Vegas?

The thrashing of flapping wings and talons scraping against metallic surfaces shot chills through my whole body. Dean and I covered our faces as claws struck out from this panicked creature. It gimbaled wildly around the cockpit, crashing into circuit breakers, switches, instrument panels, the windshield and us.

I peeked through bent elbows long enough to realize this was a bird. Black feathers floated down around me, littering the center console with mangled plumes, as if I were in the middle of a bizarre pillow fight.

Instantly, I understood the success of the Hitchcock chiller, *The Birds*.

Wide shoulder straps held me in place as I struggled to bend left or right to dodge out of the way. Obligated to keep flying our jet, we could not escape from this sealed madhouse.

Behind me, half-dozing, or chatting, or watching videos, were 147 passengers, blithely unaware of the mayhem going on here in the cockpit. So far, they were still all safe and the only thing I feared was getting my eyes clawed out.

"Oh crap!" I shouted as a wing splashed my cup of tea, as if a frantic bird made Dean hard of hearing.

"My God, how do you stop this thing?" he yelled right back.

Then the bird disappeared back between my legs. I think, by sheer accident. And there was silence.

Silence isn't supposed to be eerie.

Dean and I paused to look at each other, then shook free of our shock and dove into checking our systems. Methodically confirming everything was still in the correct position, we each slumped back into our seats and continued our approach into LAX as if nothing had happened.

But something had happened.

Our peace and routine had been invaded, and that crazed bird was still with us, somewhere. I worried it was in the E&E bay, a hollow area housing our electrical and electronic components under the cockpit. A latched access panel on the floor covers this area, but there are openings from the cockpit into it, like where my rudder pedals go through the floor. Openings big enough for a bird to slip through.

As we continued towards the runway, I may have appeared completely calm, cool as a cucumber even. But truthfully, I was on edge for every second of our descent, waiting for that bird to shoot back up from between my legs as I maneuvered our jet down to the white stripes just after the label 25L. Occasionally, I heard it flapping around, sounding like it was getting close to my feet only for its thumping to fade away with distance again.

"Well, I sure hope it doesn't screw anything up down there." Dean stated the obvious.

"So far, it's only screwed up my nerves." I tried to joke, but we both knew anything could go wrong at this point.

Finally on the ground and rolling towards our gate, I handed the controls over to Dean. He took the tiller to steer our ship in, as I dialed up our maintenance hotline on the radio and made a side call to our mechanics' hangar. We needed to give them a heads up, knowing this plane would need a full maintenance check before the next flight.

We parked, and our passengers got off, smiling, nodding and thanking us for a safe trip. Maintenance came up with the clever idea to try and flush the bird out by stuffing a powerful conditioned air hose up through our nose gear opening to blow our feathered friend out of an opening on the fuselage. It worked, and out he shot like a champagne cork on New Year's Eve. Free at last, he happily darted up to the sky to join the other birds soaring free in the warm Los Angeles sunshine.

He was where he was supposed to be, now.

I laughed to myself. I never thought *this* would be part of my dream job. I watched him disappear against the backdrop of jetliners coming and going, and drifted back to the little girl I once was, seated on the curb looking up to find beautiful, silver machines in the sky.

THE GIRL WITH
HER HEAD IN THE CLOUDS

Over, under, over, under, over, under …

I knelt on the cold tiled floor of some other person's church basement, stuck in the flock of little girls making potholders. This was my Girl Scout troop's accomplishment for the day.

Potholders.

Who knew what other activities we had to look forward to — maybe stringing plastic beads together to make necklaces.

My two older brothers were trekking through the woods and developing wilderness survival skills at their Boy Scout meetings. At ten years old, I had the childlike audacity to want more. At the very least, I wanted to get out of the cellar.

When it was over, a dozen fresh faced girls in matching green dresses giggled their way out to the parking lot to find their mothers. I followed, dragging my sweater on the ground beside me, until I reached the curb and parked myself on my usual spot. I pulled the green beret off my head, letting my pigtails go free. I knew Mom would come pick me up as soon as she had a free moment. I could be here a while.

My parents worked together in a family business. For years though, I

Elementary school—always in pigtails.

had thought my mom worked for my dad in *his* business, a mom-and-pop retail clothing store named Adams Haberdashers in our cozy hometown of New Providence, New Jersey. After sending us off to school each morning, my mom would head to the family store with my dad, racing home just ahead of him to cook dinner at the end of the day.

Everyone worked in the family business: my parents, siblings, cousins and grandparents. I spent countless hours of my childhood unpacking boxes and placing carefully folded clothing on shelves, which didn't thrill me. But the store also stocked a dazzling array of Boy Scout supplies, which did thrill me, but I wasn't allowed to touch.

I was a latchkey kid. Though our house was never locked, and I never had a key. With hours before anyone would notice me missing, I spent afternoons dawdling my way home from school. Always hungry for adventure, I spent a lot of time around the train tracks. Bored with placing pennies on the rails, I'd climb up onto the trestle overpass and wait for the train to rush by. The frantic horn would fill my ears as my clothing flapped wildly from the sudden force of wind as I pressed my back against metal beams feeling the rumble shake my feet loose as the train raced over the steel girders past my face.

I was always sure to be home before my mom rushed in the door and needed my help cooking dinner and setting the table. In old school Italian tradition, neither my mother nor I sat down until after we served the "men" of the house. When they finished eating, we remained behind to clear their dishes from the table and clean up. Before I was tall enough to reach the faucet, I dragged a kitchen chair over to the sink and peered out the window to watch my brothers running free outside while I scrubbed their plates.

My mom grew up poor in the coal mining hills of Archbald, Pennsylvania. Her mother and brother died when she was six years old, and she suffered terrible hardships as a child. After a traumatic childhood, as an adult she discovered she had been adopted as a newborn and this had been hidden from her. Opportunity was not handed to her. Breaking away from cultural norms completely on her own, she worked her way through college and became one of the first women ever to be offered a full scholarship for a master's degree in mathematics. My mom had grit. And she had a gift for calculating numbers in her head that I could only dream of. But Mom walked away from that scholarship to marry my dad and take on the time-honored support role of wife and mother. It was years before I realized how intelligent my mom was and that behind the scenes, she was the accounting brains in our family business.

In my home, my mother and father had a solid marriage with unwavering, traditional gender roles and a dogged Catholic regimen we followed without exception. I was a nice girl and an obedient child. I may not have enjoyed parts of their parenting style, but they always parented as a team and I knew I was loved. Had my life or my marriage turned out anything like my parent's, these early doctrines could have worked well for me in my adult years.

Still waiting for my mother to pick me up from Girl Scouts, I heard it first, the whine of jet engines coming up in a powerful rumble hushing the birds chirping above me. I squinted at the sky and spotted the jetliner. Somehow, I could feel the speed of the cold metal frame cutting through the soft clouds. I tilted my head for a better view. My breath quickened as a deep vibration in the air tickled my cheeks.

The girls continued to float about like butterflies, hopping and skipping around the parking lot, oblivious to the miracle passing above them.

My eyes followed the glistening aircraft until it poked back into the scattered layer of clouds and disappeared. The thunder of the jet engines faded to silence, and I was left alone again. The clouds simply ignored the jet's passing intrusion and continued to float unchanged, as if nothing had happened, and I had imagined the entire thing. I might as well have been the crazy lady walking down the street, having a conversation completely with herself.

My hometown laid under the arrival and departure corridor for Newark Liberty International Airport. Not that I had any idea at the time. My childhood was filled with airplanes passing overhead, which no one seemed to notice but me. But a jetliner had never screamed by this low before. I was fascinated and confounded that even at this moment, everyone else just tuned it out.

That jet set my imagination on fire. The match was lit and the blaze was bright.

I longed to see a plane up close. I wanted to see the inside of an aircraft. Not the cabin, but the cockpit. I wanted to see what the pilots saw. I wanted to know what the pilots knew. I wanted to feel the controls in my hands and examine every switch and button I imagined must be in there.

Up there is where I wanted to be.

But I knew that would never happen. I had never met a pilot, but so far in my life I could see for myself that pilots were not women. Whether by choice or design, there were no exceptions. I understood completely, and I didn't question it.

In my childhood world, there were all sorts of unwritten rules. Expectations. Norms. My position in life was clear and my future path was narrow. I was destined to grow up to become a nun or a housewife, at least that is what I believed. Either way I would be submissive to a man.

Nothing to see here. Just move along.

Sure, I was disappointed that my life was doomed to boredom, but I accepted it. By the fifth grade, if nothing else I was a realist in the making.

In the arena of Nature versus Nurture, for sure Nurture was winning the battle.

"Become a bride" was Santa's favorite theme every year.

A few years later in middle school, my class was administered Occupational Aptitude testing, to assess what courses we should take in high school. I scored in the highest percentiles nationwide in Mechanical Reasoning (how easily do you grasp the principles of physics) and Space Relations (how well can you can think in three dimensions). The analysis of my scores suggested the careers of engineer, surgeon or architect if I were a boy, and dress maker, florist or decorator if I were a girl. The included explanation stated that, "girls score considerably lower than boys on MR and SR tests," therefore "a girl who scores well may still be far below the average boy." These notes further advised that educational and career plans should be made considering "your family's thinking," along with keeping, "realistic thinking" and "your abilities in mind."

I took what I wanted from my test results and disregarded their career suggestions. Though the occupation of 'pilot' was not on the list for anyone, my aptitude testing gave me hope that understanding the inside of a cockpit was indeed within my ability.

As I grew, my world continued to expand and so did the way I pictured myself within it. I naturally became more self-reliant over time, and along with that developed my own opinions, but the biggest shift was my vision for my future.

I was just a regular girl, living a regular life. I may have started off with my head in the clouds, but I would end up with the rest of me there, too.

FORTITUDE — NOT APTITUDE

One of the greatest things about my childhood was that I was bored a lot. That gave me plenty of time to daydream and just figure things out. One thing I figured out was that I hated being bored a lot, and I needed a future where this would not be a problem.

Darn these wooden clogs. My footsteps echoed against the metal lockers as I walked down the empty hallway of my high school. It was the Fall of my junior year, and I was on my way to the office for my first guidance counselor appointment.

I was whole-heartedly certain I wanted to be a pilot by this point, I just had no idea how to get there. I couldn't guess the first step to take, or even which direction to turn to look for that first step. There was no internet to search. No teacher, relative or family friend to answer my questions or to help me make a plan. But now I had an appointment with Ms. Brewster, my school's most experienced guidance counselor and a working woman. I was ridiculously optimistic that finally I would find all my answers and the support I craved.

Being the child of caring and consistent parents is not something you are allowed to complain about, so I'll just say my parents had a rigid vision for my future that was conventional, practical, and oddly foreign to my every feeling about who I was and of what excited me. My parents were very much in step with the world around me, which was hitting me from every direction with the same generic messaging of traditional roles and the need to conform, fit in, and be a good girl. My mother often told me, usually as we folded laundry, mopped the floor, or as I would patiently watch her get her hair set at the salon on Saturdays, that her "duty" was to teach me my "duties," and how to act like a lady.

Bursting with youthful enthusiasm, I had convinced myself that Ms. Brewster was going to save me. She was the keeper of rotary files, index cards, and vertical cabinets full of college catalogues. I was sure she had spent her years sending the young off to tackle their dreams and break free of their parents' expectations — guilt free. I would be another notch on her belt. She had this.

If I had expected her office to have the sunny air of a travel agency filled with brightly colored posters of young adults delighting in the triumphant college-life experience and exotic life destinations, I would have been way off base.

Ms. Brewster sat behind a generic wooden desk, in a pint-sized office cluttered with loose papers and messy files stacked on mismatched bookshelves. The inadequate lighting of a single overhead fluorescent light gave her office the feeling of a dreary cave.

I slid into the torn vinyl chair on my side of her desk, eying a splattering of papers spread across her desktop with a conspicuously empty manila folder beside them. I spotted my name typed on the header of several different sheets. My God, I thought, this morass of papers must be my "permanent record."

That was a real thing?

I was embarrassed and impressed all at once. I wanted to touch it all, to be left alone to peruse each page like a teenage girl who just discovered her long-lost diary.

Perched behind this mess, Ms. Brewster looked at me from the other side of her desk with a no-nonsense, blank stare. She was a stranger, but she had my entire academic career carelessly splayed naked in front of her. She knew more than I did about my aptitude testing, my academic and extra-curricular achievements, and how I stacked up against my peers. There it all was, spilled out from one emptied manila folder.

"Hello, you must be Laura," she said after a painfully long silence. "I'm Ms. Brewster. Let's get to work." That she was the first woman I'd ever met who introduced herself as "Ms." rather than "Miss" or "Mrs.," got my attention in some strangely inspiring way.

"So, have you thought about what classes you plan to take in college?"

Before I could answer, she shot right into explaining how essential it was to pick the right courses in high school to prepare you for future college studies. She could have just asked me what I wanted as my career, but she didn't do that.

So, I volunteered it.

"I want to be a pilot," I confidently informed her.

She peered at me through her oversized fashion lenses, her magnified eyes quiet and impassive. A patronizing grin spread across her face, and she batted her mascara-caked eyelashes.

"Well now, let's look at your test scores and see what your aptitude is best suited for." She started fishing through the papers strewn across her desk until she slid one sheet out and began to peruse it.

"IQ... superior range."

What? You're mumbling.

"But," she paused, glancing at me with a half-scowl, "you have limited aptitude in mathematics."

Now that I heard loud and clear, as she cherry-picked which of my scores she gave weight to.

Instantly, she came to an absolute conclusion that not only would I need to select a career that did not involve mathematics at all, but for my senior year of high school I would need to choose classes that stayed away from anything that involved numerals or calculations.

"I would like to take physics and math next year, though," I hedged, thinking that pilots probably needed both. "What math do seniors take?"

"No, no, no. No math. That would ruin your GPA. Someone like you should not take any more math and science than you have to, and you have already met the minimum state requirements to graduate."

She was completely serious.

Her opinion of me was decided. My academic record spread across her desk was the equivalent of tea leaves that already spoke my fate to her. Why did she even bother to meet me? It's not like she was listening to anything I had to say.

"Aren't there any colleges out there where I could major in aviation?" I asked.

"No. Not that I've ever heard of."

And she was done with that subject.

Not that I didn't believe her, but she put a non-negotiable end to my dream without even taking a pause to think about it. She just dismissed me and the subject was closed.

I didn't argue with her, either.

What did I do? I nodded and smiled. I'm a people-pleaser at heart, a born obligor schooled to be polite at all costs. *Good thing she wasn't a mind-reader.*

Then she really put me in my place. "You need to be realistic and not chase something beyond your abilities."

Did she just call me stupid? No, I think she was calling me a girl.

So, one more person didn't see aviation in the cards for me. But the really discouraging part was that Ms. Brewster had proof. There it was in my permanent record, black-and-white evidence that I had no "aptitude" for math. I was insulted, but how could I refute that? I'd been tested. The state of New Jersey said so.

And so this is how my first step to becoming a pilot went.

My high expectations for Ms. Brewster had been conjured in my own mind, and I got it wrong on so many levels. She was not going to be my bridge to reach my goals after all. Walking out of Ms. Brewster's office, I didn't feel any less passionate about aviation, but I saw that this was going to be a harder road to travel than I had naively thought.

Although I did have my moments when I questioned if I actually was being stubbornly unrealistic about becoming a pilot, I still felt compelled to at least try. After all, why not pursue a far-fetched goal that nobody could tell me how to reach? To me, the idea of not even trying was far scarier than the thought of ultimate failure.

In hindsight, all of this doubt kept me wide awake to the fact that I had a big challenge ahead of me. Expecting to be crushed at any time cushioned the letdowns that would strike over and over again. But let me say, all that skepticism made the triumphs even sweeter.

I would graduate high school having taken no advanced math or science classes, and having taken no physics class at all. Senior year was marked by creative writing, art class, sewing class, and cheerleading practice. I did end up with a nice GPA at graduation, but had a perpetual uneasy feeling like I was getting away with something all year long. This feeling didn't last though, as my lack of challenging academics came crashing down on me in college.

People are quick to assume all sorts of things, whether they say it to our face or not. The thing is though, nobody knows you like you know yourself and sometimes people just get it wrong. Determination and true innate enthusiasm for something cannot be tested and scored. These are the intangible dynamics that decide where a person truly belongs in life. Have fun doing it, and you've got it.

High school did not pave the road to my future, so I compartmentalized those required hours of my day and started looking for another way to move in the direction I wanted to go.

And find it, I did.

FREEDOM CARD

On my seventeenth birthday and only months after my conference with Ms. Brewster, my whole life changed — and I didn't look back.

It was on that birthday that the state of New Jersey finally considered me old enough to drive a car unsupervised. It occurred in the dead of winter, but the challenge of parallel parking between snowbanks didn't deter me from going to the DMV for my road test to earn my driver's license on that day.

There was nothing special about getting my driver's license. Definitely a task that virtually all my peers achieved, on or right about on, their seventeenth birthdays as well. But this painfully ordinary accomplishment turned out to be my magic wand.

My super generous parents lent me the use of their old station wagon, the same one that my older brother was already driving. (He may not have been quite so pleased as me with this new arrangement.) I was growing up in a generation where parents kept little track of where their children were. Top that off with the birth of my younger sister making me into an invisible middle child of four siblings with the sheer good luck of having parents that both worked in an all-consuming family business, seven days a week — and there you had it, the perfect formula for unrestricted freedom.

With my shiny new independence, the first place I drove to during that snowy January was a small airport. I can't remember how I knew about it, or how I found it at all before the Internet and GPS, but somehow I ended up at Morristown Municipal Airport, or MMU. This felt like a pretty good first adventure, but I didn't have even the smallest inkling just how pivotal this one trip was going to be for me. A mere eleven miles from my home and fairy dust started sprinkling down on my head.

I wasn't born surrounded by people who shared my excitement for all things aviation. It was up to me to go find those people.

So there I was, finally at an airport.

I took a twenty-dollar "Discovery Flight" — a quick promo ride in a tiny piston engine airplane, offered by Cessna flight schools across the country to give potential flight students a peek at life in the sky. And in theory, to get them hooked on the idea of becoming a pilot themselves and signing up for flying lessons.

It worked.

I think Cessna stacked the deck for me, though. They didn't need to cheat to get my business, but they sure did tilt the odds in their favor.

This first flight was with a dreamy young flight instructor who went by JT. He was wearing a maroon polo shirt with a crocodile logo, tan Dockers, brown leather belt, suede Hush Puppy shoes, and naturally — Ray Ban Aviator sunglasses. His left shoelace was dragging when he walked over to introduce himself. The details of this first day remain as vivid in my memory today as when it happened.

On that day, I discovered that anyone could take flying lessons, and my dream of learning to fly airplanes became something realistic and achievable. I felt an overwhelming urgency to get started, and I returned a few days later for my first real flight as a student. JT officially became my flight instructor. But as taken as I was with the flying bug, it was an expensive hobby, and I didn't have the money to get very far.

I decided I couldn't beg, borrow, or steal, but I could find a way to earn flight time. I approached the owner of the flight school with a proposal to allow me to work at the school in exchange for flying lessons.

It turns out that Fred, the owner, quite liked the idea of having a dedicated employee that didn't want to be paid with money, and soon I was working behind the front counter of the Cessna Certified Pilot Center.

Airports are tight knit communities, and not everyone who loves flying has money. The folks that came to take flying lessons, or rent planes after they had their license, were from all different walks in their other lives. From doctors to truck drivers, at MMU we were all just airport bums on equal footing with each other and uniquely connected. Even though I was usually the only female in sight, I melted right into this crowd like butter into a hot biscuit.

Different fellows around the flight school took me under their wing and helped me out when they could.

"Hey Laura, here are the flying manuals you'll need to study." John Ryan, a Vietnam vet and part-time flight instructor, generously lent me the textbooks I needed. "Just let me have them back when you are done."

An older gentleman, who was a regular at the flight school, handed me an old plotter for navigating. "I got a new one, so you can just keep this."

I don't know if I was a charity case, or if I was more of the airport mascot, like a cute little bulldog, but everyone looked out for me and wanted me to succeed. At the airport, I was surrounded by people that understood, and even appreciated, my excitement for airplanes. I had found my people.

And so began my double-life, as I felt compelled to hide my new activities from my friends and teachers back home. I set off down a path of harboring secrets, covering up and telling half-truths, all while appearing to be the same dutiful daughter and student I had always been.

It started with little things. At first, I would smuggle flight manuals with me to school, and instead of doing schoolwork, I spent study hall tucked away at a corner table surreptitiously studying for my private pilot written exam.

Later, when football season started and cheerleading stole away my Saturdays, I impatiently waited for the big game to start, and more importantly to end, so I could get back to the airport. After the game ended, instead of joining the other cheerleaders driving around our little town honking car horns and shaking pompoms out car windows, I was now kicking off my saddle shoes and rushing to the airport to get to work and get my flying in for the day. These little things slowly grew into significant things, eventually reshaping my life and my outlook for my future entirely.

I don't exactly know why I needed my two lives to be kept absolutely separate, but one never crossed the other, and that was the way I wanted it. Maybe it was because flying made me so happy, I was afraid the fairy dust would blow away if it became something I had to explain or defend. I lived in a world where female pilots simply did not exist, and I knew my flying lessons would become a joke for everyone to laugh at. Other kids at school looked down on me as a "late bloomer," because I appeared so disinterested in drunken parties at the rock quarry and other cool teenage antics. But I was skipping past much of the typical teenage experience by choice and I didn't care how my absence was perceived. I could handle my peers mocking me for just about anything, but I was not going to give them the chance to dump on my aviation bliss. This was *my* joy and I had to protect it. It had to remain my secret.

I was slipping away from my childhood friends and all that was familiar, and it felt good. At the airport, I arrived with no background story. No preconceived ideas of who I was, or what I should or shouldn't be good at. Teenage stress and traditional stigmas didn't follow me there. I stopped asking for permission or approval to be who I was. I'd begun the transition to becoming myself and I basked in the relief of autonomy and finally feeling as though I was moving in the direction which felt right and natural for me.

MMU was an entirely new and relatable world, and nobody seemed to care that I wasn't quite an adult yet. In my business attire, I had become a forty-year-old teenager, working to keep the computers on program, keep planes properly scheduled, keep the flying students happy, and keep my boss content by insuring he had whatever he needed. I didn't even mind making Fred his hot tea every day.

There was a crazy mix of all different sorts of people at the airport, each of which I regularly bothered with my questions and eagerness to learn.

Of course, there was the expected assortment of hobbyist pilots, guys who spent their recreational time spinning around in small prop planes just for the fun of it. Although a bunch of these fellows owned their own planes or were members of a flying club, most were just renters and came right to me to check out an airplane for their excursions. Continuously surrounded by pilots shooting the breeze, I was introduced to the fine sport of "hangar flying," a pilot's version of fish tales.

"Geez, I accidentally flew into Newark's airspace, and a huge United jet shot right out of a cloud and flew straight at me. It was so close, I could see the pilot's mustache!"

I loved listening to these stories. Even better, though, sometimes I was invited to take an empty seat for real flying.

"Hey Laura, we're going for a hundred-dollar hamburger. Got one empty seat. Want to come along?"

Did I?

"Yes!"

I quickly figured out that most general aviation pilots needed a reason to rent a plane, and flying somewhere to eat was the customary reason. It's so expensive to rent an airplane, the running joke is that they are paying a hundred dollars for a hamburger. Lots of time, two or three guys would split the costs to rent a four-seat plane for the afternoon, and they'd invite me to tag along for free to fill an empty seat. I never cared where they were going or why. I was a puppy wagging my tail, happy for any scraps thrown my way — and I viewed every scrap as filet mignon.

MMU was also an Army annex, with a crew of enlisted guys maintaining a handful of transports hangared there. These soldiers had some impressive stories for my teenage ears, and they would let me pester them for hours while they worked on their aircraft and talked to me.

Perhaps the biggest surprise about MMU was the glitzy side to the airport. Conveniently located just outside of New York City, the airport catered to the rich and sometimes famous crowd, as well as important businessmen and politicians.

I rarely was eager for my day to end at the airport, but one warm Saturday I had tickets for a John Denver concert in the evening. I was counting down the hours till my workday was over, when a stunning Lear 35 jet streaked down onto the runway. Painted like a beautiful Navajo blanket, it rolled up and parked right in front of the flight school I worked at. I was sure it was the power of suggestion playing on my mind when I squinted up to the cockpit window and thought I saw John Denver behind the controls.

But then the pilot stepped out of the aircraft and it was John Denver, bouncing a basketball. Of course, I walked right over to him and introduced myself. I was struck by his openness and cheery enthusiasm as he gave me a private tour of his jet and we briefly chatted about our mutual love for airplanes. I was still pinching myself as I watched him from the crowd at his concert that night. He wrote me a lovely note with his signature on the back of a fuel card, which my mother subsequently threw away as garbage in my room — but I won't go there.

Aside from my fleeting connection with John Denver, there were other corporate and charter pilots coming and going all day long in handsome private jets and luxury helicopters. As luck would have it, a lot of these aircraft weren't just passing through. MMU was the flight base for many large companies, including Nabisco, Bell Laboratories, and AT&T. This was the early 80's and these companies spared no expense for their flight departments. It was nothing less than the most high-end and modern fleet for their senior executives.

The best part of this was that these private jets and helicopters needed constant maintenance. Needless to say, after a system was installed or repaired, the aircraft required a test flight before any of these important people got on them. So I routinely made my way around the airport, rambling from hangar to hangar, just waiting to *accidentally* run into the mechanics and the pilots of these remarkable corporate aircraft. If I played my cards right, they would let me hop onboard their sleek jet or helicopter for those maintenance test flights. Quickly, I discovered that if I was especially smiley and curious, chances were the pilot would let me sit in the co-pilot's seat and get a little hands-on flight time in the skies over New Jersey. I was just a green kid and couldn't believe how charitable these guys were to me.

Every pocket of the airport held another chance to listen and learn from somebody. I was perpetually dipping my toe in the water and getting a hint of what it felt like to be a real pilot. A professional pilot. With each flight, I was falling deeper and deeper for it all.

I had started off with my flying lessons simply hoping that someday I might be able to take a plane up into the sky, all by myself.

Wouldn't that be amazing?

It was a small dream, really. But my head started spinning the more I mixed with these different pilot groups and a new dream — a bigger dream, was taking form. I certainly didn't presume that I could ever fly for a commercial airline, and I hadn't met a professional female pilot, yet. Even so, I started thinking, private corporate pilot — maybe?

There was even a spattering of teenagers taking flight lessons, or otherwise killing time at the airport just goofing around, who I became friends with. All of them, like me, were independent kids who found their way to the airport once they got their driver's licenses. As the only girl in the mix, I seemed to have better luck hitching free plane rides than the boys did. I'm sure being female helped, but not for the reasons one might assume. Unlike the guys, I didn't need to act cool at all. I could let my

31

excitement bubble out, and these professional pilots didn't mind breathing in my admiration for their skills and sincere awe for their magnificent machines. They could see that spark in me that they had felt years back, and they could see that I wanted to learn. It was in those earliest days as a student pilot that I saw how much all pilots love to encourage and help other pilots, especially if that means making more pilots.

My teenage years weren't exactly going as normally expected for someone like me, but that is precisely why these days were so pivotal. I wasn't supposed to be there. Flying airplanes was not in the hand I was dealt at birth. But I realized I couldn't harness my dreams to what I could see in front of me. I needed to define my own expectations and pick my own direction.

Every day at MMU, I felt alive in a way I had never experienced before. Alive in a way that many people might never get to soak in, in a lifetime. I was surrounded by people who made me feel strong and capable. My spirit was unguarded and free at the airport. Everything felt right, and I couldn't imagine how life could get any better than this. But even then, I knew this was only the first step in the right direction for me.

The question remained — could I pass the real test of my independence?

I GOT THIS

"It's time," JT plainly stated.

"For what, lunch?" I was a little hungry.

"No, time for me to get out."

My eyebrows popped up. "Are you serious?"

I really was learning to fly a plane. Just a small, single engine Cessna and never without my steadfast flight instructor, JT, right there beside me … until one afternoon.

We touched down and rolled off the runway after my third successful "stop and go" and I started the ritual taxi back to the runway threshold, to take off and do it all over again.

"Pull over up there and let me out." JT wagged his finger, pointing for me to keep moving along, but in the wrong direction. I followed JT's instructions, just like I always did, but my movements felt robotic and I shifted into slow motion as it became clear that his directions were bringing us back to the ramp where he planned to abandon me.

And that is exactly what he did. We taxied to a safe spot and JT hopped out. Then he waved bye-bye to me and strolled clear of *my* airplane.

I wasn't getting out of this.

I had wanted something and had worked hard to get it, but now that it was finally within reach, I wanted to back pedal. Fear and doubt can stall out any good ambition. Here I was, alone in a plane for the first time and I was having second thoughts.

I looked timidly at the long taxiway ahead of me and the empty seat beside me. I pulled the airport diagram from the door pocket and laid it on the lonely seat next to me, taking the time to smooth it flat with my hand just to procrastinate. I never really paid attention to this piece of paper before, because I had JT to keep me from getting lost in the maze of taxiways. Now I needed it, and all sorts of other doubts started racing through my mind. But as JT walked away, I had nowhere to go except back to the runway. I eased the throttle forward and rumbled back the way I came.

"Morristown tower, Cessna 93145, runway 5, ready for takeoff. Closed pattern."

"Cessna 93145, cleared for takeoff, runway 5, stop and go approved, left pattern," the disinterested voice scratched back through my radio.

I switched the landing light on, completing the last item on the checklist to acknowledge I was about to takeoff. Tentatively, I followed the yellow lines on the taxiway onto the white stripes of the runway, every one of my movements slow and intentional. My feet patted the rudder pedals left and right as I rolled into place, until my propeller spinner pointed perfectly down the center of runway 5, and my magnetic compass read 50 degrees.

"Add a zero to the runway number and check that my compass agrees." I rambled aloud to myself because JT wasn't there to nod his head in approval and say, "Runway five should read fifty degrees. Checks good, Laura."

I took a deep breath and tasted the smell of fresh cut grass in my throat. *I got this.*

I slid the throttle forward and listened carefully for the pistons to respond to my authority. The propeller sliced through the air, faster and faster until it disappeared into a solid blur powerful enough to pull the airframe forward, accelerating it down the centerline. My little Cessna popped to life without JT there to weigh it down, and everything was racing by at an unfamiliar dizzying pace. The corner of my eyes caught the trees flowing past my wingtips and the gray pavement rushing underneath my wheels, until my flying machine jumped off the runway and everything attached to the ground abruptly dropped out of sight.

Any doubts I had dropped from my thoughts as quickly as solid earth disappeared below me. I immersed myself in making the plane do what I wanted up in the air. I watched the ailerons on my wings rock gently in mimic of my hand movements and the plane twist in sync to my feet pushing on the rudder pedals. Engine vibrations hummed into the palm of my hand, as my fingers rested quietly wrapped around the throttle lever and I smoothly slid the knob to adjust the power.

This machine followed my movements, as if it were a dress clinging to my arms and legs blowing in the wind. I was wearing the airplane. I would never be just a passenger again, detached from the machine and merely enjoying the view.

Flying a rectangular circuit, I brought the plane back around as I climbed until I rolled out on the downwind leg, placing the airport back in front of me. And there it was, picture perfect a thousand feet below me — the entire airport diagram come to life!

Air gushed through my vents, bursting over my face and blowing my hair into a wild dance. The sky tasted fresh and scentless, as if this air hadn't reached anybody or anything on the earth yet. I breathed it in deep, and a maudlin feeling of self-reliance and elation rushed over me. I might as well have had jet fuel surging through my veins.

Here I was, sitting in a seat a thousand feet above the earth. This cushioned fabric vibrating beneath my thighs could have been on any chair. With my eyes closed, I could have been at the movies resting comfortably in front of an action film. But I wasn't. My seat was in a cockpit suspended up in the sky and this was real. I was relying on unseen air to hold me up, being propelled forward at a speed I could never imagine when stuck to the ground on wheels.

Up here, gravity just ignored me and let me do whatever I wanted.

A bird floated past me, comfortably gliding by my wing as if I were his friend. I felt like a voyeur in a place that I wasn't supposed to be. For the first time in my life, I felt utterly disconnected from every person and everything I knew. I had no problems, no worries, and no dishes to wash. The world below me looked like a child's bedroom floor, with toy cars and airplanes, and construction paper cut-outs for roads and trees. How could I take anything down there seriously? That other life was all so unimportant and far away.

Most captivating for me was that I was experiencing this alone, in absolute privacy. Not a soul could see me. Not a soul could hear me. I was wholly and absolutely by myself, completely free of any constraints, any opinions … or any assistance. Sure, I had been in the air and behind the controls before, but never alone. As fun as flying lessons had been, I had never felt mesmerized like *this*.

It was a powerful moment in my young life. This encompassing feeling of absolute autonomy and personal responsibility drew me in and stayed with me. I'm pretty sure it was to my future "social" detriment, but after that day I was undeniably content and comfortable when completely self-reliant.

I circled around and carefully lowered myself back down to the ground, putting my airplane solidly back onto the runway. As soon as my wheels grabbed the concrete, I stomped on the brakes and shuddered to a stop by the first runway exit. Turning off the runway, I could see in the distance that JT had gathered a crowd of my favorite airport people, and all of them were now cheering and waving their thumbs-up — though later they did razz me for my hastened stop on the runway to make the first turnoff.

This amazing, uplifting euphoria stuck in my soul and helped form my lifelong affection for aviation. I thought of Joseph Campbell's famous quote: "Follow your bliss," and I just smiled.

The tides moved quickly, and at twenty years old I shed my "student" mindset and became the certified flight instructor. Then, I looked into the zealous faces of my students, and I felt *their* eagerness to know what I knew. Every "first solo" for one of my students became a flashback to that exciting day for me.

A feeling of déjà vu cycled throughout my career, starting with this day. I would look back at a goal suddenly behind me and remember how it had once felt impossibly far off. I guess that's how success works — one small triumph at a time. Failures proved helpful too, to keep me grounded and hungry for that sweet feeling of victory that I had already tasted.

FATHER KNOWS BEST

6

"Laura, we need to talk." My father summoned me as I walked in the door after work, and he didn't say it with a smile.

This can't be good.

Although I easily hid my time at MMU from my peers, my parents did know that if I wasn't in school, then I was at the airport. They knew I had gotten a job there, and they even vaguely knew that I was taking flying lessons — and not saving any money. Although what exactly they thought "taking flying lessons" meant, I did not know.

"Laura, you've been spending too much time at that airport. I like that you have a job, but you are throwing all of your money away." Dad looked serious. Concerned.

I knew that my mom didn't think this was lady-like, or even "normal" behavior for a daughter and had been praying this adolescent rebellion would pass. Apparently, my parents had begun to recognize that my aviation phase wasn't passing by, and I was steadily moving away from the things that they both thought were important.

I spent much of my childhood climbing into my father's lap and listening to his whole-hearted laugh at neighborhood parties, but we had very different personalities. Though my dad had a take charge attitude to life and took risks to get ahead, he is not adventurous in the way that I am. He would never ride a rollercoaster or go camping with me. He even dislikes flying on an airplane.

A first-generation Italian American, my father grew up working in his father's greenhouses, doing manual labor as a child in the early hours before school, only to return to the greenhouses after school and on weekends, working until dark seven days a week. Never allowed a day off as a kid, the first high school football game my father ever attended was my brothers' when they played, then my own and my little sister's when we cheered. As a former Marine, he showed me that success came from self-discipline, respecting others and following the rules.

"Dad, I'm not throwing my money away. I'm spending it. I'm learning to fly airplanes."

"Yes, but why? You should be saving your money to buy a car, like your brothers. You need a car." Dad's tone was so matter-of-fact, he could easily have been giving me tax advice.

I didn't know how to explain to my father that the last thing I wanted was to work towards a boring, generic goal.

"Dad, I want to *fly*."

I did a lousy job of explaining myself.

Then my dad said something that stopped me like a brick wall: "Laura, you're too immature to understand — nobody would pay a girl to fly a plane. You're throwing your money away on a fantasy."

I couldn't help but think: if I were one of my brothers doing the exact same thing, my parents would be proud, and this would be a very different conversation.

It made me sad.

I don't believe I had ever told my dad that I wanted to be a *professional* pilot, but somehow he picked up on that on his own. I hadn't thought that either of my parents were paying particular attention to my fervor for aviation, but they are my parents and they caught on.

My dad made his standard "Father Knows Best" speech, but he

couldn't turn me around. I wasn't going to give up flying and he didn't need to agree or even understand. I don't know if my dad was just testing the waters and measuring my conviction as he lectured me, or if I actually turned him around with my stubborn insistence — but in the end, he shocked me.

"As long as you stay on the Honor Roll at school, you can keep flying," he said. But he wasn't done. "And whatever you earn at work and spend on flight lessons, I'll match you dollar for dollar."

What? Did I hear that right?

I kept my mouth shut, except for a grateful "thank you!" I was afraid if I asked for an explanation, he might reverse himself again.

Apparently, Dad didn't know how easy Ms. Brewster had made it for me to keep my end of this deal academically, and he sure didn't know how many more lessons I would need before I earned my pilot certificate.

I was heartened to feel his confidence in me and thrilled for this financial boost. My boss, Fred, was a fair, but cranky old businessman. I worked for minimum wage and didn't get one second of flight time that my wages didn't add up to on my account, before I could exchange that fund for flight time. He didn't even give me any employee discount. So I was paying full pop for my flight lessons and I could only afford those at a snail's pace. After Dad stepped up to the plate, my flying lessons really took off (there's a pun in there) and doubled in pace.

Dad has often said, "I have four children and they couldn't have four more different personalities." Dad was wise enough to give us all good advice over the years, and even wiser to understand when he had done his part, and it was up to us to take his advice or not.

I'm certain my father couldn't guess what made me tick, but he didn't need to think like I did in order to support me. Though like my grandfather in many ways, my dad had no interest in his father's greenhouse business, and chose a different life for himself that didn't get his hands dirty.

It takes real strength to be wholly yourself, but even more courage to give that same gift to someone you love when you completely disagree with them. That day, Dad patted himself on the back for doing his best to raise me as a team with Mom, and realized it was time to let me go and find whatever I was looking for.

Likely he thought I would learn a hard lesson about the realities of life, but it would be up to me to find that out. And maybe, just maybe he considered that I knew what I was doing and this whole flying thing would not turn out to be the nonsense everyone predicted. Either way, he handed me the reigns to either soar — or crash and burn on my own.

Even with my dad's new implied approval, his words still weighed on me. I knew he had made this effort to discourage me and wake me up to reality because he loved me. He was worried for me. And I had to admit, Dad had a history of being right and would never steer me wrong, intentionally.

That day, my father gave a tighter grip to the self-doubt that still lingered in my mind. *Was I headed for a big disappointment?* But he also showed respect for my autonomy and confidence in *my* judgment. He opened the door for me to figure things out for myself, and that was exactly what I was going to do.

BUZZ WORDS

7

I was always the one who worried about other people's feelings and protected quiet kids from the mean girls. But this limitless unstructured level of freedom I had at the airport affected me to the core of who I was, or who I thought I was. I was brought up under the "confession is good for your soul" line of thinking. So, despite my hesitation to share a chapter of my life that I'm not proud of, I'm just going to put it out there.

I was often the last one at the flight school, working behind the desk waiting until the last airport bum and student left for the night. One evening, another teenager named Garrett stayed late to keep me company. After locking up the doors of the Cessna dealership, we found ourselves the last two left at a completely empty airport. Even the control tower had shut down for the night and the air traffic controller parking lot lay empty.

"Hey, let's walk the flight line and see if we can find a jet unlocked." That was Garrett's idea.

"Good idea," was my response.

So, we did just that. We walked the "parking lot" of ridiculously expensive corporate jets, testing each door for an unlocked aircraft, until we found one.

Leaving their door open, it was almost as if these pilots deserved to have two kids invade their exclusive jet. At least that's how we rationalized it.

Climbing up the airstairs, we made our way directly to the cockpit and

Laura Savino

settled into the pilots' seats as if we had a right to be there.

"Let's see if we can get the engines started." Again, Garrett's idea.

I had been taking lessons in propeller, piston engine planes and I had no clue how to start a turbine engine, but I did know this was a bad idea. An uneasy feeling settled into my stomach. This was going too far, and I knew it. What if the jet started rolling forward and we lost control? What if we sucked something into the jet's intake? No, this was not a smart idea at all.

"Oh, do you know how?" was all I said.

"Well, I know you don't need a key to start a jet engine." With that, Garrett started toggling switches and moving levers.

To my amazement, the left engine started to spin. It began as a deep growl, which quickly grew to a low shaking whine. A vibration grew in my thighs as my seat hummed to life. The fuselage lightened and rose up as the wheels loosened from the tarmac beneath us.

"Oh no," I shrieked, "shut it down!"

And then we simultaneously panicked, because we both knew this was going to turn out badly, and neither of us had any idea how to stop what we had started.

Garrett started pressing buttons and yanking levers. I didn't know which move did the trick, but to our relief the engine spooled down and went quiet. We darted out of our seats and scrambled back out the door onto the tarmac. I took a quick look at the left engine intake while Garrett latched the airstairs back up into place, and then we ran. The bright red engine inlet cover had been partially sucked into the turbine inlet blades. The next day not one person suspected we were the ones behind this night mischief. Though it rode my conscience, we completely got away with it and I didn't learn my lesson.

Almost immediately after my first solo, I began to play it too loose with my unsupervised flight time. I started buzzing people on the ground. To be candid, I did a little more than fly low passes over their heads. I would full out dive bomb unsuspecting pedestrians, then abruptly pull up.

My first target was a couple of guys in ball caps, sitting in a rowboat quietly fishing in an isolated part of Lake Hopatcong. They gaped at me incredulously coming down on them, then sprang out of their boat and into the water just before I shot over them and yanked back upwards. Another day,

I found a couple of golfers on an otherwise empty golf course, who dropped their clubs and ran, ducking behind their golf cart as I bore down on them.

When spring came, I went to prom with Garret, and we cut school the Monday afterwards and flew to Atlantic City for a day of sneaking into casinos. On the flight there, I took the plane just a bit off course to pass over my high school. This was the first time I had ever skipped classes, and there was something amusing about flying over my school knowing I should be there and not here having all of this fun.

"Oh look, Garrett, gym class must be having an outdoor day." I pointed out the kids running around the soccer field.

Garrett smiled because he was thinking what I was thinking. This set up fell into our laps, and it was too perfect to just let it pass. Yes, we went for it. We nosed our Cessna over and aimed right for the mass of teenagers dotting the green grass.

I kept a straight face the next day at school.

"Laura, you really picked a day to be out sick. This plane dove right at the school! The police came and everything." My friends filled me in that next morning.

"Oh really?" I shrugged. "I can't believe I missed that."

Back then, tail numbers were painted on the vertical stabilizer in very small type, and that was lucky for me. I had good timing because just a few years later the laws changed, and aircraft tail numbers were required to be huge and painted across the fuselage — exactly so that people couldn't get away with what I was doing.

Barnstorming looked really cool in vintage Hollywood flicks, but in real life a plane bearing down on someone is loud and shocking. People didn't wave as I droned past them, they ran.

This rogue behavior was out of character for me. But the power I felt in control of an aircraft was intoxicating and the independence was liberating. And it was easy to misuse this unique privilege of being a pilot, because nobody knew it was me. Anything that must be done anonymously can't be good, and it didn't take me long to not be proud of myself. This phase passed and I quit doing it, but probably not soon enough.

In addition to my developing habit of buzzing people, I was also going up alone and regularly doing barrel rolls and spins, an intentional stall of one aircraft wing with power at idle, causing me to spiral face down towards the ground, only to recover by leveling the yoke, kicking in rudder and of all crazy things, pushing the yoke forward before adding power in to swoop back up. Aside from teaching aerodynamics, this training maneuver is supposed to scare sense into the student pilot by demonstrating how easily you can plummet, even in an airplane — and should never be done without a certified flight instructor at the controls. But for me, it was a thrilling solo experience and pushed me even deeper in love with the magic of flying. I was a teenager, after all.

Having "mastered" that exercise, at least in my mind, I wanted to try out bigger and better stunts with my solo practice time. I felt compelled to challenge myself. I had never found stability or taking the safe path as any fun, and now I had the chance to really push myself to new limits. If there wasn't danger in my life, I had to create it.

One day JT and another flight instructor got the marvelous idea to fly up to Poughkeepsie, New York, and each buy an aerobatic flying lesson in the Mudry CAP10Bs. These were flown by a most remarkable French aerobatic duo traveling the air show circuit up and down the East coast, at that time. I was invited to tag along for the day on the venerable "empty seat."

As the guys strapped in under the glossy glass aerobatic canopies, I desperately wanted to go up and play, too. But all of my money was on account back at MMU, and I didn't have any cash for a splurge like this. I was stuck on the tarmac, my eyes blinking as I followed the boys zip in and out of sight, spinning and whipping about as they created the most captivating twists of torque in the sky above me with their aerobatic instructors behind the controls. Like wincing while watching a boxing match, I watched them pound the sky just to bounce back with smooth grace after each tumble and fall. It was hypnotizing.

"What was it like?" I begged JT as soon as he landed and wobbled out of the cockpit. I was relentless, wanting to hear every detail of his aerobatic lesson and nothing satisfied me but to vicariously live through every minute of his flight.

"That loop — how do you do that?" I continued pumping him for specifics at our next flight lesson, days later. I wanted to know the secrets to aerobatic tricks and JT had worn the magician's hat. He finally folded under my persistence and gave away the wizard's secrets with step-by-step instructions for the stunts carried out that day above me in Poughkeepsie. The wheels in my still developing brain started turning.

I have to try these when I'm up on my own.

Which I did. The typical hurdle, fear, was never much of an issue for me and never held me back. I was lucky like that. My wacky attempts at aerobatics probably wouldn't have been recognized on the ground as anything except a flailing airplane in distress. But to me, I was performing a beautiful ballet in the sky. The Cessnas I flew were all badly abused flight school rentals, though. Think Avis of the skies.

What I didn't do was appreciate how much stress I was putting on these worn airframes trying these stunts, and how little I actually knew about aerodynamics yet. My luck could have run out at any time. But I was oblivious to that, until it almost did.

One crisp autumn day, I rented a Cessna 152 and headed north up the Hudson River, where I came upon West Point Military Academy. Looking down from my tiny two-seater, I could see precise rows of cadets, hundreds of students all in matching uniforms moving in perfect columns across a finely manicured field. This scene was just too picturesque and flawless looking for me. Unable to resist the temptation, I drove my little plane straight down at them, to play a game of chicken. The sea of cadets scattered in all directions under my black tires, as I skimmed the length of the field like a crop duster on a mission.

When I reached the far end of the field I pulled straight up; then the excitement of it all got the better of me. On a whim, really, I decided this was the ideal time to climb higher and try an inside loop: a vertical 360 degree turn. I shot straight up into the sky above the cadets, then pulled back on the yoke to arc the plane over backwards.

What could possibly go wrong?

This was going great, and I was sure my unwitting audience below was enjoying the show — when my luck turned.

I arched backwards, and just as I reached the peak of the loop, fully inverted, my plane's momentum faded away. The airframe seemed to get stuck. Everything stopped moving, leaving me hanging upside-down in my seat belt for a very.

Long.

Pause.

My yoke turned to mush in my hands, the elevator useless without air flowing past it. My heart hesitated in perfect tempo to the engine sputtering, as the fuel drained from the lines… and I prayed for the nose to fall through.

Mercifully the nose finally dropped, my engine power roared back with a surge, and I was diving back to the ground, much like doing a backwards dive into the community pool from the high board. Accelerating shockingly fast and headed straight for the ground now, I did what any inexperienced pilot who didn't know what they were doing, would do. I yanked back on the yoke.

Trying this dicey, high-speed maneuver in my old piston engine rental was like entering the Indy 500 in my grandmother's Pinto. It was absurdly stupid. As I pulled out of the dive, gravity forcefully pinned me straight down into my seat and my worn-out Cessna reacted to the G-load with a series of startling bangs, like machine gun fire shooting out my tail.

Oh no, were those rivets popping?

What have I done?!

I scurried directly back to MMU and got my plane on the ground without wasting a second. *Do not pass go, do not collect 200 dollars.* After parking, I nonchalantly examined my little plane, trying not to call attention to my peculiar "post" flight inspection. I didn't see any damage to the airframe, and I stressed over whether this should be another secret to keep.

But like a good Catholic girl, I felt guilty and I confessed all of my sins to a mechanic, because I didn't want someone to take the plane up if I had actually damaged it. Thankfully, he couldn't find anything wrong with it and kept this a secret from Fred, our boss.

My West Point ordeal was my first real scare. I knew I had pushed it too far. But in the end, I was safe, and I loved the adrenalin rush it had given me. I *needed* adrenalin. My teenage brain was now even more convinced that I was invincible, and my need for dangerous thrills only grew. Back then, there were no extreme sports. Flying an airplane was all I had.

Just when I was having more fun than I thought possible, the seemingly impossible happened. I passed my written exam and my private pilot checkride, and the FAA granted me my pilot certificate. There it was, a piece of paper that gave me the right to take friends up into the sky with me.

As long as I had been flying, which felt a lot longer than it actually was, this development painted the experience with an entirely new and vibrant brush. "Non-pilot" people could join me in my spectacular and separate world.

I started taking friends up with me in a Cessna 172, a four-seat prop plane. Never friends from school — I still wasn't ready to give up my secret life to them—but various friends from outside of school. I even took friends of my parents up for rides sometimes, just not my actual parents, though they had a standing offer. Taking guests with me opened new doors because they had their own ideas of where they wanted to go. Up to Boston for fresh seafood, or down the Hudson River for a spectacular view of Manhattan and the Statue of Liberty.

I loved flying circles around the Statue of Liberty. I'm glad I had a camera with me this time and got a picture.

But what really kicked these new doors open wide, was that I had someone to split costs with again now that my "lessons" were over and so were my dad's financial contributions.

The pilot certificate also allowed me to be experimental in ways I couldn't before. I immediately started flying to odd airports to test out different plane models. My favorite was a J-3 Piper Cub out of Trinca, New Jersey, an old fabric covered tail dragger flown on a grass landing strip. This was a borderline primitive experience, right out of a classic World War II documentary. With my certificate, anybody would rent me a plane, not just my boss. It was unbelievable.

Just when I thought I loved something, I opened myself up to a new aspect of it and my passion only grew deeper.

On the 4th of July, my family held our regular Independence Day party in the driveway. In between hotdogs and sparklers, I threw it out there. "Hey, anyone want to go flying and circle the Statue of Liberty after dark to watch the fireworks?" The show was coming from Liberty Island that year.

I had several immediate takers, so off we went. *Fools rush in.*

It was so not-a-big-deal that we could have just as easily been a group of teenagers headed to McDonald's for ice cream sundaes with peanuts.

We got up in the air and scooted to the Hudson River, headed south and squeezed our little Cessna 172 into the raceway of small planes already buzzing around the Lady's head and torch, like bees to a hive, which was all legal back then.

Bees never collide with each other, right?

Along with every other piston-engine bug swatter who had the same idea as me that night, we watched wide-eyed as neon-colored streaks shot up just underneath us in the night air. The burnt smell of sulfur wafted through our vents, and tiny burnt paper sailed past us as we punched through lingering smoke trails. It was all great until someone screamed, "The Blimp!"

The mysterious black hole directly in front of us had suddenly blinked into a FULL-SIZED Regal-Cinema-theater screen, and we were in the front row looking directly at the Goodyear Blimp.

My knee-jerk reaction was to yank back and kick right, to avoid this massive floating screen. That saved us. We just barely passed over the top right corner of the blimp, which was lumbering along as a floating theatrical experience, entirely lighting the sky now.

"Was that supposed to happen?" Janet asked in the most sincere voice.

"Oh yeah… sure." I stumbled.

"See, it's all fine," David assured her.

Aside from almost flying into the side of the Goodyear Blimp, it was a really fun night. When we got home to our parents, we left that little detail out.

One teenager has one brain. Two teenagers have half a brain. Three teenagers have no brains at all.

RESPECT THE ENVELOPE

One summer day, I learned how quickly things can go wrong and was irreversibly forced into respecting the envelope.

Morristown Municipal hosted an airshow which attracted a crowd of 50,000 spectators over two days. For months the airport had been abuzz with everyone preparing for the show. Jimmy Dyer, a confident and handsome twenty-five year old corporate jet pilot for First Jersey Securities, was a fan of my excitement around airplanes. He understood and encouraged my enthusiasm better than anyone else and became a big brother to me at the airport. I looked up to and admired him. Fulfilling a dream of his own, Jimmy purchased a Thorpe T-18 experimental aircraft, a sleek single engine, two-seater homebuilt plane.

Generously, Jimmy asked me to come along on his final practice flight in preparation for the airshow. Jimmy ticked through different stunts, including shooting frighteningly fast low passes over the runway, as I soaked in the thrill of experiencing an airshow from under the canopy.

"Ha, here comes a hammerhead, Laura. Suck it in, your stomach's gonna flip." He laughed as he shot his aircraft straight up, only to stomp on the rudder to flip the aircraft over like a "hammer" and slam back down in the opposite direction.

The next morning at the airshow, I ran around checking on my friends

I knew were going to be performing.

"You're gonna be amazing, Jimmy!" I gave him a final wave after wishing him luck.

I was an Aviation Explorer in the Boy Scouts, and I had to say good-bye to Jimmy and go join my post. John Ryan, a flight instructor and former F-4 Phantom fighter pilot, was our adult advisor. As a volunteer activity, we parked cars and spent our morning waving thousands of visitors into organized rows in the overgrown grass turned into a makeshift parking lot. I felt like the welcoming wagon as carloads of people arrived, often surprised to see me dressed like the boys in matching Scout shirts, guiding cars into neat lines. With my high school graduation only days away, I didn't mind my secret getting out and it turned out to be fun when an occasional teacher or kid from my school riding with their family, would stop and say "hi" to me with startled looks on their faces.

I was out in the field parking cars when Jimmy's plane took to the sky that morning. From my spot, I had the perfect view of his shiny little aircraft as it darted above the airport. The heads in the crowd tilted up and turned in rhythm, following his performance above them.

"Above you now, ladies and gentleman, is the homebuilt aircraft Thorpe T-18." The energetic voice boomed over the loudspeaker system. "A sporty beauty flown by our own Jiiiimmmmy Dyyyyeeeeer!" He dragged his name out, perfectly paced with Jimmy's plane as he buzzed past the crowd.

I stood still and watched Jimmy whip by, my heart full of pride for him. I wished I was still sitting beside him and not here watching from the field.

"Sorry, the plane won't perform as well with any extra weight," Jimmy had explained to me.

He swooped by even faster on his next pass. I spotted Jimmy's profile under the glass bubble canopy as he smoothly buzzed past the crowd, following the length of the runway.

Then his aircraft's nose bobbled. Just the slightest bit, but I knew he wouldn't do that intentionally, not this close to the families watching.

My breathing seized in my throat as I watched that little bobble transition into a porpoise. The entire fuselage launched into an odd up and down wave just feet above the asphalt, snapping Jimmy's head back and forth under the glass canopy.

Both wings peeled back and tore away from the fuselage, propelling Jimmy, still strapped into his seat, onto the concrete as the entire plane disintegrated in a long shattered trail. A streak of orange fire shot down the pavement, coming to an abrupt halt in one massive fireball.

A woman's scream and crying children hit my ears.

Firetrucks wailed in the distance.

Rocked awake from my trance, I darted away from my spot in the grass and numbly sprinted through the field, around parked cars and swarms of people. I raced directly to the runway edge. Directly towards the wild ball of fire and the glowing stream of burning fuel stretched three hundred feet down the runway. The heat from the inferno warmed my bare legs, and my t-shirt wilted and clung to my back. I mixed in with rescue personnel and kept jogging, right across the taxiway, around firetrucks and an ambulance, to reach the melted cockpit.

Almost there. Almost on top of the fireball.

THUMP.

Somebody grabbed my arm, yanking me to a sudden stop. A fireman.

"Is that Jimmy?" I screamed at him.

"Stand back miss, you can't go any further." He body blocked me, putting himself between me and the fire.

"Is that Jimmy?"

"You can't go any further."

"IS THAT JIMMY?" I screamed, again and again. By any observer, I was irrational. Out of my mind.

I knew it was Jimmy, but I needed someone to say it. Something inside me was waiting for another explanation. Someone else took his plane up.

Yes, that is what happened. Someone borrowed Jimmy's plane.

"Is that Jimmy? Is that Jimmy? Is that Jimmy?" I tried squirming around the fireman, but he only tightened his grip on my arm.

"Is that Jimmy?" I relentlessly panted as he dragged me backwards.

The crowds parted to make room for the fireman, pulling along a hysterical teenager incessantly screaming into the void, "Is that Jimmy?"

A New York Times journalist wrote that a woman "totally broke up from emotion," in an article dated June 13, 1983. I was that woman.

I looked up.

Mothers were ushering their children away, while other spectators searched the flames for gory details.

Some guy in the crowd yelled, "Well, his hair really is on fire now!" and his buddies laughed out loud. I felt sick.

I calmed myself and pulled free of the fireman. He left me alone as I walked away.

I stumbled my way into the flight school and into my favorite little restroom where I had spent many football Saturdays changing into my work clothes.

I studied myself in the mirror. Grime and charred soot tinged my pink face. Mascara streaked down my flushed cheeks. *When was I crying?* I stayed in there for a long time with the door locked.

The crowds flowed out of the airport, and I eventually shuffled out to my car too, shaking off friends who tried to speak to me, or give me a hug. I drove home in silence, focusing on the cadence of my engine revving each time I shifted gear.

I performed my duties at home, helping my mom in the kitchen, until I softly settled into my chair at the dinner table, detached and emotionless. I couldn't process that Jimmy was inside of that wad of melting metal.

My parents were there at the airshow. They saw it, too. But nobody talked about it over dinner. Nobody ever mentioned it, ever, to this day.

I sat silently at the table, non-responsive to the clatter of my three siblings going back and forth with each other.

"Smile!" my dad admonished me, not tolerating a glum face at the dinner table. *Perhaps that was his way of reaching out?*

The next day at school there were kids excited to gossip about the plane crash, mostly focusing on the glowing fireball bowling down the runway. Mr. Miller, a teacher whose car I had helped parked to his absolute surprise, asked me if I knew the pilot or knew what had happened. I answered his questions briefly, then walked to my next class.

That was the only time I ever spoke about this accident, and the only time anyone brought it up to me, ever.

Stifling any outward cues that I was in pain, I smothered my feelings and moved forward.

After Jimmy's crash, I never pushed the envelope or naively took safety for granted again. His death was the first of many in my circle of pilot friends. Each death accumulated in my soul, awakening and further strengthening my commitment to aviation safety, while also quietly bringing me to my knees. But in the end, I was never swayed from my love of aviation.

EEYORE VS. TIGGER

9

"You're not delusional." JT patted me on the shoulder.

When it came time to apply to colleges, I was certain that I wanted to major in Aviation. Like all pilots, the realization that there were real dangers associated with flying small airplanes did not deter me. By this time, I had gotten to know many different types of pilots at MMU, and none thought I was in over my head. At least, not that they told me.

With only a few exceptions, word had not gotten out that I was a pilot, and this was all still a secret I had kept from my peers, teachers and school counselor. So, the only advice I received was from other pilots who thought like me, and every one of them encouraged me.

My family, who did know I was a pilot, were *not* onboard with my flying going any further than an expensive hobby. If my dad matching my earnings and fast forwarding my flying lessons was an attempt to use reverse psychology, then his plan had backfired. Allowing me to "follow my dreams" did not wake me up to reality, teach me a hard lesson, or end with me giving up on the idea of becoming a professional pilot on my own.

My mother wanted me to go to college and major in art. Seriously, art. *Okay, I was inducted into the Art Honors Society and I did like art a lot, so mom wasn't totally off base.* A Liberal Arts education is the right path for a lot of people, but everyone is an individual and at my core, art was fun, but not something I felt inspired to earn a living doing.

I knew what I wanted, and I knew to get it I needed to go to Purdue University in West Lafayette, Indiana. Purdue had the most advanced flight training program in the nation. Though aviation students were predominately male, Purdue was at the forefront of diversity and already had a handful of female students in each class.

On her fateful last flight, Amelia Earhart was on staff at Purdue and was flying a Lockheed Electra funded and equipped by the Purdue Research Foundation as a flying laboratory for aeronautical research.

Twenty-seven astronauts are Purdue graduates—that's more than any other university, including the Air Force Academy, which comes in second place. The first and last man to walk on the moon, Neil Armstrong and Eugene Cernan, graduated from Purdue.

Yes, Purdue was the place to go if you were a pilot in the making.

Like a circus poodle, I jumped through every hoop and did all that I was required to do to show my parents, and perhaps myself, that I was open minded and willing to consider all of my higher learning options. I applied and even interviewed at various colleges on the East Coast, and I slipped an application into the mail for Purdue also. I was accepted at every school to which I had applied and the consensus, of my parents anyway, was that I would accept a spot in the freshman class at Villanova. A great school, I'm sure, but the home of the Wildcats didn't have an aviation department. They didn't even have an airport nearby. So that was out.

How to tell my mother?

When I insisted that Purdue was the school of my choice, my parents were a little baffled, but ultimately conceded that it was a fine school and I would get a good education there. So, we agreed that I would head to Indiana to be a student in the mother-approved Purdue College of Liberal Arts to get a four-year degree in Art.

Yeah, right.

The Purdue arts program was hardly their flight training program, but it got my foot in the door, or at least onto the Purdue campus. I would just have to find the right door to open once I got there.

I was officially headed to Purdue. "One small step" in the right direction, "one giant leap" towards achieving my dream.

Years later, my mom told me that her biggest worry with me moving so far away was that I would fall in love with a farm boy and never come home. But I think this was actually her hope for my future. Settle down with a nice guy, stay home, and have someone take care of me while I took care of the babies. In her mind, it didn't make any difference what my actual college degree was in.

I knew that I wasn't going to college to get my "MRS." degree, though. I was going to become a pilot, travel the world and *then* never come home. So, mom got it half right.

My parents dropped me off at Newark airport, EWR and wished me luck. I had a one-way airline ticket to West Lafayette, Indiana, and a trunk full of clothes, which my Dad had to curb check because it was too heavy for me to pick up. In hindsight, just getting on an airplane alone as a teenager and heading for the middle of the country to a place sight unseen, seems a little crazy to me. But at the time it was just a "see you later, bye" send-off.

Indiana turned out to be a strange land, full of cows and cornfields and kids who hadn't spent a single summer at the shore. I settled into my dorm and academic classes quickly, and tried to lose my Jersey accent and fit in. 'Tried' being an optimistic word. I also tried to immerse myself in the culture of the Midwest by immediately pledging as a "little sister" to the fraternity Farmhouse and was introduced to peculiar and charming concepts, such as hay rides and glee club.

As different as it was from my homeland of New Jersey, I loved Purdue and all the people there instantly. But I still needed to find my niche; to find *my* people. I needed to get out of the College of Liberal Arts and into the School of Technology, specifically into the Aviation Technology/Airline Pilot program.

For all of my determination, I had no idea how to put my plan into action.

During my second week of school, I walked back to the airport to hunt down an answer. I found the terminal building that I had arrived at on that first day. That got me nowhere, so I kept walking. In the mix of the usual buildings and hangars that can be found at every commercial airport, I finally hit gold.

The door of one plain building labeled "Hangar 6" opened with a loud rasp, and I found myself in a sea of college professors, students, and flight instructors. I was suddenly in the inner sanctum of Purdue's aviation department. Jackpot!

I immediately felt a sense of awe and comfort. *This* was my home in Indiana. I needed in. I had to become a part of this.

After explaining why I was there to a random student walking by, he directed me to Professor Gross's office. Upon introducing myself to Professor Gross, I immediately began to pour my heart out.

"Please, how do I get in here, into this program?" I implored him, like a dog begging to be let in out of the rain. "What do I need to do?"

Professor Gross was a tranquil, gray-haired flight instructor. With that same polite and warm Midwest twang that I was getting used to, he explained how to "CODO," or transfer, to a different school within Purdue.

"But, to transfer into this program next semester, you will need to have your private pilot certificate. Each class stays together in their studies, and that is where the Freshman class will be in their flight training," he explained, with palatable grief for me.

"But I do have my private," I countered, doing the happy dance in my head. *This couldn't be more perfect.*

To my disappointment, this revelation didn't seem to please or surprise him in the least little bit. He nodded in acknowledgment, his face still "Eeyore" flat, in unambiguous contrast to my bouncing "Tigger" enthusiasm.

Realizing that his efforts to dissuade me had failed, he apparently decided that he just needed to be blunt with me.

"I'm sorry, but there are no openings," he continued with a somber face. "Someone would have to quit or fail out of the flight program, in their first semester, for a seat to open."

The flight program was a small and tight group to be a part of. There were only thirty students in the entire Freshman class, in a university that had 33,000 students. Each of those flight students had successfully made it through a highly competitive selection process and were handpicked with stellar qualifications. Who was going to drop or fail out of that group?

I left his office, feeling both optimistic and deflated. Now I knew what to do. I could get right to work on the CODO paperwork, and I was already planning every step that I could take to make my transfer papers rise to the top. But I also knew that I couldn't do a thing to open up a seat in the program. I would just have to cross my fingers on that one. By that I mean I hoped that someone would choose to drop out—not fail out. *But is it even possible to take flying lessons and not love it?*

Because the airport was only one mile from campus, all day long I could see small trainer airplanes painted in the Purdue colors dart about the sky. It was a constant reminder that I was missing out. So far, the students in *my* class were still behind me in their flight training. When they caught up at the end of the first semester, I had to join them.

I. Had. To.

I had come to Purdue for one reason, to find my career. I was going to be a professional pilot, because if I was going to spend every day of my life doing something, I was going to make sure it was something I had a blast doing. I was here, in this curious land of Indiana, to get into that flight training program. Period.

Professor Gross could have forgotten about me in the mix of all the students visiting his office, but I was not going to let that happen. I kept coming back. My visits became as steady and predictable as a Swiss watch. I was determined that when Professor Gross got my CODO papers, he would know the face that went with that paperwork and know my dedication.

Then on one of my regularly unscheduled visits, Professor Gross welcomed me into his office and wistfully asked me to sit down. Avoiding eye contact, he bent over and pulled open a deep filing cabinet drawer beside my chair.

"These are all CODO papers I have received for this next semester." His voice trailed off as he turned his head towards the drawer. "From qualified students, all of whom have their private pilot certificate already and want a slot." Looking up from the drawer, he paused to emphasize his final point, "if one even opens up."

I looked down at the stuffed drawer, which was jammed full, from front to back with papers and manila folders.

With kind, sympathetic eyes, Professor Gross gently burst my balloon. I felt like someone had just cracked a hole in my goldfish bowl and made me watch as the water flowed onto the floor and poor little Goldie sank deeper and deeper to the cold, pebbled bottom.

It was a long, dispirited walk back to my dorm, as I replayed his words and his "condolences" in my head. For the first time, I finally got the picture; the odds really were against me.

I needed to work even harder.

Grades and attitude: I would just have to make myself the top candidate compared to my competition. Optimism drives me. It was a long shot, but I needed to believe that I had this. A seat would open. I would be picked.

I never wavered in my resolve to get into the Purdue flight program, but I also believed that the best way to qualify for the airlines was ultimately through the military. I had learned that a handful of the students already in the Purdue flight program were in ROTC (Reserve Officers' Training Corps). They were not only attending college for free, but were getting paid an allowance to attend Purdue. But much bigger than that, they were going to fly military aircraft after graduation and get to serve our country and do something meaningful with their skills. And from there, they would be perfectly set up to slide into a career with the airlines. This was all news to me, and off I went to find the recruiting offices just on the edge of campus.

My first attempt, of course, was the Air Force.

"You are a woman," the recruiter informed me, his expression as inflexible as his crisp uniform and buzz haircut.

"I know."

"There are no *pilot* slots for you."

"I can't fly and serve my country? Just because I'm not a man?"

"Sorry, flight seats are for combat positions. Women aren't allowed in *any* combat role." He didn't appear sorry at all, though. But seeing some potential, the recruiter tried to persuade me to consider another position in the Air Force. A ground support role – "helping the pilots do their jobs."

"No thanks." I was polite, meaning I didn't roll my eyes.

I walked away and tried again with the Navy, Army, and then the Marine recruiters.

Wash, rinse, repeat.

Each time I was turned away so abruptly and unconditionally for any pilot position, I didn't pursue the military route to becoming a pilot after that.

This was 1983. It turns out that the military had opened certain limited flight positions to women before then, but word had apparently not gotten out to your average recruiter or to the public in general. It wasn't until 1993, that the military opened up combat roles to female candidates, and women could realistically compete against men for prized fighter jet seats.

I would have to get into the Purdue flight program and just figure out what came next after graduation. So, I put all my eggs back into one basket and ramped up stalking Professor Gross.

At the end of the first semester, my optimism took a deep plunge down a cold well. I had straight A's in all my classes, except for math. I had gotten a B on that final exam, and I knew that dismal B would show up in my CODO paperwork.

Damn Ms. Brewster, her assumptions, and my easy senior year of high school.

Realizing my sought-after academic perfection was shot, I did the only thing I could do. I went right to Professor Gross to confess.

"I've ruined my chances of getting in," I lamented. My grief was as real as if I were giving a eulogy. I felt like I was saying my goodbyes to Professor Gross. I was so disappointed in myself.

He listened to my admission and then smiled at me. For the first time, I wasn't a ball of sunshine and unyielding eagerness bouncing into his office. And for the first time, he bolstered my hope, instead of tamping it down.

"We look at more than just one grade, Laura. Don't worry about that." His smooth reassurance warmed my spirit and the feeling that he was hinting at an underlying message picked me right up. I all but skipped the whole way back to my dorm.

Shortly after that, I received my letter of congratulations, welcoming me into the Purdue Aviation Flight Training Program.

I had really done it.

With all of my visits to the airport, I had come to recognize most of the flight students, and I wondered whose seat I had gotten, and why? There was one tall, stocky boy who dressed in denim coveralls every day, which was not unusual for Indiana, but made him easy to notice at an airport. I wasn't completely shocked to find out I had gotten his spot. He voluntarily left the flight program after not doing well, to CODO over to the agricultural program at Purdue. He wanted to be a farmer, not a pilot. We had moved to what felt right for each of us, and we both found *our* people.

Two years earlier, I had applied to McDonald's for a job. I filled out the employment application and then I went home and waited for the call. I was so qualified for the position, I didn't see the need to do anything more.

I'm still waiting.

Filling out the application was as far as I got with the McDonald's franchise. But here I was, chosen for the Purdue flight training program, which had "winning the state lottery by using your children's birthdates" impossible odds.

It's so easy to think that life is unpredictable.

I had control over my own actions and choices, but I didn't live in a bubble. I was dependent on those around me to get to where I wanted. No one could do the work for me, but it was somebody else who recognized my work and decided whether it merited their approval or not. Yes, I met the requirements, but Professor Gross gave me my shot because he thought my attitude, or my persistence, or my pleading, puppy dog eyes— was what was really needed for success in the program.

No matter how impossible or out of reach something may seem, there is always something that can be done to improve one's chances. Do whatever it takes, and then do a little more. That's how it worked for me.

"Mom and Dad, I'm changing my major. I'm going to be a professional pilot, not an artist."

Over time, my parents got better at adapting to my aberrant interests and to being less than "informed" until after the fact. I didn't tell them about my skydiving exploits, until it was all over. I didn't mention my days repelling off of our campus five story parking garage with the Rock Climbing Club, until it was behind me.

That's how things were. I didn't particularly enjoy keeping my parents in the dark. But I loved my mother, and I found it kinder to break worrisome news to her only after I had compelling proof that I didn't kill myself.

But changing my college major was a big one. I could hardly tell my parents how this would all end up when I was still just a freshman. Of all the obstacles I didn't hesitate to find a way around, my parents' unwavering conviction that I was making a mistake was the one roadblock that I couldn't put behind me, and their disappointment continued to weigh on me.

But every step forward that brought me closer to becoming a professional pilot, always felt right to *me*.

All I could do was keep moving towards that positive feeling and try to show them I understood the world of aviation, and that I had a place in it. This was a tough sell, to them and to myself.

I had to succeed.

Today my parents fly free, and I think it's safe to say they've gotten over their doubt and disappointment.

HOTEL TOWELS ON THE FARM

"What's happens when you hit the brakes on your car?" Professor Treagor quizzed me.

"You stop?" I shrugged. Likely not the answer he was looking for.

"No, no — what's the by-product of friction?"

The blank look on my face wasn't moving our conversation forward.

"Heat! Heat! Heat!" he retorted, appearing dumbfounded by my ignorance. "You don't even know the most basic principles of physics?" He might as well have thrown his arms up in the air, he had such a look of disgust.

The blank look remained fixed on my face.

"You really weren't kidding when you said you'd never taken physics before." He shook his head in disbelief, ensuring I understood how stupid I was.

This little professor-to-student moment was the result of my seeking after class help in my Turbine Powerplant class, where it was fully expected that I had a good grasp on physics *before* I got to this class. Learning the scientific intricacies of how a jet engine worked was going to be extra challenging for me, and Professor Treagor didn't spare my feelings to make this point.

I had guessed my easy academic load in high school would come back and haunt me in college, but I really had no idea how bad it would be. I had to admit my ignorance more times than my ego liked and get the extra help that I needed. I worked myself to exhaustion, but I did catch up.

The Purdue flight training program was even more impressive than I had imagined, and so were the students in it. Everyone was like me, only smarter. Everyone knew it, too. Our grades were customarily taped outside the classroom doors for all to see, listed anonymously by the first three digits of our social security number. Much like postal zip codes, you can tell a person's birth state by the first three digits of their social security number. I was the only one from New Jersey. *One of these things is not like the others.* A definite glitch in the "anonymous" grade posting system.

I earned high marks on my papers and exams, and had a GPA I worked hard for and was proud of. But most of the students in my aviation classes were absolutely brilliant and had flawless grades. I can't say my grades were ever close to flawless.

There was a skill that I brought with me, though, that put me at the top of my class in one category. I entered the program with mad radio communication skills. I learned to fly at a demanding airport in the heart of the New York TCA (terminal control area), not tranquil Purdue University Airport. I spoke fast and efficiently on the radio, using perfect ATC (air traffic control) jargon, while effortlessly juggling whatever else I had going on in the cockpit. Holding my own with rapid-speak New York air traffic controllers was second nature to me and a skill most of my fellow flight students wouldn't acquire until years later.

Eventually, I moved out of the dorms and into a sorority house. Go Alpha Gamma Delta!

My sorority sisters wanted to make the party runs with me. Not because my bubbly personality would attract the cute frat boys, but because I didn't drink alcohol — at all. I became my sorority house resident "designated driver." That put me in-demand on weekends. My sisters would throw their car keys at me on Friday night, insisting that I stick with them for the weekend. For me, *not* partying was the key to popularity.

Since Purdue was so far from New Jersey, I rarely made it back home for the holidays. It didn't take long before my friends, practically every one from Indiana, started inviting me home with them during the holidays.

I discovered on these trips that there was more to the Midwest than corn fields and pick-up trucks. They had yards with animals roaming them.

"Here is a bottle to feed this calf." Desiree pulled the comically oversized baby bottle back, hesitating to hand it to me. "But first, you have to feel it's tongue."

"What?"

"No really, feel it's tongue"

"How?"

My first experience feeding a calf. Photo taken by Desiree.

"Put your finger in its mouth"

"Seriously?"

These farm people were something else. But I did it, and Des was right — rough as sandpaper.

One Spring Break, I went to my friend Barb's house. This was going to be a fantastic week because her dad was a captain for American Airlines and I had never had a conversation with a real commercial airline pilot before. But just as we were helping her Mom in the kitchen on Easter Sunday, the phone rang and out he ran — suitcase and flight bag in hand.

"Wait, where is your dad going?"

"Work."

He was on reserve, much like a doctor being on call, so he missed the entire holiday with his family. This seemed completely natural to Barb.

"In fact," Barb lamented, "I can't remember a holiday, birthday or school play that my dad didn't miss."

What I remember most about that visit, aside from her pilot dad not being there, is that their house was decorated in "Early Hotel." *I'm saying that with a British accent.*

Every bathroom in her house was fully supplied with mini soaps and tiny shampoo bottles, and every towel had a hotel logo embroidered on it. In the morning, Barb served me orange juice in the cutest little glass with an "H" etched on the side.

"Hilton?"

"Dad could only swipe one of these orange juice glasses at a time," Barb boasted as she opened up a kitchen cabinet, showing off an entire shelf devoted to matching orange juice glasses with an "H" etched on the side. "Do you know how many layovers he needed to collect this many?"

"Um… isn't that stealing?" That Catholic guilt thing still haunted me.

"Nah, it's part of the job," she said and grabbed a couple matching breakfast buffet plates out of the next cabinet for our buttered toast.

I may not have gotten the chance to talk to an airline pilot on this visit, but I certainly got a glimpse into the life of an airline pilot. I realized I hadn't ever looked past my love of flying to really consider the lifestyle that went with the job. I thought I had this whole career choice thing wrapped up, but there was a lot I hadn't considered. This experience didn't sway me, but it did shine a light on how much I didn't know.

I love Helen Keller's take on experience: "Life is a succession of lessons which must be lived to be understood."

BETWEEN A LOT OF ROCKS
AND A HARD PLACE

11

Flying the C182, in Leadville, Colorado.
Photo taken by Professor Donald Petrin.

I was selected for the Purdue mountain flying program while still in my freshman year. This program sent students to Wyoming, specifically to place them in mountainous terrain to accomplish their solo cross-country flight requirements for their commercial pilot certficate.

Indiana is flat. Pancake flat. This made the mountain flying program a unique and exceptional out-of-the-Purdue-box educational experience. Students couldn't request to be in this program; we were either chosen by the professors who ran the flight department, or not. I was humbled to be selected, and honestly a bit surprised. A number of students were picked for this, but I may have been the only one to regret going.

Mountain flying sounds scenic and peaceful. But navigating *between* granite slabs of rock and jagged precipices is not for the nervous pilot. Like all flying, it's about calculated risks, education, preparation and backbone.

In a specialized ground school, our group studied the unique meteorological hazards we would face, from mountain waves and turbulent eddies, to the degraded high-altitude performance of our piston engines.

I flew out to Wyoming on United Airlines, my very first experience in the Friendly Skies. Upon arriving in Laramie, I met up with the other students and our Purdue flight instructors, and we headed over to Motel 8 for our extended stay. I roomed with Desiree, my friend who had the cows in her yard.

The flying started out well and definitely began as a good experience. Initially, we took turns flying a Cessna 182 with our instructor to get familiar with the planes we would be using. We flew to Leadville, Colorado, North America's highest elevation airport at 9,934 feet, where I got to see how quickly I started to gasp for air while running across the airport tarmac. Because somebody dared me to run across the tarmac to test the thin air.

Then we were each assigned our own Cessna 172 and set off alone every morning to fulfill the cross-country requirements for our commercial certificate, flying three legs a day with each up to 3.5 hours long.

I flew to Jackson Hole, Wyoming and slipped a bit off course to do a fly-by pass of the Grand Tetons. *I get the Dolly Parton jokes now.*

I landed in North Platte, Nebraska, in powerful gusts and turbulence. The headwind was so strong that my forward speed was cancelled out and I dropped down like a helicopter to the runway. As I powered back in my landing flare just before my wheels kissed the pavement, my plane started drifting backwards, causing me to nearly roll backwards off the approach end of the runway just after my wheels touched down. I'd never experienced a touchdown where my landing rollout went the wrong direction.

I took a slight detour on my way to Rapid City, South Dakota, and ducked down to fly a few circles around Mt. Rushmore.

*Circling Mount Rushmore in my C172. I did not
intentionally buzz any of those tourists.*

One morning I departed Laramie for what was planned to be one of my shorter marathon days of solo cross-country flights. This time I headed south, to further my education by conquering the Colorado Rockies. I planned to fly right into the heart of the Rocky Mountains to Steamboat Springs, continue on to Granby, Colorado, and then head back home again to my starting point.

Successfully making it to Granby, Colorado, I refueled and then once again rolled down a gray runway and lifted into the sky. Up in the air, I banked my tiny plane and aimed straight for the grandiose mountains standing between me and my final destination, Laramie, Wyoming.
My tiny propeller airplane wasn't powerful enough to carry me over the towering peaks of the Rockies, so I darted directly between two spectacular mountain ranges until I disappeared into what felt like the fold of a postcard with fancy scroll saying, *Encounter the Majesty of the Rocky Mountains.* Naturally, John Denver was singing "Rocky Mountain High" in my head as I marveled at the chiseled granite rising up around me.

In this mountainous area, my unfolded navigational chart was a layered display of topography more closely resembling a Jackson Pollock painting than a map. Navigating became a game of artistic interpretation.

My only form of navigation—interpreting this Cheyenne Sectional Chart, with pencil lines to follow that I drew between airports.

Trying to match up the different shades of contour lines on paper with the layers of rock surrounding me, I had picked a passageway that reached all the way through to the other side of these massive rock walls on either side of me.

The deeper I flew into this craggy corridor, the narrower and more twisted the passage became. Cold stone walls tightened around me until the blinding sunshine in my eyes faded to shade, and the air grew chilly.

Wait? Where am I?

Precipitously, the pass grew too narrow for me to turn around and before I knew it, I was flying around blind curves, not knowing what I would find in front of me around the next jagged bend. Then I coasted around a stony curve and I saw it. A whimper escaped from my lips as the air emptied from my lungs.

Directly in front of me was a wall.

A solid sheet of stone rose up before me, filling my windshield. I could not see the top of it. I could not see the sky above it.

The passageway I was flying through — ended.

My God, a boxed canyon! I fell back in my seat, crushed.

I blew it.

In an instant, I understood what I had done. I had flown into a dead-end and I had just killed myself. I didn't feel afraid. I was heartbroken. I was about to die.

My socks. That is what flashed through my mind at that moment I realized I was going to die, not a look back over my life, not a look forward to all that I was going to miss, but to the white gym socks I was wearing. They were Desiree's socks. She had lent them to me that morning, because I hadn't packed enough. I would never get the chance to return them and thank her for being a good friend. This is what flashed through my mind at that very moment that I realized my life was about to end.

And then I thought, look what I've done now, my parents are going to kill me.

Oh wait.

I remained frozen in my seat. In shock. Defeated.

Then, another thought jumped into my head.

Maybe … I could do a wing-over and escape? Yes, yes, yes — a vertical turn to change direction!

No, I'm not an aerobatic pilot. I could never pull off a stunt like that. This is hopeless. It's over.

I glared at the massive stone wall rushing towards me.

Shut up, Laura. Just do it.

The immensity of my situation hit me again as a second wave of shock slammed my pounding heart. A shiver slid down my arms and my hands suddenly ached with cold. My body went rigid as every muscle tensed with anxiety and anticipation. Profound fear rippled through me as I gaped at the solid sheet of granite filling my windshield.

Now, I was terrified.

Just a teenager and still learning to fly, I had little experience to pull from. But in that moment, the fight to live became a reflex, a reaction I had little control over. A primitive survival instinct overwhelmed me, and I was flooded with indignation.

I am not just going to fly nose first into that cold rock wall.

It wasn't something I decided. I couldn't have given up, even if I had wanted to. I concentrated with an intensity, a desperation, as a bitter taste filled my mouth.

Only seconds from shattering into the gray slab, little tufts of grass sprouting from hidden crevices came into focus. I could no longer hear the drone of my engine or feel the vented air blowing onto my face. I was focused on the job ahead of me.

I yanked back on my yoke. Shooting straight upward, my plane's belly skimmed over the jagged cliffs at the end of the canyon. My seat jerked with a crackling thump-thump, snapping my neck as a wheel snagged a tiny pine sapling spurting out of a spiky crack.

With my nose pointed straight up to the sky, I dropped my right wing and fell into a steep bank while kicking in hard right rudder. My stomach flipping over with my plane as the stall warning horn blared… and then I was facing back the way I had come. I had actually shoehorned myself around. *Eureka!*

I had no idea I was capable of this maneuver, until I was forced to be capable of this maneuver. It took maybe forty seconds from my first realization that I was going to die, until I thought that I wasn't.

I heard my breath come back in a gush as my heart pulsed in my throat. My hands quivered with cold, and yet my palms felt moist under my grip on the yoke. A flood of relief burst inside of me, like a pressure cooker exploding: *I am alive.*

But my problems were not over. I was still lost.

Forced to follow the narrow canyon, I had been stuck in a maze, turning in all different directions for the past hour. I was burning through my fuel and I was still surrounded by towering cliffs. The canyon walls blocked my antennae reception and neither my radios nor my navigational instruments worked. I desperately needed to find lower terrain.

I threaded my way back through the twisted corridor, trying to spot something I had passed on my way in, to know that I was headed in the right direction to get out. Racing forward, I was full of hope that I would find open skies around the next bend, while also dreading that I would fly into another boxed canyon. I felt like I was drowning in a deep stone well, frantically trying to pull myself up the slippery rope, the glimmer of blue sky teasing me from above as cold water sloshed over my toes.

Over time, the boulders around me started widening out, giving me more elbow room between the rocky ledges.

"Denver Center, this is Cessna 65146." My radios crackled and hissed, but I stubbornly kept the microphone pressed to my lips. "Do you read me?" I repeated again and again.

Bursts of static cackled back at me, but I hung onto the thought that an air traffic controller could hear me, even if I couldn't hear him.

"Denver Center, do you read me?"

"Hello Cessna." The faint voice of an elderly man broke through the noise. "Yes, I can hear you, young lady." He paused. "I can hear Denver talking, too."

I shot straight up in my seat and squealed out loud, overjoyed when I heard his voice, and so relieved. Another pilot just out futzing around in the sky in his own tiny plane had answered me. I wanted to hug this old guy and cry on his shoulder.

I strained to listen through piercing squeals and broken transmissions as he explained there was an ongoing search for me. He wasn't surprised to hear my distress calls at all. In fact, it appeared he had been listening for me.

There's an ongoing search for me?

This fellow pilot became the middleman between me and an air traffic controller in Denver. He was my lifeline, relaying directions to me. I clung to every word he said, trembling with relief each time his soothing voice broke through the hissing clamor scratching out of my speakers.

But then things started to get strange. He began relaying messages "from me" back to the Denver controller, that I never said.

"Yup, she just told me that she can't breathe," I heard him report. "She thinks she has hypoxia 'cause she's so high up."

That's crazy! If my little plane could fly that high, I would just fly over the mountain tops.

He continued "relaying" all sorts of melodrama nonsense to the controller that was coming from some soap opera playing in his head.

"She says she's feeling dizzy now. Says she can't catch her breath."

"STOP. I did NOT say that!" I punched my microphone switch and screamed at him.

"Yes sir," he just continued. "Now she just told me her fingernails are turning blue. She really sounds like she's suffering from hypoxia."

"I did NOT say my fingernails are turning blue!" My voice pitched higher, my hand shaking on the microphone as I yelled into it. I may have been lost, but I could breathe just fine.

My "lifeline" turned out to be a crazy old man craving hero status and apparently his fifteen minutes of glory.

Eventually, I flew far enough in the right direction that I could hear the air traffic controller myself and I abruptly cut him out of the picture.

I was certain things would get better after that. I was wrong.

A cloud layer drifted into the mountain range I was shooting through, and quickly shrouded me. I might as well have been flying inside a bottle of milk.

Blindly following the controller's directions, I clung to the assumption that he could see my blip on his radar screen and wasn't just guessing at good headings to pull me through to the other side of the Rocky Mountains and into the Colorado flatlands. But I wasn't sure and I didn't ask.

Either way, he was playing it cool and calm in an unwavering deep voice, and he kept me talking.

"I need you to climb higher," he repeatedly urged me.

"This is it. I've got full power in." I whimpered, as if I didn't want him mad at me.

"Give me more, whatever you can," his voice continued on, low and intense. "Keep trying to climb. You're below most of the terrain out there."

Still snug inside a milk bottle, I could see nothing outside my windows. Nothing at all.

My heart raced under my T-shirt and my hair began to stick to my neck. Sure signs of stress. Or signs of hypoxia. But my nails were not blue. I was wearing pink nail polish, but I'm still sure my nails were not blue. Hopefully my symptoms had more to do with how closely I was playing with death, than lack of oxygen to my brain. I continued on.

That controller stuck with me until I burst out from the cloud bank and my tired eyes soaked in brown dirt and prairie grass flowing down below me. Even then, he continued to hold my hand until he pointed me directly at an airport. He aimed me straight at a runway and told me to land on it. I touched down in Loveland, Colorado, without even knowing, or caring, where I was. I was on a runway. A beautiful, wonderful runway.

His voice faded out of range as I sped down the smooth pavement.

Rolling onto the apron, I came to a stop, shut the engine off and numbly stared at the propeller come to a halt. I pushed the door open and swung my sneakers onto the tarmac. Drawing a long breath, I sucked the moist scent of Avgas deep into my lungs as warm air wafted up from the sizzling pavement.

My legs quivered as I squatted down and yanked a clump of pine needles on a shattered branch out from the wheel assembly beside my feet.

Oh crap.

I tossed the branch into the grassy edge of the pavement, shook my moist t-shirt loose from my back, and set off for the hangar across the concrete apron.

Time to find out where I was. Time to plan my flight out of here and find Laramie.

Once inside the hangar, I phoned my Purdue instructor, Professor

Petrin, who had been pacing in the flight service station back at my starting point at the Laramie airport. He was at ground zero in the search for me. I was the "missing Purdue flight student," and the aviation community was on top of it.

Receiving my phone call, he demanded that I not move, "not one muscle." He was getting in an airplane and flying to Loveland to get me. I swear, he could have been my dad scolding me.

Hours later when he arrived and had calmed down, he told me that he had already been practicing in his head the phone call he would have to make to my parents, that *he* would be the one to have to tell them their daughter was missing, or worse. He was so angry with me, and relieved. Really, just like my dad would have been.

When we finally made it back to the motel in Wyoming, Professor Petrin told me to go to my room and write down every detail of what happened that day — my version of the facts. The FAA was hot under the collar and was threatening to violate me for this incident. It's not illegal to get lost, but they had me on an altitude violation. The Federal Aviation Regulations mandate that supplemental oxygen is required in non-pressurized aircraft above certain altitudes, which I had well exceeded.

Sitting at the dingy desk in my motel room, still more than a little buzzed from the fading adrenaline high, I gripped a number two pencil and began to write. Offering silent support, Desiree perched on the bed beside me as I diligently strained to get it all down on paper, until I broke. I slipped away from the wooden chair and collapsed face down onto my bed sobbing. I was too exhausted to be strong any longer.

The fallout from this day happened behind closed doors. Aside from providing my written statement, I wasn't a part of it. Purdue stood up for me to the FAA and made some apologies on my behalf, and the violation got squelched. The Purdue Mountain Flying Program was coincidentally cancelled after this.

After that experience, I became a Christian missionary. No, I didn't have a sudden religious awakening. I had already been scheduled to leave on this missionary trip when I returned from Laramie. However, having just faced my own cold death with such drama, this trip turned out to be oddly timely. I was in a rare spiritual state of mind.

I spent that summer in Bolivia, South America, on a team building a brick church in Santa Cruz. My team then travelled to La Paz, in the Andes Mountains, and worked with the Quechua people. We ended the summer living in the Brazilian rainforest in fellowship with the indigenous people, sleeping in hammocks hung from lush trees, to keep off the ground and safe from tarantulas and red ants. I still have the frayed hammock that was my jungle bed.

I met a bush pilot during this period in the rainforest. Conversations with him opened my mind up to possibilities that I had never imagined I could do with my pilot certificate. I didn't necessarily think I was going to start flying into the rainforests of South America to make supply drops, but I became aware that there were many different ways in which I could use my skills as a pilot.

I learned again and again to not close my eyes to things I didn't expect to see or to only focus on those things directly in front of me. New ideas often snuck up on me from the most unexpected places.

THE UNFRIENDLY SKIES

I returned to Purdue for the fall semester with a broader outlook on what I thought my future in aviation could look like. I earned my flight instructor certificate in the spring of my sophomore year and returned to MMU that summer to work.

Coming back as a flight instructor to a place where everyone remembered me as a student pilot, felt pretty good. It was great to be back with my old friends, and it was fun meeting new flight instructors who worked there now.

Sue and Rick were two new instructors who had both recently graduated from competing aviation schools in Florida. They had a friendly rivalry going and our flight school was filled with laughter and practical jokes that summer.

Sue was the first female colleague I ever had, and we easily bonded as friends and allies. Just steps ahead of me in this crazy world of aviation, Sue showed me how to write a resume, how to search for a job in the aviation community, and how to handle men who didn't have faith in a female pilot. Of all the big brothers I had at the airport, I finally had a big sister to talk to. Until I met Sue, I hadn't realized how much I had missed not having another woman to confide in and to look to for camaraderie and advice.

Sue was hired by a charter company, Northeast Airways, just as I left to go back to college in the fall. Giving me a big hug on my last day, she promised to call me regularly and share the details of this next step in the journey. I was so happy for her, and her success made me even more excited for my future success.

That November, Rick was killed at the age of 24. Flying freight as a single pilot, he flew into terrain during the night in bad weather. Sue was completely torn up over Rick's death. Two weeks later, Sue was killed. Flying as co-pilot, she and her captain were flying to pick up a woman in Rhode Island and carry her to New York for the Thanksgiving holiday. Their twin Beechcraft King Air impacted the ground short of the runway on approach in pre-dawn darkness and poor weather, killing them both on impact. Sue Eason died at the age of 24. The NTSB has never found a cause for the accident.

Still in shock at Rick's death, this devastating news about Sue knocked the wind out of me and froze my heart cold. I didn't know what went wrong on that flight, but I was certain that Sue had started her morning so happy to be in the cockpit. I also knew she was a good pilot, and if her skills couldn't save her — then likely mine wouldn't have either if it had been me. I became more dedicated to learning all that I could to be the safest pilot possible and took my studies even more seriously after that.

Now getting paid to give flying lessons, I finally saved enough money to buy my first car and was able to drive myself back and forth to Purdue during the school year, which was a lot more affordable than buying airline tickets. It was a 12-hour drive, when I didn't get lost. It wasn't a 12-hour drive often.

Rand McNally became my closest friend. It was a time when unfolding an oversized paper map across the dashboard and trying to read it with a battery-operated flashlight in the middle of the night, while cruising down the highway at 70 mph, was considered "distracted driving."

When I did get lost, I would drive until I found a payphone, getting more lost in the process, to call home and ask my Dad what to do. Even super dad couldn't help much from 700 miles away.

Although my openness with my parents had somewhat improved, I still didn't tell them that I was working a third job on campus as a grader, in addition to my work-study job and my job as a Purdue flight instructor — because I had no money to pay off a speeding ticket I got on one of my long drives from New Jersey to Indiana. One lousy ticket and I had to get *another* job.

I can promise you, that didn't happen a second time. After that I drove slower than my grandma in her Pinto.

I viewed my demanding schedule and exhausting all-nighters studying, which I blame for my Diet Coke addiction, as daily deposits to lock in my future as a professional pilot. I genuinely was on the straight and narrow at college and followed the rules.

Except for that one time I stole an aircraft.

Really, borrowed it.

Without permission.

Requiring a cover-up.

One of the guys in my class had the smart idea to place a coin in the latch of an airplane hangar window at the airport, so that the window appeared closed and locked. This was how he proposed to get inside after dark, to get into the lockbox and borrow the key for an airplane. He invited me to come along. Despite my pledge to not get into trouble again after the mountain flying debacle, I still had trouble turning down free flight time. More so, I had a persistent feeling that life is short and I wanted to pack as many experiences into it as I could.

His plan worked, and just after midnight we climbed onboard and stealthily took off for the Indianapolis International Airport, IND.

By stealthily, I mean he did all the talking on the radio, because my squeaky voice was too recognizable.

On the ground in IND, we parked our plane in an isolated spot and then climbed up onto the roof of a hangar, just to enjoy the stars and watch the cargo airliners come and go throughout the night. We made it back to Purdue, putting the airplane back in the exact spot we found it and returned the key, just as the sun came up.

That next day, we quietly smiled at each other as the Aero Club members scratched their heads over how this plane mysteriously accumulated so many hours on the Hobbs meter, and question why the fuel tanks were low.

Even at the time, I knew exactly how stupid this was to do.

No need for hindsight here.

If we had been caught, we both would have been expelled from school.

I'm guessing this was a crime, too. *Grand theft aircraft?*

But why not risk throwing away our futures entirely when we could have a night of fun instead?

So the lesson is, follow your bliss — but use common sense, too. Unless you don't get caught, then just follow your bliss and steal an airplane.

Okay kidding: always use common sense.

During my junior year, my flight class took a road trip to Wright Patterson Air Force Base, in Dayton, Ohio. It was one of those exceptional opportunities that Purdue offered its flight students. We all got to experience real hypoxia in a high-altitude pressure chamber, and take part in other sophisticated training sessions that only the military has the means to offer. It was an honor to be there, and a back door into a military training experience that I had fully accepted I would never see again.

Despite how the military recruiters had dismissed me my freshman year, I felt welcomed by the Wright Patterson instructors, and was uniformly included in the entire pilot training experience. When we broke for lunch, though, there was a problem. There was no ladies' restroom anywhere in the building we were in. In fact, there was no ladies' restroom at all. Anywhere.

I was given directions to a building on another part of the airport. GPS would have been nice for this journey. It was such a long hike that when I finally got back to where I had left everybody eating lunch, our school bus had already loaded everyone up to move to another area of the airport, and had left me behind. No one noticed me missing. *That's another gripe, but I won't go there.*

I had felt respected by everyone at the Air Force base. Not to sound cliché, but I had felt equal. I was there getting an education, like everyone else. I had a future in aviation, like everyone else. Then, there wasn't a bathroom for me. This wasn't a plot against me, or a plot against women. It's just that no one thought a woman would ever be on that part of the airport, where they do pilot training. *Indeed.*

My flight engineer training at Purdue culminated with a trip down to Fort Worth, Texas, to train at the American Airlines Flight Academy. Purdue had an agreement with American Airlines, allowing Purdue students to train and earn an unrestricted flight engineer certificate at their pilot training academy. We did most of the simulator training at Purdue in DC-8 and Boeing 727 flight simulators donated by American Airlines. But we obviously didn't have actual commercial passenger jets to fly around at school. Back then a pilot could train in simulators, but had to take the checkride in the actual aircraft to be granted an unrestricted certificate.

That's where American Airlines stepped in and picked up where our Purdue instructors left off. In Fort Worth, we were slotted into American Airline's pilot training sessions, as if we were their own pilot employees in training. We shared a 727 simulator and then flew in an actual 727 for our checkride, side-by-side with real American Airline pilots in training.

This was the real deal and an experience that was more like a dream sequence for me, and I was waiting to wake up. I was enamored with and so impressed by American Airlines, their flight training professionalism, and how they treated us as students, that I was certain they were going to be the

On my first day in Texas, I went straight from the airport to the American Airlines Flight Academy in my cotton dress.

first application I put into a major airline, once I had the hours.

Someday.

For the inflight checkride on our last day there, I wore a classic navy business pantsuit, perfectly tailored to fit, with a crisp white collared shirt and neatly tied ascot around the collar. That was as close as I could get to a necktie, like the men were wearing. At 5'3", my miniature size stood out lined up with the other pilots, but my professional appearance blended in perfectly aside from that. After the successful completion of the final flight and checkride, and congratulatory handshakes from the FAA examiner and the airline pilots in my group, I walked across the airport to the passenger terminal to board my commercial flight home as a passenger on the airline.

Still in my proper and polished business attire, I checked in for my flight. I couldn't stop smiling, floating on the high of both acing my checkride and of seamlessly fitting in with the big boys — real airline pilots.

"No, I cannot allow you on this flight." The gate agent pushed my non-revenue ticket back across the counter at me.

"Why?"

"Because your attire is inappropriate"

"What?"

"You are not wearing a dress and heels."

"I'm wearing a business suit. A *nice* business suit."

"It's not a dress, now, is it?"

Because I had come to Fort Worth for flight training, American Airlines issued me an "employee," non-revenue pass to travel to and from the flight training academy. As the gate agent saw it, that made me a genuine company employee. No company employee was permitted on an airplane unless wearing "appropriate" attire. I knew I was flying on a pass and should dress nicely, though I didn't expect to be mistaken for an actual employee. Having no employee rulebook to reference, I had misinterpreted the idea of *appropriate* pass rider attire to mean business apparel or nicer. However, unknown to me, their rules specifically and without exception defined appropriate female attire as "a dress."

I patiently explained to the agent who I really was and where I had just come over from. I emphatically spelled out how I could not have worn a dress and heels while flying a 727.

As I wouldn't go away and I was holding up her line, the agent called her supervisor over and gave him my story.

"No, she is not in a dress," he pronounced without hesitation. "She's not getting on."

By sheer luck, I had worn a cotton dress on the flight getting down there days ago, which happened to comply with their rules—because it was a dress. But on that first day, I had discarded it on the bathroom floor in my hotel room, and it had gotten wet. Thinking that I wouldn't need it again, I just stuffed it to the bottom of my suitcase and forgot about it.

The agent wasn't going to budge. It was getting close to boarding time and I could come up with a dress, or I could spend the night in the terminal … and then come up with a dress. So, I went into the public restroom and in a filthy toilet stall I rummaged through my suitcase and dug it up. It had the stench of mildew and was absurdly wrinkled. But I climbed out of my clean crisp business suit and pulled the stank, rumpled dress over my head.

I went from polished, professional and clean, to looking like I had been sleeping under a bridge for the last week. I felt like Pig Pen, with my own personal odor cloud choking anyone who got close to me. I looked ridiculous walking out of the bathroom in my crumpled dress — and it was red, so I couldn't hide. But the agent seemed pleased with herself, until she noticed my shoes.

"You need heels."

Oh, for God's sake, even my fake patent leather shoes weren't feminine enough? I dug back into my suitcase until I found the pumps I had originally worn down there. The agent finally handed me my boarding pass with an unmistakable smirk of victory. I kept to myself for the entire flight home, too embarrassed and self-conscious to look anyone in the eye in the confined economy cabin.

I know this rigid idea that a female is dressed appropriately only if she is wearing a dress sounds odd now. But this is how it was in the 1980's. A woman was required to look feminine, and you couldn't look feminine if not in a dress.

It was often frustrating to get so far, only to be suddenly stopped and pushed back into the kitchen. *Why is the kitchen for women anyway? Don't men eat?* Often, it was other women who were pushing me back the hardest. This dichotomy of experiences seemed to trail me everywhere that I went. It was maddening.

It's one kind of challenge when you have to deal with close-minded perspectives or someone who personally doesn't believe you should be there. But when buildings need to be redesigned and long-standing rules rewritten, it takes a lot more than a good attitude and some resilience to get past that.

As much as I felt like I was opening doors for women behind me, it was often women who wanted those doors kept closed. It was days like these that showed me that I could do everything right, but ceilings weren't going to come crashing down just because I could do the job. One person or one act can make changes, but it takes many people sticking together, over time, to make the big changes. I needed to care about the other person's battle and help them to succeed. I came to understand that everybody's world has to change for my world to change.

PART

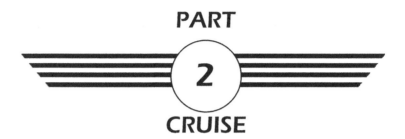

2

CRUISE

TOWING THE LINE

13

The rumble of an aged piston engine low in the sky above me broke the morning fuzz from my thoughts. My eyes followed the noise upward to a taildragger Citabria aircraft with a long banner flowing in the slipstream behind it.

JENKINSON'S BAR 5$ MARGARITA TUESDAY

I should be a banner tow pilot! *Of course.*

My flip-flops flapped across the wooden planks of the boardwalk, the warm sunshine beating onto my bare shoulders as I hustled back to my car, watching the next tow plane fly by, and then the next.

I was taking a break at the Jersey shore after finishing my junior year at Purdue, before settling back home and returning to work at MMU for the summer. As much as I loved everybody there, I was sad to go back to the flight school with Sue and Rick missing and was open to finding something different. Being a Jersey girl, towing banners at the shore seemed the next natural step for me.

Why hadn't I thought of that before?

I hopped in my car and followed the low flying planes to a tiny airstrip just inland from the sandy beaches, to Lakewood Airport. I found the owner of the aerial advertising company, Dave O'Brien, and before I could even complete my sales pitch, he hired me. As luck would have it, Dave's enthusiasm to hire me was due to my flight instructor credentials, not because he needed another tow pilot. I had just earned an additional rating and was a CFII now (certified flight instructor, instrument) and could teach both primary and advanced flight students. Dave O'Brian, and his wife, owned the entire Lakewood Airport operation. They ran a flight school and aerial advertising business out of the only building on the single strip landing field, a simple box trailer planted on cinder blocks in the sand.

Even though what I really wanted was the new experience of towing banners, I was still pumped to be hired. Although I appreciated the standing offer of employment from my first boss at MMU, Fred, I was thrilled when a total stranger wanted to pay me to fly planes. I felt validated.

That summer, I worked at Lakewood Airport assembling banners—hooking letter by letter together by hand, and then laying them out for the tow pilots to swoop down with their grapple hooks swinging, snatch them up and sweep back up into the air with a long message streaming behind them.

I got out of the way just in time to get this picture of Tom swooping down in a Citabria for banner pickup at Lakewood Airport.

I also spent part of my day as a line boy, chugging around the ramp and fueling airplanes.

However, most of my time was spent using my flight instructor certificate teaching ground school and giving flight instruction. Working as a flight instructor was just one of many absurdly low-paying pilot jobs that I enjoyed during the long process of building my flight hours. I didn't know how long this process was going to take, but I hoped that I didn't die along the way.

A number of my flight students tried to kill me daily, and that was acceptable. After all, that is the nature of teaching someone to fly a plane.

I had one student who came seriously close.

Vinnie was a brutish sort of fellow, with an almost cartoonish, condescending attitude towards women. He wasn't particularly tall or good looking, but judging by his arrogance, he considered himself to be Tom Cruise in an F-14 Tomcat. Teaching him was a challenge because he regarded me as a nuisance and ignored anything I said that wasn't unconditional praise for him and his piloting prowess.

When Vinnie reached the cross-country phase of his training, I delved into my navigation lessons. Step-by-step, I struggled to build a flight plan with him, showing him how to read a chart and plot a course calculating in winds and airspeed. We got off to an early start the morning of our first cross-country trip and took off into a warm sunrise on a calm summer day.

We flew from Lakewood, New Jersey, N12, to Allentown, Pennsylvania, ABE, then continued onto the second leg of the trip to my hometown favorite, Morristown, MMU, in North Jersey.

After refueling at MMU, we took off again heading south for our final leg back to Lakewood Airport. Our climb-out brought us over the Great Swamp National Wildlife Refuge in New Jersey. Aptly named, the land below us was miles of sticky green marsh, and I was thankful for every foot we gained in altitude that put more space between us and that mosquito kingdom.

Passing through 2,000 feet in our climb, I was shouting out my lessons over the pounding drone of the piston engine.

"Get the elevator fully trimmed out..." I waited for Vinnie to respond, until I gave up and just spun the trim wheel myself, which moved a tab on the elevator to hold it in place. "Like this, Vinnie." I leaned into the wheel while giving him the side-eye.

"Don't tell me what to do," he rebuffed me.

"Look no hands." I put my hands up in the air to punctuate my point. "See how much easier the climb is with the correct trim input." I continued to shout over the engine noise, shaking my jazz hands in celebration of a job well done, with a goofy smile on my face to catch Vinnie's attention. But he just continued to ignore me.

Abruptly, the engine stopped.

Our propeller came to a sudden halt, the black blade standing vertical in front of us, completely at rest in the most unnatural way against the blue sky.

That got my attention.

Funny how deeply comforting the racket of that old engine was, until it was gone and replaced by the hushed wind whistling past us.

I had practiced "simulated" engine failures with my students with the nonchalance of just another procedure to tick-tock through. But this was unexpected and so very real. It was shocking. A dreadful feeling soaked through my entire body, both numbing and electrifying me from head-to-toe in an instant.

I wasn't scared, I was busy. This engine failure meant that I had a procedure to accomplish, right now.

"Okay Vinnie, I've got it." I snatched up my control yoke with one hand, eying a flat spot in the green goop below us where we could glide into, while I stepped through the memorized engine restart checklist with my other hand.

```
Airspeed..........................................60K
Carb Heat........................................ON
Primer...............................IN/LOCKED
Fuel Shut-off Valve.........................ON
Mixture.........................................RICH
Ignition Sw....................START then BOTH
```

"I've got it." Vinnie's detached voice echoed back. His face was expressionless and his eyes blank, as he tightened his grip on *his* control yoke and pulled back.

"Let go." I ordered him.

Did we really need to do this *who's in charge dance* now?

"I've got it." Vinnie snapped back louder, defiantly pulling the nose up higher and higher above the horizon. I watched our precious airspeed roll back.

The plane isn't going to climb with no power, you idiot.

"Dammit, let go. Let go NOW, Vinnie!"

The stall warning horn started shrieking and a feeling of panic swept through me. Vinnie's face remained locked in a zombie-like stare at our dead propeller and the empty sky above it.

Bottom line: Vinnie was stronger than me. A lot stronger. There was no way I could overpower him and break his dead-man's grip on the control yoke. As if having our engine die wasn't bad enough, we were now frighteningly close to stalling out and spinning down into The Great Swamp. Kerrrrr-plop into mosquito heaven.

Certain that this goon was about to kill us both, I grabbed the metal gust lock resting in the seat pocket and started whacking his knuckles, until he shook awake from his trance and released his grip. We lost one thousand feet in the end, but the engine restart procedure worked and I climbed our plane back up and continued on. We arrived back at Lakewood, both equally angry at each other, exhausted and stuck to our vinyl seats in sweat.

After a full inspection, the mechanic determined some residual water in the fuel line caused the engine to quit. *So much for trusting the fuel check to my student.*

The bigger issue here, though, was the conflict between Vinnie and myself. My boss Dave, himself a big guy, fully got the picture after listening to Vinnie's version of events. Vinnie complained that I had taken the airplane away from him when the engine quit, and he boasted to Dave that he planned to show me who was in charge on our next flight.

Dave's response was to switch Vinnie from my schedule over to the biggest guy that worked for him.

Yes, Tom was a big guy. I was a small gal. Pulling me out and replacing me with this 6' 4" man was a screaming misogynistic statement and didn't help women get ahead anywhere. But in this case, it was the smartest thing my boss could have done. Even though I felt defeated, I laughed about it more. Needless to say, this smart move did solve the problem. Vinnie lost his macho bluster with Tom, and shortly after that he quit taking flying lessons.

Tom was a handsome guy, just a few years older than me with a frock of curly hair and endearing boyish smile. Our friendship grew into my first romance. Tom and I understood each other's world, and the same things made us both tick. We fit together like two puzzle pieces. When he took over flying with Vinnie to keep me safe, it felt like my knight in shining armor was saving me from the evil villager. The girl in me liked that feeling.

Sometimes, it's okay to accept tried-and-true traditional roles and limitations. We all have our strengths and weaknesses, and some of those can't be chosen. I found that I liked feeling protected and safe under Tom's umbrella. He had my back, and I had his.

I taught at several different airports over the years, and although each of my flight students had a different back story, they all came to the airport excited to be there. With an occasional exception, they were older than me. Much older. As one mature gentleman put it, he was here to finally fulfill his "boyhood dream" to learn how to fly. That felt pretty good to be a part of.

Not every one of my students had waited until later in life to get started. Several were young and very much like I had been only a few years earlier, fearless and naive. But I can only recall one student who was as crazy as I had been.

John Duetsch may have even topped me as an adventurous teenage student pilot, and I was *the* instructor who would indulge his spirited ideas.

Looking back at my old logbook, I had labeled one of John's original maneuvers the "Short Door Landing." The four seat C172, which we trained in, was the most basic of planes. John came up with a unique idea for homemade speedbrakes. Speedbrakes are the panels that pop up on the wings of a large jetliner, to create drag and slow an aircraft down after landing. Somehow, John convinced me to go along with his idea.

Okay, he didn't exactly twist my arm.

On touchdown, we would both push open our doors and hold them wide open, creating huge speedbrakes to maximize drag, and see just how short we could stop the plane on the runway. This, incidentally, was also a great test to see how reliable our seatbelts were.

I can't say how effective this technique actually was aerodynamically, but let's just say Boeing engineers were not knocking on our doors looking for new design patents. The thrill of throwing the doors open and hanging out over the tires bouncing down the runway, held in place by nothing more than our frayed seatbelts, was a fun enough reason to "test" out this aerodynamic concept.

More than a decade after I had lost track of virtually all of my flight students, I ran into John. We both started off as teenage pilots at MMU, and we both ended up as professional, commercial airline pilots for United Airlines. Who saw that coming? Life is funny like that. I'm glad I did right by people, because I just never knew when they would pop up again in my future. This seemed especially true in the aviation community.

It wasn't until after my college graduation and well into my tenure as a flight instructor that my mother came up in an airplane with me.

One quiet summer day, I finally convinced my mom to take a flight with me. She made the drive to the airport, but then she wouldn't actually get into the airplane with me unless there was another pilot onboard. By another pilot, she meant a man.

No one ever says "no" to free flight time, so it was easy to grab one of the guys hanging around the flight school to come along with us. But having this anonymous male onboard wasn't good enough. Mom sat herself in the backseat of my plane to make sure *he* had full access to the flight controls in the front seat, next to me, just in case.

To make this perfectly clear, I had way more experience and flight time than this guy, who my mom had never met and didn't know from a hole in the wall. But *now* she felt safe and would get in the airplane, because there was a man sitting behind the controls.

I took mom up and flew her over our house in New Providence. Next I headed over to Lake Hopatcong for the pretty view and then I brought her back to the airport for a picture-perfect landing.

Safely on the ground, Mom exhaled, "That was a nice flight, La La" *Yes, that's what my mom calls me.* Then she felt the need to explain to me that she was watching the "pilot's" face the whole time to see if he looked scared. He never touched the controls once and appeared calm throughout the entire experience, so mom said she felt okay then, too.

"Did you even look out the window, Mom?" I asked, trying to put my finger on what she had just told me.

"No, not really." She shook her head with a smile.

This was my Mom's version of supporting me, and I could hardly complain about her making the effort. Hoping that she would trust me enough to sit next to me, much less look out the window was too much to ask for. My mom snapped a picture of me in front of the plane we flew before heading home, and then she closed that chapter, her obligation fulfilled.

My mother took this picture of me right after her first and only flight with me.

That was the first and last time my mom has ever flown with me. To this day, my dad has never flown in an airplane with me. Any airplane. Ever.

I took whatever I could get. Feeling grateful kept me happy.

"DONNA JUANA, THE WRIGHT BROTHERS ARE CALLING"

From the moment I graduated college, I found myself perpetually mailing out resumes as I worked various jobs at different airports — flight instructing, flying charters, ferrying airplanes, New York City sightseeing tours, repossessing aircraft, and one of my favorite assignments — taking up shutterbugs for aerial photography.

A very regular client was an elderly photojournalist with the most energetic smile. "Hello, sir, I'll be your pilot today. Where would you like me to take you?" I introduced myself on our first flight together.

"How old do you think I am?" he challenged me. He was exceptionally wrinkled, and this is how he introduced himself to everyone. "Go ahead, guess." He dared me.

"Oh, I don't know … about 102?" I looked at him, poker face serious.

"Ahhh, I like you!" He roared with laughter. "We are going to get along marvelously."

I don't know how old he really was, but he certainly appreciated a good laugh over cautious etiquette. Everybody needed something different to feel comfortable with me as their pilot, and I developed the skill of reading exactly what that was.

One of the most impressive students that I ever taught was a high-level executive for Johnson & Johnson, Inc. Charles was a picture-perfect example of a successful life. He was well dressed, intelligent, had plenty of extra money, and he loved his wife. Charles was just a happy, positive gentleman to be around.

"Laura, it is such a pleasure working with you, and you are so capable." Charles shook my hand good-bye after one of our flight lessons. "I'd really like you to consider leaving your position here and coming to work for Johnson and Johnson. You would have a very bright future there." Charles went on to flatter me to no end, telling me how a young, sharp woman like myself would excel at Johnson & Johnson. I had my doubts that I deserved so much of his confidence, but with all of this praise I sure felt like soft-soap in his hands.

I could be so sure of something in life and solidly on-track to achieve it, then a shiny object would catch my eye and my head would turn. It can be a fine-line between chasing that shiny object, versus being open minded and flexible to new ideas.

I had never considered walking away from aviation for anything else, and certainly not for the corporate world. I surprised myself, though, and didn't immediately tell him "No."

Other than being a loyal consumer of Band-Aids and Tylenol, I knew absolutely nothing about Johnson & Johnson. I had no qualifications to work for this corporate giant. I had no skills or education to do anything other than fly planes. But I respected Charles and enjoyed flying with him. I knew he was high up in the company, and he seemed to be guaranteeing me a fine future, under his protective wing in the corporate world. I appreciated that although I didn't earn this offer, it was indeed an opportunity and I should think it over.

Did I really want to continue making no money, working towards an improbable dream that might never pan out? Sue, Rick and Jimmy's deaths weighed into my decision, too.

I felt obligated to at least look at other career options, and I carefully considered everything Charles put on the table for me.

In the end, I declined his generous offer.

I emerged from my internal debate appreciating even more deeply just how much I loved being up in the air. Considering another possible career only solidified my decision that I wanted to spend my days in the sky, not an office, and flying was the right way for *me* to earn a living.

I had to follow my gut.

One really never knows what is around the next corner. Life is full of unexpected chances and choices. I had always believed that hard work, combined with determination, was the only way to find success. Even though I walked away from that job offer, I learned that sometimes it really is *who* you know that opens doors.

Not for me. Not this time. But I still learned how important connections could be to one's success.

Just before Christmas, one of my floating resumes landed on the right desk at the right time. I was invited for an interview with a midnight freight company named Wright International Express.

This was a big company, based in Cincinnati, Ohio. They flew everything from twin props, up to Lear jets, moving cancelled checks around the country during the night. All of their planes appeared normal on the outside, but the interiors were completely gutted to accommodate freight, not passengers. This was a salaried position and a good job. Well, good for a pilot who was willing to do anything to build flight hours.

The interview went well.

I was hired to fly as a single pilot on a twin prop Cessna 310 during the night, hauling cancelled checks out of Teterboro, New Jersey, TEB, to about a dozen different airports up and down the East Coast.

For my flight training, I was shipped out to Cincinnati, LUK, on one of their night freighter flights. I was given a spot on the cold, bare floor of a disemboweled Lear 35, curled up in the hollowed metal tube between shipping crates in the tail of the jet. I was thrown back there with another pilot, a young guy who was also just hired and headed to LUK for flight training. With no passengers to think about, the pilots up front didn't have to concern themselves with flying smoothly, and it turned out to be a crazy rollercoaster ride for us, rolling around in the innards of this jet among the boxes in the pitch black. We roared with laughter at our ludicrous circumstances throughout the entire flight, daring the other to try to stand as we each kept falling over the boxes and each other.

I jumped through all of the written exams and flight training hoops in Cincinnati, got Part 135 certified (legal to pilot a commercial air carrier with fewer than 30 seats) and eagerly headed back to New Jersey to begin my life in the freight-dog world. Very quickly, though, I figured out that flying these stripped-down Cessna 310s throughout the night was a horrific job.

Why?

Not because my planes' interiors were eviscerated to make room for freight, and I had boxes of cancelled checks sliding around and banging into my seat as I flew.

Not because it was the dead of winter and I spent nights shivering on frozen tarmacs and flying into bleak, iced over airports.

Not because the hours were dreadful, and it felt like the whole world was asleep, except for me. *Who wouldn't want to live like an owl?*

Not because I was alone on the airplane, far removed from other people and any hope of human contact. I could deal with the loneliest and most isolated job above the planet.

It was horrific because the planes I flew were absurdly ill-equipped for the high-density northeast flight corridor, the complex airport navigational requirements, and the harsh winter weather that I was flying into.

And because these planes were falling apart.

The call sign for my company was "Don Juan." Being clever, I sometimes identified myself as "Donna Juana" to the air traffic controller. *Cute huh?* But never when things were going wrong.

"Don Juan 315. Fly direct MILTT. Expect the ILS runway 4R approach." The Boston air traffic controller directed me to fly to the locator outer marker at 3 a.m., to navigate an instrument approach into Logan International Airport, BOS.

"Don Juan 315. Unable. Unequipped." This was one of those times I was not being cute with the controller.

"Don Juan 315. Confirm, your ADF is inoperative?"

"Don Juan 315. Negative. I don't have an ADF." It felt crazy even saying this. I didn't have the most basic navigational instrument, an automatic direction finder, which is simply a round dial with a needle that points to a station on the ground. I didn't have even the most fundamental tool to find a runway. *Amelia Earhart had an ADF on her plane.*

This is how it went. It was pitiful. I was flying alone, in the dark, in treacherous winter conditions — and I had insanely inadequate navigational equipment. My instruments were Stone Age leftovers. The company should have been called Caveman Express.

"Caveman 315. The Wright brothers want their plane back."

But I still kept coming back every night to do it all over again. Until one night.

I was watching the ramp workers load my plane, stuffing box after box into the rear fuselage, until the whole plane started to tip backwards, leaving the nose wheel suspended up in the air by a few inches. That's how far aft the CG (center of gravity) was. No matter what the loader told me, this plane had to be over maximum gross weight and out of balance.

That didn't stop me.

The right engine nacelle was wrapped in duct tape. What I'm saying is, the engine housing was literally held together by sticky silver tape.

That didn't stop me either.

Not only was snow and slick patches of ice already plastered over my aircraft wings, and all I had was a broom to feebly clear them off with, but I would be flying into known icing conditions and my plane was not equipped with deicing boots on the leading edges, or any deicing equipment at all.

No, that still didn't stop me.

My good friend and fellow flight instructor, Rick, left MMU for a job just like this one, flying midnight freight for a comparable company. He was killed one night, in very similar circumstances. I thought about him.

Did he struggle with the decision to take off, like I was doing right now? Would he do it all differently if given the chance, like I was being given right now?

But, that still didn't stop me.

No, I took my seat in the cockpit, started the engines and ran through the checklist. When I checked the magnetos, only one of them was testing properly on the right engine, the engine with the duct tape. *Uh oh.*

This is why there is a checklist — to check things.

Wait a second. I have a bad magneto?

I sat there and fretted over this. Magnetos are units that ensure continuous engine ignition. They are critically important.

I had to go. I had a schedule to keep.

Hey, each engine has two magnetos for a reason, I rationalized in my head. My "back-up" magneto was working. My engines sounded just fine.

But I sat there, the engines drumming along, my propellers blowing up snow and ice behind me, the ramp workers cursing me out, waving at me to get moving.

I have to go. I have a schedule to keep.

Then, I chickened out. I was afraid.

What if that engine failed over the timberlands in Connecticut or Massachusetts?

What if on my way to Boston I lost my engine over some forest, while overweight?

I would auger-in. That's what would happen.

I could not maintain altitude on one engine, while overweight, in icing conditions. I would go down fast. And how could I ever find a clearing to make an emergency landing in the dark, if I even got the chance to try for an emergency landing?

The melodramatic "made for TV" re-enactment was playing in my head. It was a Why Planes Crash documentary on stupid deaths that involved fire.

What if I pulled a Rick? The thought shuddered through my heart.

I shut down the engines, climbed out of the plane, and walked to an airport payphone to call my boss in Cincinnati.

I was completely honest with him.

"I can't do it."

"What do you mean you can't do it? That's the job. This isn't United Airlines, missy. You're a freight dog!"

I apologized and hung up the phone, then walked straight to the employee parking lot, got in my car and drove home. I simply abandoned my fully loaded plane on the ramp.

What did I just do?

I walked away from my aviation career, that's what I did.

It was over.

I would be blacklisted as a pilot. I could already picture myself covered in red spots, from future employers touching me with a ten-foot pole. But that wasn't my biggest problem. No, it was the painful self-realization that I didn't have the guts to be a pilot. I didn't have the right stuff after all. I felt ashamed for being scared. I was a quitter. I hated myself.

I should have taken the job at Johnson & Johnson.

The next morning, I checked the news for any small plane crashes. Nothing.

In my absence, someone else took my seat last night and made it. I cried like I have never cried before. I was a failure.

I had felt fear before, but only as a response when something bad was happening. Fear had energized me to act in an emergency. It had kept me alive. But fear had never deterred me from going up in the air to start with. Fear had kept me on the ground this time, and that had never happened before.

I can't recall ever feeling so beaten down. I was deeply disappointed in myself.

For a solid week, I just wanted to be left alone as I grieved the loss of my dream. All the negative self-talk inside my head kept me from sleeping. I punched my pillow out of self-loathing, all night long. I sobbed in the shower every morning. I rehearsed how I was going to admit defeat to my parents, and I cursed myself for not having a backup plan.

I was in mourning. I was pathetic. Ben & Jerry became my midnight buddies.

My self-confidence had been badly thumped. Quitting felt unsettling and defeating to the core of who I was, and I allowed myself to wallow in it. My feelings all came up to the surface until they spilled out of me.

But failure is a funny thing. I cried until I was done. Then I was empty and I got bored with myself, and I got over it.

Hell no, I wasn't going to quit. The plane was falling apart.

I was going to find a better job.

WHATEVER IT TAKES

15

I can promise you that nobody's "dream-come-true" ever just fell into their lap. We all know and expect to have to put forth hard work, to get what we want out of life. And yes, it's commonly understood that "who" you know can make a difference, too.

But what I didn't see in the self-help books or college brochures, is that sometimes I would need to just suck it up and live however I had to live, because I was "getting" to where I wanted to be.

After I updated my resume with my last place of employment, I started mailing it out again. Though I was no longer employed as a freight-dog and I did not want any future employer to call my last company for a reference, those twin Cessna 310 night hours were right there in my logbook, and I couldn't hide them. I would have preferred to bury this period of my aviation career. But in the end, I knew I had to own it and put it out there to get on with my life.

After hugging everyone good-bye at MMU when I had quit to go fly freight, my ego could hardly go back there for my old job. I found a new position flight instructing at an airport where I hadn't worked at before, Caldwell Airport, CDW, in Northern New Jersey. This turned out to be the airport which John F. Kennedy Jr. based his own airplane and departed from on his last flight.

This wasn't exactly a better job. I hadn't found that, yet. But it was a job. I was still building flight hours, and I soon fell back into the comfortable routine of flight instructing.

Quicker than I expected, I received a phone call from the chief pilot for Precision Valley Aviation at the Manchester-Boston Regional Airport, MHT, in New Hampshire. Precision was a regional airline that operated as Eastern Express, feeding the mainline carrier Eastern Airlines from remote locations. Their planes were painted in the Eastern Airlines livery, seats were marketed and purchased through the Eastern Airlines reservation system, their printed tickets were labeled Eastern Airlines, and their employee uniforms said Eastern Airlines. As far as the public was concerned, this was Eastern Airlines. That's how regionals work: the smaller aircraft painted in major air carrier livery are actually separate companies.

"Your credentials are just what we are looking for." The chief pilot got right down to business. "I see you are already Part 135 qualified. I'd like to schedule you to come in for an interview."

"Um, well yes ... not really. I quit that job."

"But you had that job. You passed the Part 135 checkride, yes?"

"Well, yes I did, but ... " I don't know why, but I felt guilty that the job I walked away from was turning out to be the job that this Chief Pilot liked best on my resume. It didn't matter, though, because he didn't let me finish my sentence.

"I don't care. I wouldn't risk my life flying that freight garbage, either. If you passed the checkride, then you can fly a plane. So, can you come in for an interview?" he continued, sounding as if he had pen in hand to write me into his calendar.

"Well, yes."

And with that, I dug my navy-blue business suit out of the back of my closet and headed to Manchester, New Hampshire for an interview.

I was hired.

Although this airline wasn't my ultimate goal, I was indeed an airline pilot now. For real.

I went to ground school, flight training, and successfully qualified in the Dornier 228; a German built, twenty-one seat, twin turboprop, passenger transport aircraft. Not only was this an amazing aircraft to operate, but for the first time I wasn't flying the plane all alone. I was one of two pilots in the cockpit. On top of my workload being cut in half, I finally had someone to talk to.

Eastern Airlines Express Dornier 228

To add icing on my cake, I soon found the real charm of working for an airline was how much was done behind the scenes to make the pilot's life easier. I had professional schedulers, licensed dispatchers, gate agents, and mechanics all working with me, and I became a part of a system of people.

In addition to the other pilot sitting beside me, I quickly learned to depend on hard-working colleagues and could drop my Superwoman, do it all myself, attitude. Another bonus was that I was flying humans, not boxes.

This was undeniably a better job.

I had to pay for my own uniform and flight bag, as I would for every airline I would ever work for, but for the first time I was issued the contents that went *inside* my flight bag. My plane might have been smaller than what the big boys were flying, but my official "airline pilot" flight bag was just as heavy, coming in at thirty-two pounds.

What exactly is in this black leather box that all pilots hauled around? It's part library; stocked with engineer-worthy technical manuals, approach plates and navigational charts; part Home Depot with an assortment of tools, flashlights and duct tape; and part personal survival kit for those long days with Band-Aids, granola bars and Pop Tarts. *Hey, even Amelia Earhart had to eat.*

My base assignment was Lebanon Municipal Airport, LEB, in New Hampshire, which meant that was where my flight schedule began and ended each day. I arrived broke and I made pitiful little money working for a regional airline, like everyone else. My previous pay for hauling boxes was literally twice what I was earning now carrying people. Our salaries were below the poverty level, and we were eligible for food stamps, which I never collected, though a number of the pilots did.

I needed to find someplace to live, and group living was the solution. Having virtually no money was not my only problem. I was the *one* female pilot in Lebanon, and the guys in my new hire class had already grouped up with each other into "bro-cliques." To find housing, I had to fit into an all-male group of strangers comfortably enough to live with them.

So, I thought, here we go — not sure if disaster or adventure lay just ahead.

I found my group and pooled my money together with three other homeless pilots from my new hire class. We rented a neglected cabin on the side of a small, picturesque ski mountain in Quechee, Vermont. This little wooden house was in such a remote setting, there was no mail delivery and we had to invest in a P.O. Box in town to receive our paychecks.

We were all so laughably short on money, we smuggled "free" supplies from the airport to take home. We swiped toilet paper from the public restrooms, garbage bags off the janitor's cart, we filled our kitchen drawer full of condiments in little packets, and the only silverware we had was the plastic kind we pilfered from the airport snack shop. Ramen Noodles and Kraft cheese slices on Wonder Bread became my core diet.

Sanitation workers were not municipal employees in our area, so you had to hire a private garbage collection service to pick up your trash. In no way did we have extra funds for that luxury, so we let the garbage pile up in our kitchen until eventually moving the trash to a heap in our basement … and let it rot. It was disgusting.

All of these little inconveniences paled against the brutal cold temperatures we endured. In the winter, it regularly dipped to thirty below zero at night on our little mountain. Our heating bill was insane, so we turned the heat on just enough to keep our pipes from freezing. I could

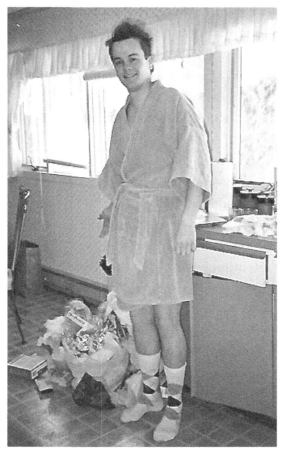

My roomie Chris. We were garbage proud.

never escape the cold and went to bed fully clothed in my winter parka, hat, gloves, snow boots, and I wrapped myself like a burrito in the only blanket that I had.

As cold as our cabin was, my car was even colder, icing over in the driveway each night. I would routinely drive to work in the pre-dawn hours with my windshield completely caked in snow and ice, except for the tiny circle that I would chisel clean to peer through.

As numbing cold as my car was, our hollow alloy planes were even colder, resting on the sub-zero tarmac overnight. It wasn't until after takeoff and we had climb power, that the engines could pump sufficient warm air into the cabin and I could finally take off my hat, scarf and gloves and fly the plane unencumbered. I would already be up in the air when the sun finally rose and chased the cold and dark away, bringing the freshness of a new morning.

We flew excruciatingly long days at Eastern Express, six days a week, feeding Newark, LaGuardia, Boston, and Philadelphia from remote mountainous airports in the upper states. One typical day of flying started at 5:00 a.m. and looked like this: LEB-RUT-ALB-EWR-ALB-RUT-ALB-EWR-ALB-RUT-LEB. I would fly this day without once getting off the plane. We had no flight attendants, no auto-pilot and flew raw data approaches at every airport. This means we flew everything by hand and had no magenta line to follow, leaving us to find that tiny piece of paved runway by interpreting swinging needles on rudimentary round gauges and reading paper charts. Most days our attention was divided between our instruments inside the cockpit, dangerous weather outside our windows, and refereeing whatever chaos was brewing among our passengers seated behind us.

If we didn't have low visibility, we had low ceilings, or icing conditions, or thunderstorms, or snowstorms, or turbulence, or crosswind landings with gusts to thirty-six knots. With constant takeoffs and landings, we didn't have time to get above the weather, so we just powered through it. In the middle of all this, we had passengers climbing out of their seats and walking around the cabin, pitching the CG (center of gravity) of our aircraft back and forth. We didn't have cockpit doors, and sometimes they would wander up front just to see what we were doing.

"Excuse me sir, you need to sit down." I leaned out of the cockpit as far as my headset cord could reach.

"I'm looking for the bathroom," the passenger yelled back, then walked up to me as if I desired to have a conversation with him in the middle of our approach into Newark, EWR.

"We don't have a bathroom. Please sir, I need you to sit down."

The captain gave me *the look* as he struggled to keep our nose from pitching down as this two-hundred-and-thirty-pound man shifted his weight from the rear of the plane, where I had strategically placed him at the beginning of our flight to balance the aircraft, to the front.

"So, what's that lake we just flew over?" The passenger decided that since he had my attention, this was an invitation to chat.

"Please sir, sit down now!"

And with that, this passenger settled himself into the front row, exactly where I had told him he couldn't sit when he boarded the plane.

When one person got up, other passengers generally viewed this as permission for them to get up, too. One passenger talking to the pilots would become a free-for-all, and soon everyone would start wandering up to the cockpit to strike up a conversation with their pilots.

Maybe flying boxes wasn't so bad?

Even if people stayed in their seats, we were perpetually on display in the cockpit, with eyes watching our every move. That may have been the most stressful part of the job. Depending on the moment, I felt like a celebrity or a trained seal.

Once on the ground, I needed to race around the cabin to clean whatever mess our passengers left behind, before the next group of passengers climbed onboard. I was regularly stunned by the trash stuffed into seatback pockets and cushion cracks, everything from dirty diapers to filled vomit bags. Years later flying for United Airlines, I had a deep appreciation for our cabin cleaners — who swept through each aircraft between flights, taking care of all of this after the passengers and flight attendants had emptied out. As much as I disliked my cabin cleaning duties, the truly repulsive part of my job was chasing the oily, bacteria-infested rats away from our plane at LaGuardia airport. These city rats would get bold at night and aggressively come out in packs with their noses twitching to swarm around our planes, which were parked by the side of the terminal building. Our passengers had to walk outside to board our Dorniers, and my job was to shoo the rats away before our passengers stepped onto the ramp. No joke, this was a serious responsibility. I felt like I was saving my people from the Bubonic Plague.

The flying was phenomenal hands-on experience. Every flight required constant mental calculations blended with physical coordination that energized all of my senses. I loved the challenges, and I even loved the inane distractions that would pop up. I was living an amazing life, but there were definitely moments that I could have done without, and that was about to become clear.

RIDE 'EM, COWBOY

For some of the guys who had been at this for years, the long days and intense flying led to some crankiness. Or maybe it was cockiness. Or maybe it was just exhaustion that gave way to feeling entitled to make their own rules and take short cuts.

Maybe it was all of the above.

Our routes from big city civilization to the sparse upper states were always over treacherous landscapes. Except for some tricky approaches into several remote airports in mountainous terrain, not much thought was given to the land below us, though.

While still a newbie first officer (co-pilot) for Eastern Express, I was enroute from LaGuardia, LGA, to Rutland, Vermont, RUT, one late night after an extraordinarily long day of demanding flying. Reaching the outer boundary of the busy New York airspace, my captain, Reece, cancelled our IFR (instrument flight rules) flight plan and dismissed the air traffic controllers from tracking our flight any longer. In clear weather, this was common and routine for "Express" flights to do. As Part 135 carriers, we weren't bound by the same tight rules as our Part 121 major air carrier counterparts, though the flying public wouldn't know this.

Now free to do whatever we liked, Reece left the published airway we were tracking and pointed our aircraft directly to our destination. Flying a straight line is always nice. *Who doesn't like a short cut when you're super tired late at night?*

With nothing but rural mountains and forested countryside flowing beneath us, there was no hint of civilization, or any light, rising from the ground. A thick layer of clouds drifted in and filled the dark abyss above us. The overcast sky blocked out the moonlight and stars, putting us into blackout conditions as the sky turned as dark and shapeless as the rural terrain below us. Having no outside cues, our eyes focused on our instrument panel to tell us which way was right-side up.

But if you are *not* on a published airway and you are *not* talking to an air traffic controller, then you don't want to get cavalier about the topography when you can't see it. You want to keep your distance from the ground and anything rising up from the ground.

Reece was at the controls. Since he had cancelled our flight plan, by law we were required to stay out of the clouds. Trying to stay beneath the overcast layer thickening above us, he was cruising along below the minimum terrain elevation figure on our sectional chart.

"I've got this Laura," he assured me. "I know this terrain and this route to the airport like the back of my hand."

Hey Reece, it's too dark to see the back of your hand.

Unlike Reece, I did not think I had every detail of the terrain memorized. I also did not know this route, because it existed solely in Reece's head. What I did know was that my flashlight was highlighting high terrain on my sectional chart, with peaks and valleys. And by high terrain, I mean higher than us.

"Reece, we're too low." I was starting to get that worried feeling, but with no door between us and our passengers, I kept my voice hushed and my facial expression blank.

"No, we're good." He dismissed me.

I tapped my foot nervously and bit on my lip as long as I could, which wasn't long. "Reece, I don't know where we are." I was definitely sounding worried now.

"Don't worry. I do."

Apparently, we were on the "Reece Highway" in the sky.

Again, I restrained myself as long as I could. "Reece, we really are too low. We need to climb." I was nagging him now.

"No, Laura," he scolded me, not sounding nasty, but more like he was exasperated. "If we climb into the overcast, we would have to get an IFR clearance." He continued to speak to me as if he were a tired parent correcting a toddler. "You see that light there in the distance. That's a beacon, and I know exactly where that is. I follow it every night. I know precisely where we are. We're good."

Yes, there was one lonely light visible at eye-level up ahead. It was nothing more than a single isolated beacon, miles off in the distance.

"I don't know. We're really low. I can't see the terrain around us at all."

"Laura, I've got this." Now he was getting irritated with me.

My foot was tapping furiously. "Reece, please, we need to climb. I don't recognize that beacon."

Finally, Reece snapped at me. He didn't yell. It was more of a "you don't have my experience, so leave me alone," kind of frustration.

"Okay, Laura, listen to me."

I listened, and I never forgot what he said to me at that moment.

"Sometimes you just need to shut your mouth and take it for granted that your captain knows what he's doing."

I had no comeback for this.

Actually, I thought that made sense. I did not have the experience that he had. He'd been flying these routes for a long time. He was an "old salt," as much as you can be at twenty-six years old. Maybe I was being a Nervous Nellie? Who wants to fly with her? Do I want *that* to be my reputation?

"Oh Shit!" shot out of Reece's mouth, as he slammed us into an intense climb with full thrust.

"That's the wrong light." He grunted through clenched molars.

Reece shot our aircraft straight up into the cloud layer, and I reflexively radioed air traffic control to put us back on a flight plan and back into radar contact. Reece didn't apologize to me, but I did apologize to our passengers.

There really is no hiding things when the passengers are looking right at you.

I turned and smiled and nodded as I spoke, as if this was the normal way us cowboys fly these little ol' planes. "Sorry about that abrupt climb, folks." Then I continued my announcement with a weather update and expected arrival time, as everyone cocked their head to stare at me. I found that almost anything said while completely calm comes off as believable to people, despite whatever evidence may be screaming the opposite around them.

Although Reece had been outwardly ignoring my concerns, my incessant badgering actually did push him to rethink our situation. I'm glad I'd spoken up, but I also grasped how I had allowed Reece to sway me away from my confidence in my own knowledge, and from my gut feelings.

After that night, I never took it for granted that the captain "just knew what he was doing." I never just "shut my mouth" again. And years later, as a captain myself, I always listened to what my first officer had to say. That night made me a safer pilot, and a better and braver person.

I carried this lesson that "my voice counted," and "everyone's knowledge and input mattered," with me everywhere in life.

BIG ZERO

17

"Two dollars says my first officer can juggle these eggs." Reece jiggled an egg in his hand as if he were holding dice.

I played along and made a stupid look. *Who me? I can't juggle.*

"No way, she can't juggle," snorted Stan, one of the captains from another domicile who didn't know me. "Okay I'll take your two bucks. But you're going to be in trouble when she drops them." He rolled his eyes. "You're not allowed to touch the freight, but it's your job, not mine."

I actually had mad juggling skills and could juggle just about anything my captains could pull out of our cargo hold, including eggs. This was another easy two bucks for Reece today.

"I want my cut," I chuckled as we walked away, but Reece just tucked the dollar bills into his shirt pocket.

As worn out as all of us pilots were, we still had the energy to keep up with inside jokes and running gags, especially if it meant making a little money. Reece never did give me a cut from his wagers, but he was always happy to fly with me. My piloting skills earned me respect, but I kept my captains laughing too, and that kind of approval was worth a lot more than two dollars.

There are exceptions to everything, though. One pilot hated me. Somebody regularly vandalized my company cubbyhole, sticking gum inside my headset or cutting up my uniform tie when I left it in there. This anonymous pilot would tear ads out of magazines for fat reduction pills or deodorant, and stuff them in my box after labeling them with marker — *Laura, this might help you.*

One afternoon, I was walking and talking with a mechanic when I stopped at my cubbyhole to pick up my company mail. I reached in and pulled out a book titled *Zero,* with a handwritten note stuck in between the pages reading, *Laura's memoir.* I knew that book had come out of the passenger lost and found box.

"Oh, that's just mean," the mechanic reacted. Everyone in the station knew this was happening to me, but no one would tell me who was behind it.

"Who is doing this?" I found myself pleading with this mechanic, yet another colleague who claimed to know who was behind this but wouldn't tell me.

"That's not right," he responded sympathetically. "This isn't funny any longer. I told him to stop already." This mechanic felt for me, but he still wouldn't give up the bully's name.

I never did find out who was behind this harassment, or what this person had against me. But I always assumed it was one of the male pilots who did not like the idea of a female pilot invading his territory, and I was the only one in the base. Whoever it was, I bet I got hired by the majors before he did, and I got my revenge without even knowing it.

We serviced dramatically varied destinations from major international airports to tiny little air strips hidden in the ski mountains of Vermont, and the government had a hand in controlling that. Our company was subsidized to fly to certain airports that were non-profitable to service. They were non-profitable because the traveling public had little interest in flying to them. Providing required scheduled service, we often ferried empty planes in and out of these remote locations. This led to tempting circumstances for young venturesome pilots.

A rumor raced through our pilot ranks one afternoon.

"Did you hear, a couple of our guys flew under a bridge on their way to Montpelier this morning?"

"Are you kidding me?" I thought that was cool.

No, wait. Not cool.

"They are going to be fired," I lamented.

I was impressed, but I also knew this was going to end badly for these guys.

They were fired.

Not only that, they also received violations from the FAA. Just like that, they would never get a job as an airline pilot again. They were finished.

I had always pushed the limits when I could myself, but I knew where the line was. I wasn't even tempted to try a trick like that in a commercial passenger aircraft, even an empty one.

Well, maybe I was tempted — but I knew better.

I felt bad for these pilots, but I scratched my head over how they could have possibly thought they would get away with a stunt like that.

Once every ten weeks, we got a scheduled break of five days off from flying. This was a very anticipated reprieve from our exhausting schedules. Once my rotation off just happened to fall over Christmas, so I flew home to New Jersey to visit my parents for the week. I was happy to spend the holidays with my family. But undeniably, I was more excited to sleep in a warm house, take a shower without shivering, and have a kitchen fully stocked by mom with actual silverware to eat with.

After Christmas trying to hop on a plane back to the Lebanon airport was a nightmare. Personally knowing the pilots flying these planes had no pull whatsoever, and I was bumped from every flight departing EWR, until the last flight of the day left without me. You would think flying free is a great perk … until you try to fly standby over the holidays.

My parents charitably offered to drive me back to my house in Vermont the next morning. They are helpful like that, but I also think my mom was curious to see where exactly I lived and who exactly I lived with.

We made good time on the drive up. When we arrived, I invited my parents to come in for a little tour of our humble cabin. It was the middle of the day and none of my three male roommates were home. To my relief, the cabin looked pretty cleaned up in my absence, at least to me.

Until we walked into the kitchen. I admit, there was more garbage than usual spilled across the kitchen floor, and the smell was nauseating.

"This kitchen is a mess!" my mother exclaimed; a bit overly dramatic for the situation.

"Oh yeah, somebody forgot to carry the trash down to the basement." I shrugged it off.

And with that, my mother's eyes swelled with tears and she sputtered, "You lack natural female instinct," as mascara puddled beneath her eyes.

"I wasn't even here, Mom. How could *I* have kept the kitchen clean?"

"Keeping a clean kitchen is *your* duty. You should be upset," my mother stammered, obviously deeply troubled over my lack of concern for this situation. I should have been traumatized to walk into a messy kitchen. I should have felt instinctively compelled and duty-bound to clean up the mess left by the boys, with not a thought to the fact that it wasn't my mess.

That's how strongly my mother felt about time-honored, conventional gender roles.

I respect my mother and admire her success in achieving what she wanted out of life. But much like I had outgrown buzzing people or the desire to fly under bridges, I had long grown to understand that I would never cry over spilled trash in the kitchen. I was working towards something larger.

THE CASE OF THE MISSING LUNCHMEAT

"I'm missing a slice. Definitely missing a slice."

My roomie Chris looked across the kitchen, waving his plastic package of Oscar Mayer bologna in the air with a look of irritation on his face. "Who got into *my* bologna?" he demanded, eyeing each of us.

You would think this was horseplay. But no, this was serious business. Just how poor do you have to be as an airline pilot to be this upset over one missing slice of bologna?

Answer: Pretty darn poor.

It may seem crazy that the loss of a single slice of processed meat was such a big deal, so let me tell you how we got to this place.

One late afternoon in early March of 1989, I landed back at LEB, dog-tired and content after an eleven-hour duty day which included eight hours of hands-on flying. After I said bye-bye to my passengers and watched the last of them deplane, I packed up my flight bag in my usual mindless routine, then stayed behind to clean up the cabin as the captain also left. Stiff and bleary eyed, I finally climbed out of my airplane relieved to be freed from the cramped cockpit. Inhaling the fresh air as I stepped down the airstairs, a burly man shuffled past me dragging heavy metal chains. I paused on the bottom step and watched him squat down and wrap cumbrous chains around my aircraft landing gear.

"Hey, what are you doing?" I protectively barked at him.

"Didn't you know, Eastern Airlines went on strike. You, my dear, are out of a job."

"What are you talking about?" I was feeling defensive now, and perplexed. Of course I knew there was strife at Eastern, but I was so removed from it I never imagined it would touch my life.

Then, I saw them all.

Looking across the ramp, our entire fleet of Dornier 228s were lined up along the apron, as they would be if it was the end of the day and late at night. But it was too early for this scene. Then I noticed, they all had chains wrapped around their tires.

The walk across the ramp to our maintenance hangar felt like an eerie trip through a cemetery of dead and forsaken airplanes. Before entering the building, I turned around and took it all in, because I had a queasy feeling that I would never see my beloved Dorniers again.

The hangar was spookily deserted. There were no mechanics buzzing around, tools in hand, working on our airplanes and laughing out loud at dirty jokes. The emptiness was creepy.

I treaded through the abandoned maintenance hangar and swung the door open into the passenger terminal at the other end. My flight bag fell from my loosened grip, landing at my feet with a dull thud as I peered through the door and a shiver wiggled down my arms.

Our entire wing of the airport terminal had been stripped bare. The passenger terminal was blank and naked. The huge Eastern Airlines logo on the wall behind the check-in counter, had been torn down, leaving the scarred drywall underneath it uncovered and exposed. Bare wires and plugs sprouted out from empty countertops, where the computer monitors had been. An empty metal bracket awkwardly jutted out from the wall, where the big screen posting flight arrival and departure times had hung.

There was nothing left.

The eeriest part was the stillness of it all. The silence. There were no people. No gate agents gathered behind the counter, chatting away with each other. No passengers milling about, killing time before their evening departure to some major city. No shop keepers standing behind cash registers or janitor pushing his cart between bathrooms. I felt like I had just stepped into an episode of *The*

Twilight Zone, and I had somehow missed the end of the world.

The Eastern Airlines machinists had gone on strike, and all operations had ceased earlier that day. Everything was cancelled, but my early morning flight had already departed before this happened. Technically, we were Precision Valley Aviation, recognized and operating as Eastern Express. But with no Eastern Airlines, that was indeed just a technicality. When Eastern Airlines stopped flying, our services were no longer needed. Just to ensure our little company didn't continue flying under the Eastern Airlines name—Eastern collected everything at each airport that we operated out of that used the Eastern Airlines colors, logo or reservation system, including our computer terminals with their proprietary software installed.

Eastern Express was erased from the airport.

In an instant, I had nothing at all to do. I huddled with my roommates in our cold cabin, waiting out the strike while trying not to spend any money. Along with our flying schedules, our tiny salaries also came to an abrupt stop. Our airport-supplied toilet paper quickly ran out, and food became sparse in our bare kitchen.

And so it came about that a single, missing slice of bologna was grounds for war, and a package of Ramen Noodles might as well have been a gold brick.

The 1989 strike at Eastern Airlines was the employees' last stand to stop Frank Lorenzo, a ruthless corporate raider who had taken control of the airline and was selling it off in pieces for his own personal profit. Lorenzo had pushed the machinists to strike, so as to replace them with cheap scab labor. But he miscalculated his employees' unity and was taken by surprise when the pilots and flight attendants supported their colleagues with a sympathy strike. The entire airline shut down in the blink of an eye as the three unions pulled together as one.

Soon it was apparent that there would be no return date for us. And just like that, I was unemployed and looking for work, again. Now you might think I shouldn't have felt quite so devastated, since everyone lost their jobs. Misery does love company, and I had a lot of company. And it's not like I was fired or wimped out and quit because I was scared. I had no bouts of self-reproach this time around.

But I still felt doomed.

I was suddenly a pilot looking for work, and the market was suddenly saturated with pilots looking for work. Aside from all of the unemployed Eastern Express pilots out there from multiple companies, every mainline Eastern Airlines pilot was out of work, too.

Every. Single. One.

These mainline guys had more experience and flight hours than me, and there were thousands of them. Quite simply, their qualifications were superior to mine in every way. Almost all of them lived up or down the East coast, and that's where they were looking for work. Exactly where I was looking for work.

I was at the bottom of the airline pilot food chain. I wasn't the antelope that the lion eats. I was the leafy plant that the antelope eats, that the lion eats. I was doomed, alright. Rock-bottom, Shakespearean Hamlet doomed. The realist in me was rolling her eyes. This was a disaster.

This time around, I didn't have the luxury to spend time feeling sorry for myself. Landlords are funny about letting you live in their house when you don't have any money to pay them rent. So, we all had to vacate our little cabin. We cleaned out the refrigerator, packed up our belongings, and finally found a place to unload about fifty bags of rotted trash. (We took turns driving to the JC Penney's dumpsters in the middle of the night.)

Hey, I wasn't planning on staying at Eastern Express forever, right?

I had to keep telling myself that.

And I wasn't going to get very far in the airline industry living in Vermont either, now was I?

Also had to keep telling myself that.

So, this was an opportunity.

It was hard convincing myself of that one.

I could see how people get comfortable and just hang on to something good. It's hard to walk away, to hopefully find something better.

I thought I would get to decide for myself when it was time to move on, but it was a white-collar thug named Frank Lorenzo, who Barbara Walters called "the most hated man in America," who made that choice for me and everyone else at Eastern Airlines.

This turn of events was startling, and it was serious. It was sad, too, because I loved my Dorniers. I loved my colleagues. I even loved my little frozen cabin on the side of a ski mountain, and I definitely loved the guys who suffered living there with me. But all of that was over now.

Whether it was my idea or not, it was that time again.

Time to find something better.

REAL PILOTS DON'T FAINT

"Sorry for what you're going through up there, but we're looking to fill some pilot seats here at Pan Am. Can you pass the word to your pilots?"

Pan Am had their thumb on the pulse of the entire aviation industry. Shortly after Eastern Airlines went on strike, Pan Am Express, the regional arm for Pan American World Airways, called our chief pilot with word that they were hiring. Every suddenly jobless pilot at my company, including me, was ready to climb into whatever life raft we could find.

We mercifully had one thing going for us, at least temporarily. Our union, ALPA (Air Line Pilots Association), set up a strike fund to financially support the mainline Eastern Airlines pilots. So those more seasoned pilots remained busy walking the picket line and weren't out job hunting, yet. ALPA, however, gave no financial support to us Eastern Express pilots, even though we were all dues-paying ALPA members now furloughed and out of work, too. But that's another story.

I was in the first wave of pilots to flood the Pan American World Airways International Flight Academy in Miami to interview, which was a multi-day process. The world's best pilots trained at this high-tech facility, including the pilots who carried the President of the United States on Air Force One. It was an honor to walk those halls under any circumstances, but I was beside myself with both excitement and trepidation knowing I was here to have *my* mettle tested as a pilot.

Having learned my lesson from American Airlines, I purchased a navy pencil skirt business suit for my non-revenue flight down on Pan Am. As impractical as this was, I decided to stick with the conservative skirt for the interview process. Pan Am was our nation's flagship air carrier and was a venerable and traditional company. I didn't want to rock the boat and affront any good ole boy by wearing pants, or look too feminine by wearing pleats or ruffles.

On the first morning of this process, I walked out of our hotel with a handful of my fellow out-of-work colleagues from Eastern Express, including my former roomies, and together we headed down the sidewalk to find the correct building for our interviews.

Every major airline seemed to have a building on this one long boulevard beside the Miami airport. The Pan Am pilot training center stood just one block down from the Eastern Airlines pilot training center, and I felt like I was strolling down fraternity-row of the airline pilot training industry.

Shuffling down the block in our business suits while clutching our logbooks and gawking at these iconic buildings, we definitely looked the part of young pilots arriving for interviews. Just before pivoting off the sidewalk for the entrance of the Pan Am building, a group of Eastern Airline pilots in full uniform and carrying picket signs, dropped out of their circular formation down the street and hustled over to us.

"Good morning." They politely broke into our conversation bubble, short of breath from trying to catch up to us. "Are you all here interviewing?"

"Yes, we are." We replied in clusters while nodding our heads.

"Please, you don't want to cross the picket line," one of the uniformed pilots implored us. "You don't want to get a job *like that*," another one added with a sense of urgency.

"Oh no, we aren't interviewing with Eastern," I shot right back.

"We're here for Pan Am," someone else in our group chimed in.

The picketing pilots dropped their signs with a look of relief, and wide smiles spread over their faces. After some polite exchanges, they shook our hands and wished us the best of luck.

I would never cross a picket line. None of us would. Stealing somebody else's job is cheating. People with solid qualifications don't need to cheat. Besides, safety is dependent on us working together and having each other's back in the cockpit.

I made it through the first round of interviews and advanced to Day Two of the hiring process. The next morning, I arrived at the medical building for my physical exam, looking sharp but feeling restricted in my tight stockings and heels, and hungry from the required 12-hour fast. I stepped into this generic looking building to find it jammed full of pilots neatly placed in organized queues, and I quickly realized this was no ordinary office building on the inside. I was directed to take my place at the end of one of these lines.

Like cattle being led to slaughter, my group progressed through each stage of the medical evaluation. Moving from one door to the next, I was the only female in my herd, which grew awkward as we stripped down to various stages of dress for different exams. Thankfully, I did get the room to myself for the topless EKG. I signed away my right to any medical privacy, including a consent form to be tested for HIV, with the results to be sent directly to Pan Am. I was asked all sorts of peculiar and irrelevant questions.

"Tell me, Miss Savino, how does menstruation make you feel emotionally?" This was followed up by, "What form of birth control do you use?" The doctor assumed I was having sex. *That made me laugh.*

The good part was that I got to skip over the prostate exam entirely, and there was no comparable cancer check for me to deal with. I guess the only cancers that matter are the ones men fall to.

I considered myself to be in perfect health, except for recurring headaches and the fact that I was a bit underweight. But both seemed expected considering my lifestyle, and I assumed I'd skate through this part of the hiring process. Getting poked and prodded was fairly mindless work, so I spent my time thinking about the simulator evaluation coming up next. That, I knew, was not going to be mindless work.

They gained my full attention though, when I passed through one particular white door, which deceptively looked like all the other white doors. A nurse waiting just inside, waved for me to take a seat as she shut it behind me.

"Take off your jacket and roll up your sleeve," she instructed me. I quickly figured out that her task was to draw my blood.

Now this is where things started to get a little muddled for me.

I dutifully complied and offered her my skinny arm, which she started to flick manically looking for a fat vein. I hung in there while she clumsily sucked six vials of blood out of me, clanking each one onto a metal tray. Feeling a bit freaked as she kept going, vial after vial, I concentrated on talking myself out of feeling lightheaded and on avoiding eye contact with my tubes of blood stacked on display in front of me.

Finally, she was done.

"Okay, you can put your sleeve back down," she instructed me as I climbed out of my chair. Then she promptly dropped the tray holding my blood, shattering the glass tubes on the tiled floor and spattering my blood over my ankles and shoes.

"Oh no!" she yelped, "I'm so sorry about that." She frowned at the mess on the floor and then looked up at me. "We need to start over."

"Are you kidding me?" I can't remember if I said that out loud or if that stayed in my head as I shouted it to myself. But I was incredulous.

She was comically jittery the second time around, even more so than the first. She couldn't find a vein that made her happy and she kept switching back and forth between my two outstretched arms, stabbing me here and there in search of at least one cooperative donor spot.

I had a feeling she felt badly for putting me through this, but by her twelfth apology, I was sure. I was doing my best to put on a cool "no problem" kind of face as I leaned onto my armrest to hold me upright.

After she finally scored another six vials, I pulled my sleeves back down. Without even attempting the coordinated maneuver of buttoning my cuffs, I picked up my blazer and strolled out of the lab as casually as I could pull off. I nodded to the pilot entering the room after me and headed down the sterile hallway to the end of the line at the next white door. I could see where I wanted to go, but with each step my legs melted beneath me and then my vision warped into a blur. I wilted against the corridor wall, desperately grabbing at the smooth white paint for something to hold on to as I gracelessly slid down the wall into a heap on the polished linoleum floor.

Out cold.

I woke up on a table in an examining room, with a gray-haired doctor I didn't recognize rubbing my hand to wake me up.

"Did I fail the medical?" I swear these were the first words from my dry lips.

"No, no. Some people faint after having their blood drawn. No worries young lady, this just happens sometimes." He smiled at me reassuringly.

But I was worried. Most definitely worried. I was certain that Pan Am wouldn't want a pilot who faints. I kept rewording my question so I could continue asking the same thing over and over again without sounding like I had memory loss.

"This won't count against me? Or will it?" I kept going. "Are you going to tell Pan Am I fainted? Is *this* going in my medical report?" He indulged me with more reassurances, but I wasn't done. "Are you really sure this won't count against me?"

My pale white hands returned to a rosy pink, and after a short rest I got up off the table, straightened my skirt, picked up my blazer once again and got back in line where I had left off. While standing in the hallway, pondering over how to get blood off of nylon stockings, a big hulk of a guy stumbled out the blood lab door hyperventilating and made the same walk down the hallway that I had failed to complete. He took his place behind me in line, then topping me, he crumbled onto the floor with a thump. A couple of pilots standing in another line jogged over to him as if they had marched in this parade before and helped him into the same room I had just emerged from.

Dang, is that nurse dropping everybody's blood vials?

Watching that beefy guy topple over after getting his blood drawn felt more reassuring to me than anything the doctor had said. Just when I thought *This could only happen to me,* I realized, *No, that's not true. Whatever it is, I can promise that you are not the first and you will not be the last.*

On my way to my simulator session next, I ducked into the ladies' room and furtively tried to scrub myself clean with wet paper towels, which only shredded over my ankles and shoes. The white crumbled mess looked worse than the dried blood.

I can't win here.

My valiant effort to clean-up only made my sore arms ache more as I muscled my way through the simulator ride. Not one person seemed to care about the disaster on my shoes, though, and I wished I had known that sooner.

I was living back home with my parents when the "Welcome Letter" from Pan Am arrived in the mail, offering me a pilot position. My dad was next to me when I opened it and for the first time since I was a little girl, I jumped into his arms and hugged him like I was ten years old. This was far more than a *better* job. I don't think my dad ever envisioned me actually getting hired as a pilot by a large air carrier. He was truly happy for me, if not more surprised.

This was it!

I was a pilot for a major airline, an international flagship carrier. I was thrilled to be picked up by Pan Am, and I was also simply thankful to no longer be among the unemployed. Of the entire group of my colleagues whom I had arrived with for this interview, only myself and three others survived the ups and downs of the stressful four-day process and ultimately were offered a job.

Like pledging a fraternity, I had suffered through those four days of hell week, torn between a sense of pride and sheer misery. I was relieved to make it through to the end, but sad so many of my friends weren't moving forward with me.

We were all competent pilots, but sometimes you have good days and sometimes you have bad days. Like so many things in life, there are no do-overs in the interview process.

SPACE MOUNTAIN ABOVE BUFFALO

Children behave!

I started off as a first officer on an ATR 42 flying for Pan Am Express, a sleek turboprop born from a joint French and Italian aerospace venture. This regional aircraft seated fifty passengers, plus a crew of three, including a flight attendant. Although this was a smaller plane than most that Pan American flew, Pan Am Express was not a separately owned company, and we flew under the venerable Pan Am call sign. All pilots flying for Pan Am and Pan Am Express were on the same seniority list, assuring that I would move up that list to the first officer seat in the Boeing 727 next, and then keep going from there for a lifetime of progressing through the ranks at this massive international air carrier.

I believed my career was set for life at Pan American World Airways.

After my new-hire class finished ground school, I was paired up with a couple of other young pilots for the flight portion of our training. We were sent to Buffalo, New York, BUF, and spent the next couple of weeks staying in a garish hotel that had previously been a Playboy Bunny Club resort. The irony was not lost on me that this hotel, intentionally built right across from the airport, had counted on a steady flow of pilot clientele that Hugh Hefner never predicted would look like me.

All of our training was scheduled in actual aircraft, not simulators, so we flew throughout the night when the planes weren't in service. Taking turns behind the yoke, we swapped in and out of the pilot seat mid-flight, as our instructor put each of us through the paces in the moonlight. When it wasn't our turn in the hot seat, we gladly left the cockpit to go and "rest" in the passenger cabin. Set loose in the back, we raced up and down the aisle of the empty cabin, falling over each other as the plane took off, landed, bounced through simulated engine failures and spiraled in steep bank turns as the pilot in training practiced different maneuvers.

I took my flight training very seriously, memorizing operational data and practicing emergency procedures in my head all day long when I wasn't sleeping. In the cockpit, I was a perfectionist and expected nothing less of myself than a stellar execution of every maneuver and berated myself whenever I failed at this. But when I was released from the pilot seat for a break in the cabin, I let my stress go and soaked in as much fun as I could. We all did. How often would I have an empty aircraft all to myself and my friends? It was like renting out Disneyworld every night and getting to ride Space Mountain unlimited, while standing on the seats. *If the public could only see their pilots now.*

As soon as training was complete, I was fitted for my new uniform and

Standing at my Pan Am ATR 42, waiting for my passengers to arrive at JFK.

jumped right into my schedule with Pan Am.

Flying at Pan Am was a walk in the park compared to what I had been doing at Eastern. The routes were similar, but the ATR 42 was much better equipped with an autopilot and advance navigational technology in a smart glass cockpit. Our smooth LCD screens were cutting-edge compared to the traditional analogue gauges still in use on the larger Boeing aircraft, and in military aircraft.

The most welcome safety enhancement, though, was the cockpit door. We had a flight attendant who cared for our passengers and cabin cleaners who cared after our passengers. I could focus completely on flying the plane.

I flew with a whole new variety of pilots, from all different backgrounds and age brackets.

"Flying here is so much easier than my last job," declared Armando, my captain for the day, as we cruised over the Adirondacks headed up to Rochester, New York, ROC.

"It sure is." I couldn't have agreed with him more.

"Nobody is trying to shoot me down. Piece of cake."

"Ah, okay. I was just thinking about the cool nav package on this airplane," and I gave Armando my sideways please-do-tell dimples.

Armando had been a fighter pilot in the Israeli Air Force. He spent our long lulls at cruise altitude reminiscing about his youthful scrapes during the Six-Day War and other military horror stories, which he oddly thought were funny. I listened to his "John Wayne" anecdotes with nothing I could add. Nothing at all. Flying with him put my sheltered flying career into perspective.

All pilots have their story about how they got here, and no two pilots have a matching tale. But pilots are not individualists. We take turns on shared airplanes, rotating in and out of the same seat. We know the feel of the same curved walls cocooning us and electrical smell of the same warm instruments guiding us. We reach for the same switches and twist the same dials. We banter the same enigmatic aviation language over community microphones, while listening through passed-around headsets cradled over our ears.

We train together with the purpose of mastering full conformity, tamping down any individualism that might hinder consistency and predictability. We endeavor to master procedures identically to the next guy and exalt in responding to the most surprising of circumstances as a reflective mirror of each other. When we go to work each day, chances are a pilot will be flying with another pilot she has never met before that moment. Our training assures that this makes no difference.

Each commercial airline pilot has their specific position, on their specific model of aircraft. Generally, when a pilot moves up from first officer to captain, or from one aircraft type to another, they are no longer qualified in their previous seat and simply leave it behind. They have to intentionally drop those marbles out of their head and make room for different ones, in order to learn a completely new set of facts and figures and retrain their subconscious and muscle memory to reflectively find every switch in the dark all over again.

Although the captain is ultimately in charge and the final authority on a flight, the two pilots on any commercial aircraft trade off flying duties equally. One pilot flies the aircraft, while the other takes care of everything else, such as running checklists, communicating with air traffic control and company dispatch, checking weather and programming the onboard computers. It's always a fair exchange of work on the flight deck, and flying-pilot versus non-flying-pilot duties diligently rotate each leg between the captain and first officer.

The ATR 42 may have been the lion in the technology chain, but flying into JFK our small aircraft was the runt of the pride. We knew how to keep up with the big boys, though.

We were often assigned 250 knots (288 mph) by the air traffic controller, but our ATR 42 could hardly reach a speed of 250K without some help. Knowing how the game worked, the air traffic controller concurrently assigned us a lower altitude, so we could strategically make this airspeed happen in a dive.

Time to land at JFK. As the flying-pilot on this leg, I double-clicked the autopilot disconnect switch on my yoke. A brief alarm chirped, making sure I knew what I had done. I slid the throttles to idle and waited for our power indicators to roll back and the drumbeat of our engines to fade away to near silence. Pushing forward on the yoke, I pointed the nose down until the clear sky outside our windshield moved away and I was looking forward at the ground below us.

I will admit now to the sly thrill of feeling my hair floating upwards and my thighs rising into my seatbelt with the negative G load, as our airspeed built up to 250 knots in a controlled plummet. Yes, we did get panicked passenger and flight attendant complaints every time we did this, which was often. *Hence, we loved our cockpit door.*

Accepting an arrival procedure that required 250 knots was a challenge for my smallish aircraft. But we knew we had to take it, or we would be assigned *another* arrival, one meant for the minions. If just one Pan Am ATR 42 declined this clearance into New York, then all of us would be relegated to the little league of small aircraft routes and deemed not up to mixing with the big boy traffic flow into an international airport. We always accepted this clearance, not only out of practicality, but out of pride.

A grin of excitement passed over my face as we accelerated into the sea of large jetliners streaming in from every direction in the clear blue and coming together into a single line for our assigned runway at JFK. To the outsider, this might look like a school of helpless fish seemingly caught in the same strong current, being pulled together into one flowing river. But to a pilot, this scene was all part of a carefully choreographed dance, powerful and beautiful.

It felt good to slide into our place in line. We became part of something bigger. I felt a brotherhood with each pilot in the aircraft ahead of me and those behind me, all of us in the sky and collectively responsible for each trusting passenger sitting in our aircraft cabins. This responsibility was not a weight, it was a privilege.

SHENANIGANS IN THE COCKPIT

I enjoyed bringing people together and safely delivering my passengers to their destinations. But another great part of working for Pan Am in the late 80's, was the perk of riding as a passenger myself, at no cost. There was a built-in social life that came with being part of this company, and sometimes a few of us pilots would join up with a flight attendant or two and randomly hop a flight to somewhere exotic for an impromptu group getaway. If a seat went empty on any Pan Am flight, it was ours for the taking.

One afternoon, four of us walked onto a Pan Am 727 headed to St. Thomas, Virgin Islands. As the passengers boarded, we hung around the cockpit door chatting with the pilots working this trip, waiting to see what seats remained unfilled in the cabin. In the end, the gate agent handed the final paperwork to the captain and told us, "Sorry ladies and gents, but we are completely full."

I leaned into the cockpit to thank the captain for his courtesy before we headed off to try our luck on another flight.

"I don't care if the cabin is full." The captain smiled at me. "I'm not leaving anyone behind, even if you have to sit on the head for takeoff and landing." We stayed, and yes we sat on the toilets. The captain made the rules back then, and nobody was uptight about it. *Times have changed.*

I had no problem fitting in as one of the guys at Pan Am. So much so, it was borderline insulting. One day hanging out in the pilot lounge in between flights at JFK, a few of our flight attendants strolled in for a visit. Comically, half the guys jumped up from their resting spots and started fanning their feathers and flirting with these women.

I didn't move from my comfy spot on the sofa. After the ladies left, my captain resumed his slouched posture and settled back into the cushion in the spot next to me.

"Hey, Luke." I shot him a sarcastic crossed look. "Not for nothing here, I might not be in a skirt, but I am a girl. How come you never stand up when I walk in the room?"

"Oh no, you're not a girl." He continued without even bothering to look up from his newspaper. "You're a Pilot Pig Dog, like us," and he resumed completely ignoring me.

I think that was a compliment.

Not everyone could ignore the fact that I was female, though. One afternoon, I received an envelope in my company mailbox. Our chief pilot had forwarded a letter to me which the company had received from one of my passengers. He was kind enough to include his response back to this customer.

Dear Sirs,

I had a nice flight from JFK in New York to Norfolk in Virginia. The flight was smooth and timely. However, I feel the need to inform you that only one of our stewardesses provided us with drinks and snacks. She was a lovely young lady. The other stewardess sat in the cockpit for the entire flight, and I even saw her playing with the knobs. Both my husband and I are very concerned that this put us all in peril. Perhaps there was some Shenanigans going on between the pilot and this stewardess. We feel obligated to inform your company that this is happening on your flights.

Sincerely,
Mrs. Old Lady

(I changed her name to protect the clueless.)

Our Chief Pilot promptly wrote her back.

> Dear Mrs. Old Lady,
>
> Thank you for your letter. At Pan American, we take safety very seriously and welcome input from our customers. The female crew member which you observed on the flight deck, was the pilot.
> I am happy that you had a smooth flight and hope you return to fly with us again in the near future.
>
> Sincerely,
> Pan Am Chief Pilot

This had me in stitches for days. As incredible as this misunderstanding was for me to comprehend, it did make me wonder; if this one woman took the time to actually write a letter and search for the correct address to mail it to, then just how many of my passengers were alarmed when they saw me in the cockpit and I just never heard about it?

I didn't have to wonder that for very long, as this incident was just the beginning of "mistaken identity" occurrences which would replay throughout my career.

Many years later as a Captain for United Airlines, I often welcomed passengers into my cockpit for a quick visit before departure. *FYI, pilots love when passengers visit.*

"Knock, knock" I heard a motherly voice behind me, tentative, saying knock-knock while standing on the other side of my open cockpit door.

I paused my preflight flows to welcome a young mother onto the flight deck, with a little girl about four years old, clinging to her side.

"Hello." I smiled at the small child. "Would you like to sit in the pilot's seat?"

Wide-eyed, she emphatically nodded "yes," and climbed into the empty co-pilot's seat beside me. My first officer was outside doing the aircraft walk around, and I knew he wouldn't mind a little visitor in his seat.

I put my uniform captain's cap on the little girl and had a short chat with the mother, as she eagerly took pictures of her cherubic child holding the sidestick in her tiny hand pretending to fly the plane. When they were leaving, she leaned down into the little girl's ear and whispered, "Say thank you."

Walking back out the cockpit door, I overheard the mother bubble to her daughter, "The nice pilot let that flight attendant sit in his seat, but when he gets back, she is coming back here to bring you a snack."

This whole time this young, adult woman thought I was the flight attendant, even though I was wearing a pilot uniform, with a tie and epaulets while sitting *in* the captain's seat. That simply didn't make any sense, but this was hardly an isolated episode.

On another occasion, after landing, a gentleman poked his head into my cockpit before disembarking and enthusiastically queried me with some technical questions about my aircraft, such as what forms of navigation I used to get us here today and what company manufactured the engines on this aircraft. He then asked me about my personal background and training to be here.

After answering all of his questions with straightforward, albeit technical, explanations, he concluded our conversation by saying, "Well, tell the pilot *he* did a great job with that beautiful landing."

Then his wife, patiently standing behind him added in, "Oooh, when did you girls get those cute hats," pointing to my uniform hat with the UAL wings emblem attached to the front and the golden chicken-scratch captain insignia across the brim.

My first officer quietly seated beside me in the right seat, had to turn his head out of courtesy to hide his eye roll and wide grin. But he made sure I saw his face. For this entire conversation, while I was sitting in the cockpit, in the captain's seat answering technical questions about my aircraft and my personal flight training, they thought I was a flight attendant.

Just how?

On another trip, a passenger leaned her head into the cockpit and quite seriously quipped, "Oh is this 'bring your daughter to work day?' You two look so cute dressed alike," referring to myself and my first officer.

One afternoon, a man stepped into the cockpit to take a peek before exiting the aircraft after a long international flight and exclaimed, "Wow, this plane only has one pilot! Technology really has come a long way." There were two of us sitting in the cockpit, but only one of us was male. To this day I wonder just exactly who he thought I was sitting in the pilot seat.

Over the years, I've observed that people can rationalize anything in their minds to make a situation fall into line with their beliefs and what makes them feel comfortable.

Let me just add, this confusion wasn't unique to our passengers and the flying public. On more than one occasion, I've had flight attendants actually make the exact same mistake, along with other aviation professionals.

On one flight departing Reagan Washington National Airport, DCA, a husky Sky Marshall dressed as a typical passenger in jeans, Nikes, and a Yankees Cap, stepped into the cockpit, presented his ID, and gave his entire security briefing to my male first officer.

After he finished his spiel, my co-pilot just nodded and said, "Okay, now you might want to tell the captain." Even a trained Sky Marshall thought I was a flight attendant … with four bars on my shoulders, while sitting in the captain's seat. It's not like he hadn't been on a flight deck before and didn't know where the pilots sat.

At times, passengers would poke their heads into the cockpit as they were boarding my flight before departure to say "Hi," or perhaps really just to check us out, and there would be *no* mistaken identity.

"Are you our pilot today?"

"Yes, I am," I would say as I held out my hand for a welcoming shake.

And with that, these passengers would walk off of the aircraft.

As we pulled into our gate with an on-time arrival at our destination, I would remember those passengers who didn't trust me, and were likely still sitting at our departure airport trying to find another flight.

So, how did that work out for you? I would wonder with a smile.

Some people handle their fears with denial, while others just walk away when reality does not match their expectations. But most people just need an adjustment period. I've experienced this hesitation with other pilots, flight attendants and mechanics, as well as from passengers. Often people just need some time to adapt to the idea that their pilot is not a broad-shouldered, gray-haired man. They need a moment to convince themselves that it's all going to be okay when they realize there's a woman up there in control.

I never took this as an insult or felt disparaged. I was simply in a position that some people had not seen before and could not believe. That felt good.

Although it could be frustrating at times, it was also exhilarating having a front-row seat to the groundswell of change as it came over the aviation industry through the 1980s until today. I was lucky that the doors were opening for female pilots at the same time that I came of age to fill one of those seats. I could only feel grateful to not only be a part of that change, but to get to experience it up-close during those early years.

LAST UNIFORM IN THE CLOSET

22

"I swear the name of our company has changed," Pete moaned. "We aren't Pan Am, we're Troubled Pan Am." He dropped our community *New York Times* back down onto the grimy coffee table in our break room.

It was true. There were a lot of news articles about us lately, and you never saw the name Pan Am without the word "troubled" in front of it. To stave off bankruptcy, Pan Am had sold its most lucrative Pacific routes to United Airlines, and rumors were flying their European routes were next on the chopping block. After only a brief honeymoon with the company, a sinking feeling started setting in. Sinking, as in sinking ship and the rats were starting to jump.

It was that time again. Time for another application spree looking for that elusive *better* job. My flight time and credentials were growing rapidly as I flew for Pan Am, and I was a strong candidate for a major airline now.

I thought I'd have a leg up with American Airlines because I could cite my successful training experience with the company during my senior year at Purdue. But to my disappointment, American immediately rejected my application. Their eight-page application focused on the "health" of a candidate to a point bordering on the ludicrous. *In my opinion.*

Just to apply to the company, I had to answer vague questions such as, "Have you ever been treated for a female disorder?" There were questions about pregnancy, and menstruation pain and regularity—right down to self-assessing how heavy my flow was and for how many days each month this affected me. As bizarre and arbitrary as I felt this was to evaluate my qualifications for employment, I think what eliminated me from consideration was that my mother was adopted. American Airlines required the pilot applicant to build a family tree denoting the current state of health, medical history and the cause of death (when applicable) of every biological relative going back to their four grandparents. Having no knowledge of my mother's gene pool, I could not provide this medical information. American Airlines never invited me in for an interview. *They might as well have eliminated me because I wore shoe size six.*

However, I was invited to interview with Trans World Airlines, or TWA, followed by United Airlines. Both companies set up their pilot interviews to be accomplished in separate phases, with each phase lasting up to three days. The pilot would show up for the first day of a phase, and with each test they would continue to move forward, day after day—or be sent home. These two companies had remarkably similar interview processes, including administering the same written exams. As it happened, each phase for TWA was scheduled first, which served as good practice for the subsequent UAL version.

After each phase was completed, I flew back home and stood watch over my mailbox waiting for a letter containing either information that would move me to the next phase or a rejection with no explanation. This put a couple of months between each phase, dragging the process out over the year. Mercifully, I kept moving forward with both companies. So, while flying for Pan Am, I was perpetually sneaking off to either St. Louis or Denver to complete written tests, medical exams, interviews, and simulator evaluations as I progressed through the hiring processes.

Phase One contained a preliminary personal interview and an enormous number of forms to complete, along with a collection of personal documents.

After that all went well, I continued on to hours of written exams which looked similar to college entrance SATs. This assessment was to test the candidate's general level of knowledge, intelligence, and education.

I was competing against older and often more experienced pilots, but surprisingly I found myself at a real advantage over them for this academic testing. At twenty-four years old, my college years were not that far behind me, and this sort of academic drivel was still fresh in my mind.

I did well and progressed to the next phase with both TWA and UAL.

For Phase Two with TWA, I walked into a room to find a single chair isolated in the center of a horseshoe arrangement of tables which seated a daunting panel of men. I awkwardly sat down in the empty seat, surrounded as they each zinged questions at me. However, talk is cheap, and the most demanding part of the interview process came next.

The test of the pilot's flying skills.

I stuck with a skirted business suit through all of this, purchasing several different skirts in various dark colors, as I learned this was the requisite interview attire for females. I rationalized I could fly in a skirt just fine, but I worried that heels on the rudder pedals would be the real challenge. If Ginger Rogers could do everything Fred Astaire did in heels and backwards, I could do this.

The flying skills evaluation at TWA was in a Boeing 707 full motion flight simulator, which was a behemoth-dinosaur of an aircraft to fly.

"Sit down, young lady. Make your adjustments and let me know when you are ready." The examiner welcomed me into the simulator, hugging his clipboard while shaking my hand. I had never been in a 707 cockpit before, but I had to hide my awe and settle right into my seat, as if this was just an ordinary thing for me to do.

I clumsily adjusted everything down to my 5'3" height, shrinking the cockpit by reeling the rudder pedals in towards me and sliding my seat full forward, placing the control yoke close enough that my short arms could push and pull it full range forward and aft. I raised my seat up ridiculously high, bringing the overhead switches within reach while opening up my view over the nose.

Despite the simulator being a big hydraulic fake of the actual aircraft, the pitching, rolling, engine noise and visual effects were real, making it no less intimidating while sitting at the controls than if I were in the sky.

You might think the most difficult part of flying this old ship would be controlling the four massive engines, interpreting Jurassic-style analogue dials and deftly controlling the massive steel rudder pedals with my size six pumps.

But no, none of that is what got me.

The testing began and I took off, following specific maneuver requests from the examiner. I adapted to the feel of this foreign cockpit quickly, except I found myself distracted by a most embarrassing situation. Commercial airline cockpit seats have a wide cut-out between the pilot's thighs for the yoke shaft to move in between the pilot's legs. This didn't go over so well in a pencil skirt, especially since I'm short and had to slide the seat full forward.

The yoke shaft hiked my skirt right up to my crotch every time I pulled back, giving the examiner a peep-show of my panties with each maneuver. This gray-haired gentleman politely glanced away each time I grabbed for my skirt to yank it back down with one hand, while maneuvering the jet with my other hand. At one point during the flight, I pretended to need my aeronautical chart and gracelessly spread it over my lap to cover up. I wasn't fooling anybody, though we both pretended not to hear the incessant sound of crumpled paper crunching between my inner thighs.

Somehow through all of this mortification, I managed to fly the jet with precision and moved onto the final phase of the interview process with TWA and was ultimately offered a job.

Before I answered TWA, I wanted to see how far I would get with United Airlines, but I was only halfway through their interview process. The best strategy I could come up with was to put my head in the sand and ignore the congratulatory letter from TWA, and then their subsequent follow-up letter warning that their offer would be rescinded if I did not respond.

Putting off my response to TWA was a big gamble. I was taking the very real risk of ending up with nothing. But United Airlines was now the premier air carrier in the United States and serviced sixty countries worldwide. It had taken over Pan American's most prestigious and profitable international routes. If I was hired by United, it wouldn't get any better than that. It was hard to believe this was even a possibility. Perhaps because it felt like such a pipedream, I held out for UAL and continued to keep TWA on hold until they really did rescind their offer two months later.

After that letter came, I quickly got past my panicked reaction and became even more laser focused on my goal to get hired by United. I was determined to make this huge gamble pay off. That brass ring was within my reach and I was going to fight for it with everything I had.

Although we interviewed individually at United, I was perpetually in a queue of pilots waiting in line for something, and often I would spot guys who I had gotten to know. Usually, we were seated in a waiting area making nervous polite conversation with each other while waiting for our name to be called by a woman carrying a clipboard. There was an unspoken camaraderie between us. We were all going through the same stress and all had the same hopes. It was only natural that we bonded, in an oddly competitive, but supportive way.

We watched as each pilot was called from their seat, with a cheer of "good luck, kill 'em in there." But the candidates walking out of their interview got more of my attention. Some exited the room standing tall and triumphant, while others quietly exited with slumped shoulders, looking defeated.

Unique to the United Airlines pilot selection process, pilot applicants were given written psychological personality profile tests, followed up by a one-on-one interview with a psychologist, which laughably really did take place in a dimly lit room with a doctor taking notes on a clipboard while the pilot rested in a comfy chair.

Unlike any other part of the interview process, time in this room varied hugely between candidates. One guy might reappear after only ten minutes, seemingly relaxed and relieved, while others remained behind that closed door for thirty minutes or more. When one guy didn't emerge from the room for forty-five minutes, I was compelled to get up from my seat in the waiting room and approach him as he walked out.

"What happened to you in there?"

It wasn't until I stepped up to him that I noticed the shine of sweat on his upper lip.

"Aww, I'm in the middle of a bad divorce and he kept asking questions about that," he sighed. "It took a long time to get through it all."

"Okay, that's cool." I gave him a pat on the shoulder. *Oh, that doesn't sound good.*

He was not back the next day.

For several hours, I fidgeted in my seat watching for the door to open and for my name to be called, until I was the last one left alone in the waiting room.

"Ms. Savino, your turn."

I finally walked through the mysterious door and took my seat in front of the psychologist. Before my eyes could adjust to the dim windowless room, the doctor delved into personal matters having nothing to do with my ability to fly a plane.

"Do you have a boyfriend?"

I hesitated. "Yes." *Was that the right answer?*

"Do you want to marry your boyfriend?"

"No. Well, maybe." *Wouldn't a normal person want to get married?* "If things keep going in the right direction, yes … someday."

"Do you plan to get pregnant and have children?"

"Sure, once I'm married." *Where is this going?*

"What religion do you practice?"

"I'm Catholic." He didn't immediately respond, so I clarified. "Roman Catholic." *Wait, I'm talking too much.* Who needs to clarify what sort of Catholic they are?

"Oh, you're Catholic … so you plan to have a lot of children then?"

"Maybe," I edged. "No, not really. I have three siblings. I don't want that many kids."

"Do you go to church every Sunday?"

"Yes, I do," but I quickly added, "unless I'm working, then I don't."

Sure, I can be Catholic, but not so Catholic that I would mind working Sundays, Christmas, and Easter.

"Tell me how your Catholic upbringing 'made you feel' as a child."

The doctor was insistent that growing up Catholic must have been stifling and I must have feelings of guilt all the time, about everything. Of course, I told him growing up Catholic was a dream, citing our annual church carnival as the pinnacle of my happy childhood memories. Apparently, I'm not as good an actor as I thought because he remained stuck on this whole Catholic thing and didn't buy that I enjoyed a childhood of catechism classes. It took him a while, but he eventually let it go and moved on with his questioning.

"Tell me about your relationship with your mother?"

"And your father?"

"What is your father's occupation?" He never asked me my mother's occupation.

"How many hours of sleep do you need daily?" *Quick, what would be the right answer?* I said, "six."

"Do you stay in bed when you're not still sleeping?"

No personal question was considered off the table. There are not too many occupations where an employer could get away with this line of questioning, but there would be no civil rights outcry over this. There were no personal rights when it came to public safety. I didn't hesitate to answer anything, no matter how intrusive the question, because I understood this was how the game was played, and I wanted the job.

The psychologist must have concluded that I was not an axe murderer because he checked all of the right boxes and jotted down "healthy, mature female" on the comment section of my form. The interview only lasted twenty minutes, which I thought was a good sign. Despite the embarrassing questions, the only thing I really felt was relief. I left the room feeling comfortable that I must have passed this psychological test. Sure enough, I was invited back for the next morning, and weeks later I received a letter inviting me back for the last phase of the hiring process scheduled about two months later.

The final phase started out with the simulator flight evaluation. For this test, I was in a holding area with only one other pilot. Coincidently, Malcolm and I were staying in the same hotel and had become fast friends, comparing notes and background stories over breakfast that morning.

The simulator ride took about an hour for each candidate, so when Malcolm was called in first by a clipboard lady, I settled into my seat for the wait and used the quiet time to review procedures in my head. I was completely floored when after only fifteen minutes, Malcolm walked back into the waiting area, escorted by the same clipboard lady.

"Ms. Savino," she announced, "Please come this way."

"Malcolm, what the heck?" I grabbed a quick second to talk with him. "You only just went in there."

"I know." Malcolm beamed. "I did so great, the examiner didn't need to see any more." He appeared delighted with an awkward grin painted across his face. I couldn't tell if he really believed this. *Oh no, Malcolm, that is not the way it works.*

"Oh, wow, Malcolm, that's great." I gave him my most supportive squeeze on his arm.

I turned my head before disappearing through the door with the clipboard lady. "Wish me luck, Malcolm. I'll talk to you back at the hotel."

I never saw Malcolm again. He was gone.

I hid my relief when I was escorted to a Frasca training simulator for the evaluation, but I was bouncing through a jubilant tap dance inside my head. I had been both a student and a flight instructor in a model similar to this at Purdue. This was a wonderful unexpected advantage. But that bit of luck was not what gave me the biggest comfort.

United's simulator flight evaluation was computer graded, which is how Frasca flight trainers work. There was no human opinion involved. There was no bias. The computer did not know my gender or height, could not hear my higher pitched voice, judge how I wore my hair, know if anyone could see my panties or if I had a paper chart trapped between my thighs.

It was a tough evaluation, but it was fair. I knew I needed to earn a high score because the Eastern Airlines pilots were dropping back into the workforce in droves now, like hungry locusts wearing pilot uniforms. I didn't have their muscular stature and deep authoritarian voices, so I was counting on an evaluation of my flying skills that was completely blind to level the playing field.

Like my previous simulator evaluations, the test consisted of precision and non-precision approaches using Jeppesen approach plates, shifting crosswind takeoffs and landings, holding patterns, unusual maneuvers and a surprise emergency with a jarring alarm specifically intended to startle the pilot and observe their reaction.

It all went well and did indeed take a full hour.

Climbing out of the simulator, the instructor looked at me and with a slight nod of his head said one word, "Nice." He was not permitted to give me any results, but that simple gesture was as revealing as if he had given me a high five, followed by a slap on the back.

I moved on to the grand finale of the pilot hiring process at UAL, which consisted of a panel interview and a medical exam the next morning. If this final day went well, then I would have made it successfully through every test over these past six months and get the job. With TWA out of the picture and Pan Am on the edge of bankruptcy, this was it for me. I had no fallback plan.

On this last day, another clipboard-toting lady escorted me to a room for the last interview. I walked through the door to find an isolated chair placed in the center of a stark white room, with two men seated behind a table on the far end of the room. There were brief introductions; one gentleman was from Human Resources and the other was a senior captain for the airline.

The captain started off.

"I see you have a 727 flight engineer certificate. So then, you just went out and bought it?" There was definitely disdain in his voice. Since I had never been employed as a 727 flight engineer, he presumed I had purchased 727 simulator time to get this, which was a common backdoor approach to pad a resume by wealthy pilot candidates.

This wasn't starting out well.

"No, the 727 flight engineer ticket was a requirement to graduate from Purdue. We also trained on the DC-8," I explained. He looked a little chagrined and nodded in approval. *Phew.*

"And you were on work study in college?" I wasn't sure if that was a question or statement.

"Well, yes. My dad had three of us in college at the same time." I hesitated, a little embarrassed to explain my situation.

But he moved right on. "No, I get it. Very good."

After a while, the questions switched from general background to aviation specific and technical.

"What is the difference between a microburst and a macroburst?"

Easy. Meteorology 101.

"You have a high engine vibration indication at cruise altitude and a flight attendant has informed you of smoke in the passenger cabin. What do you do?"

I recited the proper procedure. But he didn't seem satisfied with my answer and followed up with, "Why?" So, I gave him a more specific answer. This is "why" the checklist says to do this and this.

"Why?"

And I gave an even more specific answer. Because this is "how" that system works.

"Why?"

With each more detailed explanation I gave, he immediately shot me another "Why?" followed by, "Why?" then another, "Why?"

There was no end to it.

All right, I was starting to catch on.

Sure, he was testing my knowledge. Did I understand what I was doing? How technically in-depth could I explain aircraft systems? But he was looking for something more. Like a toddler testing his mother's patience, he was trying to push my buttons. He was measuring my temperament. Assessing how I handled pressure. How did I adjust, when I ran out of answers? What was my ingenuity? My disposition?

So I preempted his next "Why?" by concluding my last answer with "And I don't know anything more than that," and grinned at him.

He gave a hearty laugh at my moxie and moved on.

The Human Resources guy questioned me next, and he came at me from a completely different angle.

"What would you do if your captain was talking too much and getting on your nerves?"

"Turn down my volume." I replied and didn't go any further. And with that the captain let out a big snicker, but the HR fellow didn't get the joke.

"They wear headsets. She is going to cut him off. Ha, that's good!" the captain chuckled, as he explained pilot humor to his colleague.

"How would you handle flying with a captain who was arrogant or demanding?" he continued on.

I pondered that for a second and thoughtfully responded, "I can get along with anybody for a week." He nodded at me, as if he felt reassured by my answer.

The interview continued on like this, in a comfortable tone. I took my time with each answer, speaking deliberately and succinctly. Nothing exudes confidence more than someone who does not appear rushed or too chatty. I left giving them each a firm handshake and direct eye contact, and I thanked them with a sincere smile on my face. I strode out of there with such a good feeling,

I felt victorious. I was certain I had done well.

All I had left was the medical exam, and then I was done with the entire process.

I was warned the medical evaluation would be comprehensive, and it was. In addition to everything I had previously experienced at my Pan Am and TWA exams, United required each applicant to provide a copy of their motor vehicle record from DMV, and to fill out a questionnaire with a fixation on injuries.

Have you injured your head?
Have you been injured after drinking?
Have you been injured in an assault or fight?
Have you been injured in a road traffic accident?
Have you had fractures or dislocations of bones or joints?
Have you ever had surgery performed? (eg. tonsillectomy, hernia, etc)

This was before I was in any accidents or had broken any bones, so I started off the medical evaluation feeling confident. But I knew better than to feel overly comfortable, considering my unfortunate Pan Am fainting debacle.

And of course, something ridiculous happened to me that didn't seem to happen to anyone else. I failed the hearing test.

Wearing headphones, I was instructed to hold a corresponding hand up when I heard a tone in each ear while sitting in a booth. I performed this task perfectly. I could have been a dog.

Noticing my paperwork did not appear to be moving forward to the next station after the test was completed, my panic antennae issued a red alert.

"Is everything okay with my hearing test?" I nudged the nurse.

"No, I'm afraid you failed it," she stated, as if she weren't ruining my life.

"What?" My voice got a little higher. "I'm sure I can hear just fine."

It turns out the issue was a misunderstanding of the instructions. I had raised my hand when I heard a tone, then put it back down. Apparently, I was expected to raise my hand and *keep it raised* for as long as I heard the tone. For this failure to understand the instructions, she failed me for having a hearing impairment. Because I spoke up and protested just a bit, *okay a lot,* she allowed me to retake the test. I performed better than a trained poodle the second time around.

Other than having a shy bladder and taking an extraordinarily long time providing a satisfactory sample into a narrow test tube, I made it through the remainder of the medical evaluation uneventfully. The flight surgeon even appeared bored during my physical exam, which I took as another good sign.

It had taken six months, but I made it to the end of this grueling hiring process and I knew I had done my best. My eyes sparkled with tears in the bright sunlight as I strode back to my hotel. I felt powerful, as if the whole world was on my side.

I was sure I had the job. I was on such a high, I fluttered about my hotel room packing up, and headed to the airport for my flight home with a beaming smile plastered across my face. I remained on a high, floating on my own little cloud for the entire flight back home.

That day was Sept. 11, 1989.

Shortly after that, I received a letter in the mail from the United Airlines Flight Officer Employment department:

> Dear Miss Savino,
> We are pleased to advise you that our Pilot Selection Board has accepted you for our Flight Officer training program...

The rest of the words blurred together as my heartbeat raced in my ears, and I skimmed through the long letter until I reached the bottom of the page.

Your final acceptance to our program is subject to your continuing to meet our selection standards. Our congratulations and we look forward to seeing you in our Flight Officer training program.

It was real. I would be leaving for Colorado to begin my flight training with United Airlines. My entire life was about to change. I felt like I had just won the lottery.

Sept. 11, 1989 was the most pivotal day in my aviation life. Reaching back to my earliest childhood memories, this one day was the culmination of all of my days of wistful dreams, hard work, determined hope and big gambles. This day was the pinnacle accomplishment that exceeded anything I even dared to hope for as a little girl. If I could go back and tell her this day was coming, she would never have believed me. The unequivocal triumph and gratitude I felt was overwhelming and pure.

I made it.

I knew this would be the last uniform in my closet. There was nothing *better* to go for.

For the next twelve years, I would fondly think of 9/11 as the happiest day on the calendar in my aviation world.

My final interview schedule:

Dear Candidate: *Laura Savino*

On *Monday*, *Sept. 11, 1989* you have been scheduled for:

* Medical Exam at *10:30 A.M.*

Report to the Medical Department in the basement of our Flight Center, 5-10 minutes before the time shown above.

* Interview at *8:30 AM.*

Report to the 5th floor of the Stapleton Plaza Hotel Office Building at 3333 Quebec Street. (Across Quebec Street from the United Airlines Flight Center.) Please report there 15 minutes before your scheduled interview time.

Good luck to you in the remainder of processing!

Flight Officer Employment

\jem

Laura Savino

154

PART

3

ARRIVAL

WARNING: WOMAN IN THE COCKPIT
the kitchen is hot

Nothing ever turns out exactly as we expect. Until something is tangible and real, right there in front of one's eyes, there is no way to really know what it will be like.

Flight training in the simulators is realistic, in a sanitized disaster movie sort of way. Everything technical is practiced and perfected, but there are so many more aspects to the real world of aviation than just flying the airplane. There are just so many times you can have your eyes opened before you are wide awake. For me, it took more than one rousing.

My awakening began on my very first day of ground school at the United Airlines Flight Training Center. My new hire class was a mixed group of furloughed Eastern Airlines pilots, military vets, corporate pilots and regional airline pilot pig dogs like me. As vastly different as our backgrounds were, we were all basically cut from the same cloth, and we were all equally thankful to be on the property and to be the up-and-coming pilots of United Airlines.

"Did you hear?" The group was already buzzing with company rumors on that first day. "A *female* pilot has complained about how she was treated by some captains." Said as if the word "female" was scandalous in itself.

Like all corporations, there was company gossip. And like all the other pilots, I disregarded her complaint. I will even go so far as to say I was disappointed that anyone who had the grit to make it this far, would be a whiner. Right from day one, I saw how this rumor fostered suspicion towards female pilots, and I worried that I would be looked at in that same light. I resented that she was making the path harder for those of us behind her.

There is a lot of stress that comes with being a pilot. A type of stress that most pilots thrive on. The stalwart attitude that women are too soft, or emotional, or just overly sensitive to do this job or to fit into the virile mold was ingrained in this culture. Any little thing could be used to prove this point, but I didn't quite understand this yet. The overriding sentiment among the ranks was clear to me, though. If women can't take the heat, they better not blame their captains.

I knew I was a competent pilot, so my only real concern was not fitting in. I didn't want guys who were paired with me to secretly worry that I was out to accuse them of something, or to feel skeptical that I didn't deserve to be here at all. But I understood that I could not demand respect, I could only earn it.

I decided then, on Day One with United Airlines, that my approach would be "one brick in the wall at a time." My behavior could help shape attitudes and opinions, one pilot at a time. Not just toward me, but toward all women who would come along behind me. Do a good job, be a team player and love aviation just the same as any other pilot—that's what I could do to shape my own work environment and what my colleagues thought of me.

Then I was assigned the Boeing 747 as a second officer (flight engineer) and sent to the New York domicile as my first position with United. Almost every new hire started off as second officer on the 727 fleet, the single aisle, domestic workhorse of the airline. But in my new hire class, a few of us were sent to the 747, a widebody aircraft and the ruling Queen of the Skies on our international routes. This was an unusual new-hire position.

Most of the captains flying the 747 were just there for the last year or two of their careers before retirement. Likewise, the most senior first officers in the company sat in the co-pilot's seat, many also in their final years before retirement. I was the third in command on the aircraft as the second officer.

The flight engineer, endearingly called "the plumber," was the pilot who sat behind the flying pilots and manually controlled the aircraft systems, such as pressurization, fuel crossfeeds and engine thrust, and radioed in position reports on oceanic crossings. This was a critical and busy job before computers took over and streamlined these systems. This seat traditionally

My first seat at United on the Boeing 747, cruising at 40,000 feet over the Pacific Ocean. Photo taken by Captain Robert Bragg, 1990.

had professional flight engineers, pilots who spent their entire careers in this position until retirement.

So, my first seat at United Airlines was in a cockpit of senior citizens, a generation from the Golden Age of aviation where pilots were referred to as Sky Gods. I quickly figured out that most of these guys had assumed they would retire before ever sharing the cockpit with a minority, much less a female, much less a "girl" younger than their daughters. To call these guys good ole boys from a bygone era would be to stereotype them, and would be an understatement.

The respect and admiration I had for these gentlemen was immeasurable. Everything about working on the 747 reeked seniority and experience. I felt privileged to be there, like I had cut to the front of the line.

It turned out to be a baptism by fire.

I arrived for my first flight overly studied and prepared. But it's the things that you don't see coming that teach real lessons. Studying did not help me learn these ropes.

My first trip was from New York's JFK to Tokyo, Japan, NRT, a long haul flight of fifteen hours on duty. Once passengers began boarding at the gate, time rushed by at a frantic pace until we reached cruise altitude, and everyone slowed down and settled in for the many hours ahead.

"Hello boys." Gloria, the Purser (lead flight attendant on international flights) for our flight stopped into the cockpit. "I'm just doing a coffee check. I want my boys to stay awake up here," she rasped out in a smoker's voice.

Gloria apparently didn't care if I stayed awake. She didn't offer *me* any coffee, but rather turned in my direction and added, "You, I'm going to bring a bottle of milk. You little brat were born after every flight attendant and pilot on this ship was hired." Gloria wagged the crew manifest in my face as she spoke, which lists every crew member's date of birth and company date of hire. I wasn't certain if she was being friendly, or if she truly was irritated by my baby face.

Finished with me, Gloria turned her attention to the captain and smiled at him, as if they were old friends and I was invading her turf.

We had just reached the point in our workday where the pilots start to find out about each other, and our conversation continued to flow around Gloria's presence.

"Vern." I continued my chat with the captain, who I had only met at the beginning of this flight. "Weren't you just going to show me pictures of your family?"

Vern seemed hesitant now to keep talking with me and Henry, the first officer. I assumed it was because he didn't want to be rude to Gloria, who looked somewhat impatient standing there in her heels apparently expecting the captain's full attention.

So, I thought I would include her then.

"Gloria, are you married?"

"Ahhh, yes," she hesitated, without turning her head to look at me.

"Oh nice," was my usual friendly response. "Kids?"

"Yes, three," Gloria offered, but without any enthusiasm.

"Pictures?" I continued. "Vern was just going to show me pictures of his family, too."

Including Gloria was a cinch.

After some cajoling, Vern opened up his wallet and showed off his family pictures. "Oh Vern, your wife is beautiful." I handed the pictures to Gloria. "And your grandkids are adorable." I passed those pictures over to Henry.

Gloria left and never did return with any coffee.

Hours later, it was the captain's turn for a rest break. The relief pilot quietly rotated into Vern's seat as Vern took his turn in the cockpit bunk bed.

Vern methodically removed his tie, belt and uniform shirt, and hung them neatly in the cockpit closet, placing his shoes on the floor underneath them. In just his white V-neck undershirt and unbuttoned slacks, he disappeared through the privacy curtain and into our communal flight deck bed.

Shortly after that, Gloria silently let herself into the cockpit with her own key, and without saying a word she unzipped her dress, kicked off her shoes and climbed into bed to join Vern, pulling the bunk curtain snuggly closed behind her.

After she disappeared, my eyes flew open and met the other two pilots. We exchanged knowing wide-mouthed gapes, although their looks of surprise did not come close to mine.

"Great job, Laura. You made the captain show pictures of his wife to his girlfriend." Henry scolded me with laughing eyes.

Holy crap!

Awkward things like this kept happening. I didn't think to be offended or to take any of these uncomfortable situations personally. But I did realize, again and again, that flight training only partially prepared me for my new position in *this* world of aviation. Being an insider was indeed a new experience and I had a big learning curve ahead of me.

HE-MAN WOMEN-HATERS CLUB
girls keep out

24

I pushed through the metal security door and trod my way down a dozen concrete steps, rolling my bags behind me. A rhythmic thump-thump echoed against the bare cinderblock walls as the wheels on my suitcase dropped onto each cold step. Down in the restricted area beneath Newark International Airport, EWR, the stairs brought me to a deep underground hallway that led to a door placarded: Pilot Operations.

I entered a room of humming fluorescent lights hanging over rows of plain white tables, each cluttered with papers. Men stood around the room, all dressed in the identical uniform that hung on me.

I edged from table to table, smiling and nodding at the men gathered around each until I found the cluster of paperwork with the number 801 stamped across the top sheet. I joined this group.

"Hi, I'm Laura Savino. I'm FE to Narita today." I introduced myself as the flight engineer, extended my hand to each of the gentlemen I would be flying around the globe with for the next week.

Paul and Hank, the first officer and the international relief pilot cordially introduced themselves, reciprocating my handshake. However, the captain remained hunched over the table, pen in hand intently scrutinizing and scribbling on the flight papers.

"And that's Dick," one of them offered, smoothing over the snub. Note: The captain's name actually was Dick. It was too fitting to change.

When Dick finally raised his head to natter with Paul and Hank about the flight plan, he made a performance of ignoring me. He flagrantly looked right past my outstretched hand and didn't respond to my repeated, "Hi, nice to meet you," attempts to introduce myself, as if I were a ghostly manifestation that only some people in the room could see and hear, but not him.

Another pilot, Rick, a check airman for the company, walked up and joined us at the table. Dick looked up without hesitation and shook Rick's hand. "Hello, I'm Dick." He welcomed him in a hard, gravelly voice.

I was still in my first year with the company and Rick was onboard my 747 today to observe and evaluate my performance as part of the probationary process. It was important that I was able to demonstrate not only competency in performing my job, but my ability to fit in and work together with the crew. As the captain, Dick knew this. All too well, it would appear.

Flight planning completed, we all walked through the airport terminal and down the jetbridge to our widebody aircraft as a group. Preflight, passenger boarding, and takeoff progressed like clockwork. All this time, Dick continued to shun me. I remained the invisible crew member to him. When he introduced the other pilots to the flight attendants, but skipped over me as if I wasn't standing right there, it was awkward and confusing for everybody. I could see the flight attendants were getting weirded-out at Dick's odd behavior towards me. The captain sets the tone on the airplane. Clearly, I was to be ignored.

Tension took its toll on our teamwork. Chatter usually kept us all engaged on long flights, but uncharacteristically each pilot grew quiet and self-isolated in their seats as we took flight and settled in at cruise altitude. There was an elephant in our cramped room.

With thirteen hours of flight time ahead of us, I didn't dare think about the clock. As a matter of habit, I try to avoid a countdown until the last several hours before landing, so the trip doesn't feel so long. But in this uptight environment, it was overwhelming to think about the number of hours stretched out in front of me, trapped in this tiny space with Dick.

After an hour numbly at cruise altitude, I had settled deep into my seat and all of us in the cockpit fell into a silent lull as we circled the planet. Hour after hour passed, and a meditative, warm feeling of security settled into the cockpit as we languished quietly in the emptiness of being nowhere, high in the vacant stratosphere. I sipped hot tea in the quiet sunlight, eventually relaxing into my own pensive refuge as my eyes dully monitored fuel flows and I calculated fuel burn for each engine. My breathing smoothly fell into sync with the tranquil rhythm of the engines droning over the silence on the flight deck.

Out of nowhere, like a startling slap of thunder, Dick violently swung around in his seat to face me. My eyes sprang fully open as he jutted his chiseled face into mine, glaring at me with intense wild-eyed fury, his lips tightly pressed together in a powerful, quivering rage.

"It's people like YOU who are keeping people that are qualified from getting hired, like MY SON!" He seethed, his breath rapidly pulsing with anger into my face.

Dick released a heavy exhale, the veins bulging in his forehead, and his face flushed red from built-up fury and bitterness. He drilled a look of absolute disgust and contempt into me, panting, waiting for my reaction. He was looking for a fight. Hoping for a fight.

I just looked back at him. I'm not sure what emotion he perceived from me or wanted from me, but I was empty. Blindsided, I was completely unprepared for this random flail of emotion spit in my face. I could find no facial expression to label my reaction.

Dick had absolutely no idea what my qualifications were, but apparently his condescending assumption was that I had none. I was handed this seat. I was the thief who stole away his son's dream. Whatever problems he had were all my fault.

And I represented change. Some people just aren't good at change. But the change I represented was change that Dick vehemently did not want. From his perspective, his self-image and importance were taken down a notch. The world could see that being a pilot didn't take a big strong virile man, but someone who looked like me could do his job. Dick was indignant. He was vindictive.

He wanted the airline industry, our country, his world — to go back in time. He wanted a return to that fading Golden Age, where people who looked like me served coffee to people who looked like him.

Paul, the first officer, also snapped to attention at Dick's startling outburst. He sprang upright in his seat, an innate response to the captain's unexpected burst of energy in our quiet cockpit. Though he shot me a quick glance of sympathy, Paul turned his head back around to the instrument panel at the front of the plane and allowed the captain free reign to berate me behind his back, unchallenged. Paul knew his place in this hierarchy.

Dick finally turned back around in his seat, repulsed by my silence and vacant face. Nobody spoke a word after this. The cold air between us in the cockpit grew more chilling than the deadly temperature on the other side of our windows. I had been aware that some pilots thought I didn't fit in. Until this day, though, I had no idea there were some who hated me and were eager to get rid of me.

I remained in my seat, in a state of alert for another hour until I broke the silence and quietly whispered a request to leave the cockpit for a blue room break. Dick ignored my request, but I knew he heard me. I gently unbuckled my seat belt and got up from my seat to leave.

I cracked open the cockpit door and quietly slipped into the darkness of the passenger cabin on the upper deck, where the flight attendants had drawn all the window shades shut to simulate nighttime for our sleepy passengers. Because we were flying west, the sun lingered in the exact same spot in the sky as we traveled around the planet against the earth's rotation, and the brightness of day remained unchanged for the entire flight.

"Laura, I need to talk to you." Rick, the check airman, quietly rushed up to me as though he had been monitoring the cockpit door waiting for his moment to grab me. He had left the cockpit hours ago to relax in a passenger seat on the upper deck, for the long cruise portion of the flight where there was little for him to grade me on.

I greeted Rick with a dim smile. "What's up?"

As my eyes adjusted, I caught the grim look on his face and my mood shifted to match his.

Careful to protect our conversation from the lounging passengers, Rick leaned in with a hushed voice, "The captain wants you fired." He delivered this news with the most serious, yet incredulous expression across his face. The company can let a pilot go for any reason in their first year of probationary employment, and our pilot union is powerless to protect a newbie pilot until that year is up. It was Rick's job to evaluate whether I was company material or not — and to recommend either dismissal or my continued employment to management.

"Wait, what?" I looked at his face, impatient for my eyes to adjust fully to the darkness. Rick had an easy, good-natured disposition. We were both from New Jersey and had quickly fallen into razzing each other with Jersey jokes, so I might have thought he was just messing with me. But Rick's expression didn't leave any doubt that this was not a joke.

"Dick, he wants you gone." Rick seemed at a loss to make sense of it himself. "He wanted me to find grounds … to put it in my evaluation. He wants me to make sure you don't make it to the end of probation."

I smirked, "On what grounds?" It was absurd, but regardless a wave of anxiety rushed through me. I had felt the captain's anger towards me, but I was still shocked by what Rick was telling me. *I didn't do anything wrong.*

"That's what I asked" Rick shrugged in agreement. "He told me to 'find a reason.'"

"Can he do that?" I mouthed to him with worried eyes, aware that our conversation had caught the attention of a few passengers.

"You're in a tough spot." Rick looked exasperated. "Dick told me that if I didn't find a reason, he was going to report you for violation of the Ops Manual, 'grooming noncompliance.'"

"What?" We had strict grooming rules. I knew that. With some creativity, I imagined it wouldn't be hard for Dick to come up with something. "What does he have me on?" I was worried now.

"Your hair," Rick gave me an exasperated look. "Your hair touches your collar."

"My hair is pulled back!" I whispered in protest.

Our Operations Manual did say hair must be "neat and trimmed above the collar." But, that wasn't written for me. The part about keeping your mustache neatly groomed and having a clean-shaven face didn't apply to me, either. But clearly, common sense didn't apply in this situation.

Rick was great, though. He was on my side and enlisted the flight attendants for help. They put me in their elevator, and we dropped down into the privacy of the kitchen galley below deck. Beauty school opened up just for me at 38,000 feet, hidden in the belly of our jumbo jet among the stores of food and beverages. They magically converted my ponytail into a bun, using lots of bobby pins to hold any loose hairs from falling onto my collar. I looked silly.

Rick sent me back into the cockpit with the stern warning, "Laura, just sit on your hands and keep your mouth shut. Dick isn't fooling around."

In the end, Rick gave me an outstanding performance evaluation for my probationary line check, so that bridge was crossed. But I flew with Dick for the entire month, long past this trip with Rick as my wingman. Before my next trip, I made sure my hair didn't touch my collar. That was a very long month of sitting on my hands, but at least Captain Dick couldn't come after me for my hair any longer. Honestly, he had nothing else.

For months I had anticipated this probationary line check as my biggest professional hurdle to get past. But it turned out the real challenge to my career was flying with angry Captain Dick. What really mattered was how I wore my hair, not my competency as a pilot. It was all so ridiculous to me.

No matter how much I anticipated and prepared for something, the unexpected would happen. Who would have thought that Rick, the check airman I was supposed to be worried about, would be the one who kept me cool and turned out to be my biggest ally? And who would have thought that I would turn to the flight attendants for their help and clever ingenuity to get around the captain's plan to have me fired?

Dick had unsettled me in a way that I was unprepared for. I lost a sense of my enthusiasm on that trip and became regrettably aware that I needed to be careful, because he was not the only 'Dick' in position of authority over me. Though he was an extreme example, there were a number of pilots who expressed their displeasure with working beside me. These men would endlessly nitpick my flying, disregard my input, or bitterly compare me to their ex-wives or out-of-control daughters.

As hard as it is to not take things personally, I've seen time and again that it really isn't about the person on the receiving end. Over the years I've crossed paths with a handful of pilots who were just blatantly unhappy individuals and biased against me, and biased against others too, though for different reasons.

It takes a lot of time and ardor to get past powerful people with biases and strong opinions. But for me personally, I found a way to shut them out and not worry about these captains and their egos. I learned to keep my distance, to sit on my hands—and patiently keep moving forward. As long as I did my job well, they had no power over me.

I didn't let the Dicks in the world bring me down. And I stopped making assumptions about who was and who wasn't on my side. When needed, I reached out for whatever support I could dig up. I knew I could get through anything.

While many captains did accept female pilots working beside them, those same men often didn't have as easy a time adjusting to men who were beginning to take flight attendant positions.

As a courtesy, the captain traditionally offered one of the cockpit bunkbeds to the flight attendants to share amongst themselves however they saw fit. Our flight attendants had a curtained off area in business class for their crew rest periods, but having a bed was a step up. Everyone loosened up their uniforms at nap time, but as the culture changed at United, this courtesy took on new challenges.

Knock — knock, knock, knock — knock — knock, knock.

I got up and answered the door, which was my job as the pilot sitting closest to the door, whenever I heard the secret knock.

"Heyyyyy, I'm Jordy." A young man bounced into the cockpit, as I returned to my seat. His flight attendant uniform was starched to stiff perfection. A blond mop of hair swooped down over his forehead, while the back was trimmed short above his collar.

"So, I'm walking down the street in New Delhi and this guy comes by riding his elephant." Jordy went right into story telling mode, bubbling away with enthusiasm as he loosened his tie, pulled it off and tossed it onto the upper bunk bed.

"I said 'how much do you want to let me ride your elephant?'" He unbuttoned his white uniform shirt and stripped it off, standing bare chested in the center of the flight deck, continuing to bounce his one-man comedy routine off of us three silent pilots.

"The guy tells me five rupees, and like magic the elephant gets down on one knee and this guy hops off and I get on."

Jordy unbuckled his belt, and with a yank, it whistled through his belt loops until it was off and swinging in his hand.

"There I am, riding down the street on the back of this elephant." His hands flew up into the air to act out how he balanced on the elephant. "Did you know that elephants live so long, they get passed down in the family to the next generation?" He stepped out of his shoes.

I watched awkwardly as my captain sat rigid in his seat, irritation rising in his face as he watched this grown man pull his clothing off one piece at a time, in *his* cockpit.

"I was done with the elephant ride and I said 'Okay, you can stop this thing and let me down now.' But he wouldn't stop the elephant."

Then he unzipped his fly.

Don't do it Jordy!

Jordy was oblivious to his audience's lack of appreciation for a good story, or for a one-man burlesque strip show.

"He said to me, 'five more rupees to make my elephant stop.' Do you believe that!"

Down came his pants, which he kicked off and hung in the closet on the only remaining hangar, next to the Captain's London Fog. Jordy stood there completely naked, short of his Fruit of the Loom tighty-whities and navy socks. Intense unfiltered sunlight from the upper atmosphere streamed right through the stretched thin cotton, leaving extremely little to the imagination. Jordy turned his back to us, bent over to pick up his shoes and set them on the floor of the closet.

He spun back around and finished his story. "So, I had to jump from the elephant."

The captain remained tight lipped and the first officer had a smirk pasted across his face. I sat in my seat, smiling at Jordy while eying the two grayed hair veterans occupying the flying pilots' seats, each about to explode.

"See you all again in three hours." Jordy chirped his farewell and climbed into the upper bunk to sleep. We wouldn't see him again until his rest period was over, and then his burlesque show would play for us again, in reverse.

"What the hell is happening here?" The captain burst out in a loud whisper. "I did *not* need to see his naked ass." He shook his head in disgust. "I sure didn't sign up for this shit." He took a breath and calmed down just a bit. "And we have a lady in our presence. I'm sorry, Laura, you shouldn't have to endure that sort of display here in the cockpit."

I'm not sure if my captain was embarrassed, angry, or just shocked at what his world had become and how little control he had over his flight deck at that moment. I know this, though: he never saw this day coming when he signed on at United three decades earlier.

In 1990, the first year I began flying for United Airlines as a second officer on the 747, it seemed the world had gone mad to many of these senior pilots whom I flew with. Women in the cockpit were a big adjustment and infuriating to some of them, but men in the cabin were insanely bewildering to many. As much as some captains were dismayed, or even mad that I wanted a man's job, they didn't know how to react to a man wanting what they considered to be a woman's job.

Their perspective was formed at a time when stewardesses served them coffee wearing go-go boots and mini skirts, and touted slogans like *Fly Me* with a wink of the eye. However, by the 1980s, airlines were finally opening their doors to whomever was qualified, in whichever position they chose.

Pilots generally love flight attendants. A lot of them married flight attendants, multiple times. This gender role reversal was head spinning for even the most open minded among these macho men.

Although I didn't always know where I stood with our female flight attendants, I felt a natural fellowship with our male flight attendants, and I didn't expect that. We were both outcasts in a cool sort of way. Those gentlemen were creators of, and were blamed for, this upside-down gender changing world in the airline industry as much as I was.

Most pilots who were unhappy with these changes, unhappy with my presence, kept it to themselves. With some exceptions, like Captain Dick, their resentment towards me was expressed behind my back. And like Jordy, I was never the wiser.

Thankfully those pilots who treated me with animosity were few and far between, and easy to figure out. It was simple to just stay out of their way, even when I was seated next to them. More of these senior pilots took me under their wings and teasingly called me Baby Einstein, because they had never envisioned a 110 pound girl with a round face running their engineer panel.

Fortunately, I always felt like I had more supporters than enemies.

WAR

25

Sometimes we are all just Americans and everything comes into perspective. Sometimes our passengers aren't on business or pleasure. Sometimes our passengers are going off to war.

United States airlines are an integral part of our national defense. Commercial passenger aircraft are our nation's Civil Reserve Air Fleet (CRAF). This program providing long range military air transport, initiated by President Truman, was finally activated in 1991 when Operation Desert Shield and then Operation Desert Storm required rapid and massive deployment of military personnel and equipment overseas. Pilot and flight attendant participation is strictly voluntary on CRAF missions.

I may have been turned away from a flight slot in the military when I was in college, but I did get to do my small part when the Persian Gulf war began in 1991. This was a deeply emotional experience, and I only participated in the smallest way. I helped deliver our troops to war.

Flying soldiers, not the public, put our flights under different FAA regulations. Basically, there were no rules for our passengers. CRAF flights are treated as a charter service, much like having your own private jet. This meant our cockpit door remained open during the flight, and the flight deck was easily accessible to all onboard. Throughout the trip, courageous, athletic soldiers flowed in and out of the flight deck, jokingly pushing each other out of the way to hang out with me and the other pilots. These were the most pleasant hours I have ever spent droning over the Atlantic Ocean.

"What are all of these buttons?" one handsome Private asked me.

"Circuit breakers."

"Dang, how old are you? Are you single?" Ask about my circuit breakers. Best pick-up line ever.

Then like a flip of a switch, the moment turned melancholy and the realization of where we were bringing these young men and women hit us hard.

"So, headed off to serve our country?" The captain, an affable, wrinkled man with a round pot belly, struck up a conversation with a Second Lieutenant peering over his shoulder at the instrument panel. "Are you looking forward to putting your training to use?"

The young officer didn't respond with a smile. "My wife is eight months pregnant." His voice quivered. "I'm going to miss the birth of our first child." He ran his sleeve quickly over his tearing eyes. "I don't know if I'm ever going to meet our baby."

The smile quickly dropped from my captain's face as he looked towards me for some help. I could only shoot him a grimaced look as he stumbled over what he should say next to this heartbroken soldier.

After his group cycled out of the cockpit, the co-pilot didn't waste a moment. "Way to go boss," he ripped on the captain. "Just make our soldiers cry."

"That's it. I'm done talking," the captain flatly shot back as he slumped into his seat.

We all awkwardly laughed, but the light-hearted mood was gone after that.

A year later when our troops started returning, the feeling in the aircraft was powerful and exhilarating on these CRAF flights, now flown in reverse. After landing, the soldiers threw open the cockpit emergency escape hatch, flailing their arms through the roof, waving the American flag in frenetic joy to be home.

I received a Civilian Medal of Honor, awarded by the Air Force, for my small contribution during the Gulf War. It was a humbling privilege.

Community News

LAURA SAVINO, daughter of Mr. and Mrs. Joseph Savino of New Providence, recently received the Civilian Desert Storm and Desert Shield Medal of Honor. This honor was awarded by the Department of Defense and presented by the United States Air Force in a ceremony in Washington, D.C. As an airline pilot for United Airlines, Ms. Savino was a member of the Civil Reserve Air Fleet, and she participated in civilian missions to transport military troops to and from the Persian Gulf War. The award was to recognize United Airline's pilots for outstanding achievement and contribution during the Gulf War.

From the Summit Herald, Berkeley Heights and New Providence Dispatch, dated 1993.

We all want to have meaningful lives and to feel challenged and responsible throughout. I didn't do much, but I was grateful that I could play some small part in helping those who do make great sacrifices for our country. Leaving the soldiers behind, I returned home from that trip ever grateful for the freedom I had to live my life as I chose.

LOST IN LOVE
life changes

26

"We got a call from the tower supervisor," our dispatcher anxiously radioed us shortly after we landed at JFK. "They want the pilots on your flight to report to the tower." His tone grew even more serious. "The chief pilot wants you to call him as soon as you can."

Our approach and landing had been unremarkable, yet it sounded like there was a violation in the air that maybe a "talking to" could squelch. At least, this is how our dispatcher and chief pilot perceived this request for our appearance at the FAA control tower.

Hopping on a Port Authority bus, I rode over to the tower with the captain on my flight, both of us searching our memory for what had gone wrong on our landing that we didn't know about.

An air traffic controller named Dominic met us at the base of the tower and proceeded to give us both a tour of the facility without a mention as to why we were there. At the end of this visit, Dom asked me out.

The entire "violation" was a ruse to get me to the tower to settle a bet among the controllers regarding my looks, weight, and sexual orientation.

Dom, apparently the only one who wagered that my tiny feminine voice over the radio would match my appearance, won the bet and he got to ask me out. It was an obnoxious abuse of their authority as air traffic controllers, which required my captain to explain repeatedly to the chief pilot — while I got a date out of the ordeal.

On our first date, Dom swooped me up on his Honda Goldwing motorcycle and off we went to Jones Beach on Long Island, New York.

"Do you want to drive it?" he casually asked as we came to a stop in the parking lot.

"No, I've never operated a motorcycle," I explained to him. "I can't even touch the ground on this one," I pointed out, as he seemed to shrug off my first decline of his bold offer.

"That doesn't matter, just ride up to me when you want to stop and I'll grab it." With that, he climbed off, I slid forward and off I went. Like promised, he caught the heavy bike as I rolled to a stop next to him after I was done zipping around cars in the massive parking lot.

My last and only other boyfriend, Tom, rode a motorcycle. I was never allowed to drive it because, "You would only hurt yourself. Motorcycles are dangerous," he would explain. I appreciated his concern for my safety, but *he* rode a motorcycle.

I was sold on this new guy. Soon I had my motorcycle license and purchased my own bike — one I could reach the ground on.

My very first motorcycle – Honda CB Custom.

Dating Dom had unique perks at a time when air traffic controllers abided by fewer rules, especially New Yorkers. My flights were never delayed, regardless of gate holds or how long the lineup for the runway was. Other controllers in the system joined in on the game and my plane was cleared "direct" to any destination once airborne.

Everyone had great fun, especially the captains who flew with me. "Eat my dust," they would rub in to other captains over our company frequency, as we taxied around them headed to the front of the line for takeoff.

I began spending time in the JFK control tower. Dom would let me give clearances over the radio to pilots that I knew, and I would record the ATIS (automatic terminal information service), the hourly message every pilot operating at the airport was required to listen to.

Dom regularly did what he wanted, flipping the bird at authority. The rules didn't apply to him, or to me when I was with him. When ATI (Air Transport International) crashed at JFK in 1991, Dom called for Port Authority to pick us up at the control tower and bring us to the crash site. We had absolutely no legal grounds to be in this secured area, but nobody questioned Dom's authoritative demands.

ATI crash site – JFK International Airport, 1991

When TWA 837 crashed two years later, a widebody L-1011 with 292 crew and passengers aboard, we again were driven directly to the crash site upon demand.

*I was stunned examining the burnt out L-1011 fuselage of TWA 837—
JFK International Airport, 1993.*

Dom was older than me, a bad boy and powerfully self-confident. He filled my need for excitement. Much like I saw in others around him, I lost my own voice and bent to his authoritarian personality. I had met my match, and I was attracted to that.

I ultimately married Dom. We moved to Virginia where we could both be based out of Dulles International Airport, IAD, and we started a family. The irony is, I had become my mother, in my own way. I had married someone I felt subservient to.

With life as normal and routine as it could be for an airline pilot, one afternoon I was thrown in a way I never saw coming. Returning home from a trip to London, the captain set a tone I admired. He showed me how to combine the good old days with today's working woman in a way that kept everyone happy.

I peered down at Reykjavik, brown fields and green mountains backdropped city buildings lining the coast of Iceland.

Knock, Knock, Knock — Knock — Knock, Knock —Knock

"Hi Shelley." I opened the door and smiled at our Purser. Despite her neatly pressed uniform, her slumped posture and drained face revealed how she was truly feeling.

"Now, now Darling," the captain, Roy, welcomed Shelley into our space with a deep southern drawl. "You just look weary. Sit down here and let me rub your shoulders." Roy was one of the old-school captains who had come over from Pan Am when United bought their Pacific routes and aircraft. His concern and appreciation for our flight attendants was sincere and paternal.

Shelley dropped into the empty jumpseat closest to Roy. He told her stories about his family, as he kneaded the stress from her shoulders. She left with a small smile on her face. After that, first class cheese plates and warmed nuts streamed into the cockpit. After Shelley had closed the cockpit door behind her, I cocked my head and looked straight at Roy.

"You know Roy, my neck is pretty sore too." I may not have been pushing a serving cart for the last hour, but one of my chronic headaches had taken hold in the back of my head.

"Well of course darling." Roy smiled. "Spin your seat right around." Just as he placed his hands on my aching shoulders, he paused and tugged down the back of my stiff collar, now loose with my tie removed for the long flight.

He peered at the back of my neck. "My, oh my, I bet you get a lot of headaches, now don't you?" he stated in the most matter-of-fact tenor one could pull off with a southern twang.

I swiveled my head and looked at him, both puzzled and impressed. "Yes, I do." I gave him a raised eyebrow. "How did you know that?"

"Your neck is really somethin' out of alignment." He tapped a spot on the back of my neck. "You have a big bump right here."

He continued on to tell me all about his daughter's neck problems and her lingering headaches. He suggested I make my first visit to a chiropractor and assured me this should put an end to my headaches.

I had long since attributed my persistent neck and shoulder pain to my irregular schedule, heavy flight bag, poor nutrition, and chronic exhaustion. It was impossible to have a healthy lifestyle as an international airline pilot, and I accepted the physical costs of my chosen profession. Two days after this trip ended, I would be making a long-distance motorcycle ride with Dom to Lake George, New York, to get my newest motorcycle measured for a custom Corbin seat at the annual Americade Bike Rally. If a chiropractor could make my neck pain go away before that long ride, I was all in.

I did make the trip to a chiropractor, but I did not make the trip to Americade. Actually, I didn't do much of anything at all for the next year. In a medical scenario too outlandish for a Hallmark movie, the chiropractor discovered I had broken my neck. My first two cervical vertebrae, the Atlas (C1) to the Axis (C2) were crushed, and shattered bone fragments had traveled through my spinal canal and were lodged in my medulla oglongata, or base of the brain. To simplify; my skull had been severed from my spine.

After multiple neurosurgeries, three bone grafts, eight pieces of 22 gauge stainless steel wire tied through my cervical vertebrae, excruciating physical therapy, and the battle of my life to regain my medical certificate, I was back in the cockpit. This unimaginable nightmare is an entire book in itself, so let's just say that Captain Roy, one tired flight attendant, and a scrupulous chiropractor, ruined my life — and saved it.

LOCKER ROOM IN THE SKY
where no woman has gone before

27

I returned to work and moved up to the flying pilot seat as a first officer on the domestic, narrowbody 737 fleet, leaving the historic Queen of the Skies 747 fleet and its gentleman's club of Sky Gods behind. On my first flight with United Airlines as a first officer, I took my seat in the 737 cockpit, confident and prepared. Having completed weeks of ground school and simulator training, I was ready for the real thing.

First officer on the Boeing 737, United Airlines.

Every preflight begins with an exterior aircraft inspection, followed by a methodical systems and emergency equipment check inside the cockpit. Commencing my cockpit checks, I flipped open the small doors of my emergency oxygen mask compartment, and there it was — my introduction to the real world of aviation. *My* world of aviation now.

Folded and hidden underneath that closed door was a scrap of paper. A message in a bottle neatly tucked away, clearly meant for the pilot to uncover.

I was curious and enthused. This message was meant for me?

I unfolded the paper and discovered that my welcome card to the brotherhood was a pornographic shot between a naked woman's spread legs. No head, no body, just her fleshy honeypot torn from a magazine.

I reflexively crushed the loose paper in my fist and pitched it into our trash bag, stuffing my old *USA Today* on top to make it disappear.

Some disturbed individual had a bad sense of humor.

I took a breath and continued on with my normal preflight flows, flipping open caps that covered switches and opening access panels. Then I began to look a little deeper than my preflight checks required, checking *behind* the crash axe and *inside* the smoke goggles.

It was everywhere.

Bits and pieces of nude female body parts torn from magazines, painstakingly and shrewdly stuffed into every possible crack and crevice in the cockpit. Not just in the spots where the pilot would normally be looking to do their job, but everywhere a deviant imagination could fathom to hide something as slight as a piece of paper. If you could slide it, uncap it, lift it or unscrew it, there was a paper treasure to be found underneath.

I was being harassed by a man I had never met. Some pilot had left a cornucopia of dirty little surprises for the next pilot taking his seat to find.

But it wasn't just this aircraft; it was the next and the next. Day after day. Flight after flight. Every trip started off with an Easter egg hunt for the pilots. Find the hidden egg in the most clever hiding spot, and crack it open for the treasure inside. This was a thing.

When I stumbled across that first vulgar photo, I was baffled. But as the days went on and the erotica just kept going and going, my inner lightbulb switched on and I got the picture. Just exactly where I was, finally sunk in.

I was in a world where women did not go.

This was a secret. Their secret. I was being inducted into an exclusive club that I never imagined was there, and that never imagined I would be here.

Being a member of this club now, there was apparently no need for the other pilots to be discreet around me. They were careful to cover-up their latest porn discovery if a flight attendant walked in, but there was no consideration like that for me. I was brought full onboard and soon recognized this was a juvenile competition of sorts between the boys.

"Look what I got," one pilot would show the fellow seated next to him.

"Oh, I can top that," the response was to one-up him, and win. "Look what I found here." It was a sort of bonding ritual between the guys. I'd say a tradition.

This friendly competition included not only finding the porn, but also hiding the porn. Who could come up with the most clever and unexpected hiding spot? Sometimes I wouldn't stumble onto a particularly explicit photo until I lowered the flaps for landing, or at some other unfortunate time to feel mortified and distracted.

This is the thing, though. More than shocked and disgusted, I was disappointed. But I was not angry. In a way, I felt special. I felt successful. I was an insider now. Who knew what really went on behind the cockpit door? I did.

Now don't get me wrong. I didn't condone this nauseating behavior. Once I figured this whole game out, I made a show of ripping out every single piece of porn from its hiding spot in front of my captains. I cleaned up the fleet one jet at a time.

"Whoa, whoa, whoa! What are you doing, Laura?" Captain X, Y, and Z would bark at me, distressed by my mad cleaning skills.

"PUT. THAT. BACK." They would order me, like I just didn't understand the rules of the game and needed a tough coach to set me straight. But I continued ruining the game for them.

Some captains would warn me, "You want to be here, then fit in, dammit! Don't think you can just screw with things and not make enemies." They would joke in the way that one jokes when they are completely serious.

"Sorry Captain Z, the world is changing. This is disgusting and I'm cleaning up, so get over it." I would laugh back at them, even more serious. And just what could Captain Z say to that? Who could he complain to? No one. He was defeated. This was my seat now, and we women were here to stay.

But I wasn't done. I didn't stop there. I began replacing what I had removed with my own folded magazine clippings of men from Jockey brief ads, the kind with the obvious sock stuffed in front. Or maybe I'd find a European magazine with muscle men in teeny-tiny wet speedos. That always freaked my captains out. My material was not exactly risqué by definition, but it was effective just the same.

"Hey, you can't do that. That's gross!" My captains would shudder with disgust.

"What's the next guy going to think, lifting that cap and finding THAT under there?"

The objections were remarkable to me.

"Well, I hope the poor fellow isn't offended." I would look my captain directly in the eyes, cock my head and smile with as much sarcasm as my dimples could pull off.

On the inside now, I could be the change I wanted to see.

This was the early 1990s, and thankfully those days are long past. Over the years as more women trickled into aviation, porn-laced cockpits became frowned upon by management. Pilots eventually were instructed to cut it out. Reluctantly, they did. Times had changed. Their bachelor pad in the sky had gone co-ed, and the ladies were redecorating.

LOOK, BUT PLEASE DON'T TOUCH THE PILOT
NDA behind door number one

28

As much as the Captain Dicks and Captain Zs did not want us ladies invading *their* flight decks, there were some captains who were delighted to have us female pilots locked inside the cockpit with them. They were all too pleased to have us sleeping just on the other side of their hotel room connecting door on layovers, too. These captains who just loved us female pilots were challenging in an entirely different, and I think a worse way than the ones who hated us.

Captain Herb was one of these men. On the surface, he was a friendly and I'd even say a jovial captain to work with. But soon after we started flying together, he began making lewd comments to me inflight, that I wasn't quite sure how to take.

"Oh, I see you got some cookie crumbs on your shirt," he started one day at 36,000 feet. "I flew with Sarah and she got crumbs *down* her shirt," he tilted his head to look at me. "She let me clean them up for her." He finished his sentence with a bawdy grin and a wink.

Did he actually wink at me?

"Okay, good to know." I brushed the crumbs off my tie. When the flight attendants liked us, we got hot Mrs. Field's cookies leftover from first class.

But Herb didn't stop. "Just saying, she liked it when I helped her clean up." Yes, he was going somewhere with this. Somewhere I wasn't going.

"Thanks, but I've got it."

I thought I had made myself clear, in a subtle and non-confrontational way. *Good job Laura.*

I could not have been more wrong.

Rather than accept that I was not at all interested in this topic or in his 'assistance,' Herb took my disinterest as his cue to work harder to convince me. Moving past just hinting that something naughty went on between him and Sarah, in coincidentally similar circumstances to those in which we found ourselves now, Herb exploded into a full graphic description of a sexual encounter with Sarah and her misplaced cookie crumbs. As appalled and disgusted as this outburst made me feel, I stayed calm and continued to maintain my complete disinterest in the topic. Still not getting the reaction from me which he was reaching for, I was certain this would put an end to his crude overtures.

I was landing the plane into San Salvador, El Salvador, dodging an active volcano, when Herb raised his cookie crumb obsession up a notch.

My left hand gripped the thrust levers, my right held the yoke, and my five-point seat belt harness squeezed me firmly into my seat as the runway rushed up to meet us—when Herb placed his gross, sweaty palm over my hand on the throttles. Wrapping his pudgy, hairy fingers over the back of my hand, he declared, "Let's make this a coupled approach."

A "coupled approach" is a real term involving coupling up autopilots in bad weather, which had absolutely nothing to do with this landing, on this day. Bad pilot humor aside, he had me good. I could not move my hand away. I could not get up and walk away. I couldn't even speak to him about what he was doing. I was completely occupied landing the plane. My thoughts and actions could be on nothing else.

Herb's repulsive hand remained firmly cupped over mine. Then just as I was pulling the throttles back to flare the aircraft at touchdown, Herb finally released my hand ... only to slide his slimy fingers up my arm to my body.

Holy crap, what is he doing?

He was assaulting me is what he was doing. And I had to sit there and just take it. Because, if I wasn't perfectly clear, I was landing the plane.

After we reached our gate, I raced through the parking checklist faster than I have ever gotten through that list before. I desperately wanted to get out of my seat and get away from him. I didn't get very far, though, because our flight attendant was standing just outside our cockpit door, blocking my escape route while saying bye-bye to the steady stream of passengers exiting our plane.

"Bye-bye." I stood behind her and joined in, nodding and smiling to our passengers. "Bye-bye."

Then Herb got up and stood behind me, adding his own deeper voiced, "Bye-bye," as the passengers filed out.

And then I felt it.

This cannot be happening.

Herb was standing behind me, grinding my rear end with his stiff … *You have the picture.*

I was sandwiched in the doorway, with the flight attendant in front of me and Herb behind me. I couldn't move. Herb could not have been more pleased with himself.

He got me again.

Maybe there really was some truth behind that rumor I heard on my first day?

Maybe that female pilot who complained about how she was treated by her captains knew something that I didn't know? My eyes were opening, and I felt ashamed that I had gone along with everybody and just dismissed her story without a second thought. Now here I was, in her position, and I was the one who no one would believe.

I didn't know what I could do to stop him. But, the one thing I was certain of, was that I could not let my problem with Herb get out among the ranks or I would be the one the next new hire class was gossiping about.

It was a long ride to our hotel that evening in El Salvador. A painfully long drive. To get from the El Salvador airport to our hotel in downtown San Salvador, it took an hour of driving through deep jungle, cruising past guerrilla soldiers holding AK-47s, hunkered among the trees along the roadside. We usually had an equally armed bodyguard in the van with us, as a group of nuns had been stopped and assassinated on this road. But we didn't on this night. I sat in the isolated back row of the van with Herb, as the flight attendants customarily boarded the hotel transportation before the pilots and took the front seats. As usual, the back bench was the only spot left in the van when it was our turn to climb in.

I'll just say it. Herb groped me on that rear bench seat. His big, heavy, sweaty body pinned me into the corner, and he grabbed every body part of mine that a man does not have. I pressed myself against the window, into the corner of the bench seat, but Herb just slid over to me. There was no getting out of his reach.

Yes, the flight attendants were aware of what was going on behind them. At one point, I struggled with Herb as he wrapped his arm over my shoulders and pulled my head down into his crotch. The one male flight attendant in our crew turned around to see what the commotion was behind him. Herb gave him a wide fraternal grin, while I tried to relay my distress with an opposite "please help me" look. The flight attendant took his cue from Herb, the captain, either disregarding or not understanding mine, and quickly turned back around and minded his own business after that.

I felt so alone.

As part of the ensuing investigation, I would later write in my formal statement that I was "embarrassed and humiliated" during this van ride. But through all of it, I was "very concerned about making a scene" in front of the flight attendants and the van driver. Looking back on my twenty-something innocence, I just shake my head today. I was worried about making a scene?

Just unbelievable to me now.

When we finally reached the hotel, Herb stuck to me like glue and followed me to my room. That in itself wasn't so unusual, because lots of times the captain will see his crew safely to their rooms before he finds his own room. Except when I got to my room, he wanted to come in with me.

Herb didn't just ask to come in, he pleaded with me to let him in. When I stood firmly at my door, refusing to open it until he walked away, his pleas turned to whimpers, until he was blubbering like a hurt child.

I was ready to vomit at this point and cry myself. There are just so many times you can say the word "NO."

"Please, I just want you to watch me undress," he begged. When that didn't work, he tried, "We could just lay down and hold each other. Please, please, please I just want to feel your soft cheek pressed against my chest hair." And with that, he rubbed his shirt suggestively, his eyes brimmed with tears.

I quite honestly thought he was having some sort of a mental breakdown. It was all so bizarre. It took a long while, but eventually he gave up. His departing words were to let me know that he was feeling suicidal and he needed to be with me, or else he might not make it through the night.

Unfortunately, there he was, healthy as a big sweaty horse that next morning.

Things did not get better as our trip went into the next day, or the next. No, things got significantly worse. Herb continued his physical assaults in the cockpit, but it did not take him long before he spread his wings. Like a virus, he infected everyone with his fantasies regarding me. He constantly made comments to hotel personnel, flight attendants and other colleagues at work, implying to them all that he was having sex with me.

At hotel check-ins he would instruct the receptionist to cancel my room, while pushing my room key back across the counter to them, blocking me from picking it up.

"You can keep this. *We* only need one room." He would crow to the receptionist.

"No, please give me my key." I would implore the receptionist. And back and forth this would go, with the hotel clerk stuck in the middle, not knowing if we were a cute couple, or if one of us was a psychopathic liar.

Walking into flight operations, Herb would loudly groan to announce his entry, then dramatically boast, "I've got blue balls." He would pause for heads to turn his way, then with the palm of his hand point to me and declare, "Look at my first officer!"

This would give him the attention and approving laughs that he craved.

But what left me the most shaken and hurt of all of this was what came next.

Before the passengers boarded on one particular flight to Los Angeles, LAX, Herb bubbled about the quiet aircraft cabin, spewing his usual sexually explicit remarks about me to our flight attendants. For the first time, though, one of the ladies was alarmed and acted on it.

Kay made the point to get me alone and express her concern for how the captain was treating me. I really cannot express in words just how comforting this was to finally feel that someone cared. I always felt confident and emboldened when flying the aircraft, but I inexplicably felt powerless regarding Herb and what he was doing to me. Everyone could see how he treated me, yet no one stepped in to help.

Pilots get a new schedule each month, so we are generally paired up with the same cockpit crew for one month at a time, flying multiple trips in a row together. I felt like I was underwater holding my breath, waiting for this month to be over so I could resurface and let out a big exhale. When Kay approached me with empathy, it was an overwhelming relief.

Kay and I became fast friends and we got together on our layover. We ate and walked around shopping. Kay was the same age as my mother, and it was such a comfort walking and talking with her. I felt a trust growing between us. She wasn't a pilot and she had no allegiance to their boys' club. She wouldn't doubt my story and spread rumors about me. I felt she was a safe person to confide in. She cared about me, and soon I felt close enough to her to let my walls down. I opened my heart to Kay entirely, about what was happening with Herb.

I rarely spent any time with other women and this "girl talk" meant a lot to me. Just her listening helped me feel like I was not so all alone any longer. Kay made me feel better and encouraged me to hang in there, assuring me it was his problem and not mine.

The next morning, Herb confronted me once we were alone in the cockpit. "Kay told me you said terrible things about me." Herb pounced on me. "Kay told me I need to watch my back around you. Kay told me you were out to get me." Herb then accurately relayed back to me everything I had told Kay in confidence the afternoon before.

She had been playing me.

I was devastated.

After that, Kay iced me out and Herb was her new best friend. Of everything that had happened and everything that was still to come, in the end this stunning betrayal left the deepest pain and lasting mistrust of others.

Did Herb at least leave me alone after this? No, because that would require common sense and self-awareness. My trips with Herb finally ended, but his fixation on me did not. He regularly looked up my work schedule and kept perfect track of me for well over a year after our last flight together. He would call me in my hotel rooms, always knowing where and when I arrived. He would leave me small gifts and dirty notes in my company mailbox, and on my car in the employee parking lot. There must be a thousand cars in the employee lot at IAD. This would have taken a Herculean effort to find my one tiny car, which was white and generic. Apparently, Herb had a lot of time on his hands to stalk me.

Even when I didn't see him, his trail was always one step ahead of me everywhere I went. It was disturbing. It was pathetic.

Until it all came to a head and imploded on him.

I never did report Herb to management. I knew, or at least believed, I couldn't. Herb was a senior captain with a stellar reputation and lots of friends. He had a wife and grown sons my age, who were also pilots. They were a respected military family. No, I kept my mouth shut. Especially after my one attempt to confide in Kay backfired so spectacularly. I didn't trust a soul after that.

I thought Herb had just gotten away with it all, until one day I was called into the chief pilot's office in IAD. Every female pilot who had ever flown with Herb was called in, one at a time. Herb had apparently used a graphic story *about me* to manipulate another female pilot into cooperating with his fantasies. That was the same trick he had tried on me, using Sarah and the cookie caper.

But the truth was all coming out now. To say the least, my experiences with Herb weren't unique. As one of his other female first officers put it, "He just zoomed in on me!" Herb obsessed over *each* of us ladies beside him in the cockpit.

Herb lawyered up.

I was sent to interview with a company psychiatrist in Denver, together with one of his other victims. Then we spoke with the EEOC (Equal Employment Opportunity Commission) in downtown Washington, D.C. The investigation kept getting bigger and bigger; more women, more stories and more attorneys got involved. Until one day, Herb quietly went missing from work. He stayed out on sick leave, supposedly getting "counseling" for months.

Sometime after Herb disappeared, FedEx delivered a large envelope to my door. Inside I found a multi-paged NDA (non-disclosure agreement), and by that I mean a gag order for me to sign. I was not the only female pilot to receive this package. Our company legal department thought us ladies should keep silent regarding this course of events.

With names redacted or changed, the agreement read in part:

> Ppg 2. *Savino agrees that during her employment with United and at all times thereafter, she will not make any statements of any kind to any person or entity regarding 'Herb'...*

The agreement continues to state:
> *The parties unconditionally release one another, jointly and/or severally, from all claims, lawsuits or causes of action both known and unknown which they have or may have against one another, arising out of or relating in any way to the employment of (my name and others), by United Airlines."*

> Ppg 5. *"The Parties agree that they will not initiate or participate in any discussion of this Agreement, its terms or their own involvement in or knowledge of the events which prompted the making of this Agreement..."*
> *If asked, the Parties agree to respond: "The matter has been resolved to the satisfaction of everyone involved." Any other response will be considered a breach of this Agreement.*

They wanted a legally bound vow of silence from us female pilots and from Herb. Breaking our silence regarding the assaults was punishable by disciplinary action and payment of $15,000 to the damaged party in addition to their legal fees and expenses. The company's position was that we were partially to blame for Herb's behavior, and an agreement where nobody involved could speak about what occurred was in our best interest to protect our reputations as ladies. It seemed obvious to me that the company only cared about protecting their reputation to the public.

As you can see, I did not sign it.

It was decided that this was a medical issue and Herb would receive "help." No disciplinary action was taken. I can't judge that, even if I don't agree with or understand that decision. My union-appointed attorney did explain to me, though, that asking for discipline would invoke a fight from Herb and his attorney. That would mean more employees interviewed, leading to more widespread stories about us female pilots among the ranks. Gossip would be rampant. Our reputations would be smeared, as Herb's defense. She explained to me that all of us female pilots "would pay a higher price than Herb." So, this was kept quiet and Herb got a paid vacation for therapy—and the matter was closed. At the time, I was infuriated that he got away with this, especially after realizing I was not the only female pilot he had been abusing. But, I was also relieved it was over, understanding that my attorney was right.

Those were the times we lived in.

Herb returned to work after several months. My request to never fly with him again, was denied. I was told that as a professional, I should be able to compartmentalize personal problems and fly safely with anybody. Shortly after this, I changed fleets, moving from the 737 up to the 757/767 aircraft, and I never did fly with him again. All Herb could do was shoot me sad eyes and a pouty face whenever we crossed paths at the airport.

Going back to that first day of the investigation, when I was being questioned in the chief pilot's office and the can-of-worms was just opening, the assistant chief pilot threw out something that stuck with me.

Trying to understand the situation while scratching his neck he said, "Why would an old guy with a bad toupee think all you young girls were hot for him?"

I don't think he meant this as an actual question. It came off more like an observation or even a joke. But he summed up what was going on in a way that I had not thought about it before. Herb really did believe we all wanted him and enjoyed his crude attention. That is how delusional he was. I've flown with a few other delusional captains, the ones who genuinely believed in their own over-the-top virile image with the ladies, but none were nearly so far gone as Herb.

How exactly was Herb caught? After years of assaulting his first officers, what finally brought him down? No, none of the other female pilots spoke up. We were all strong, gutsy women, and we were all on the same page when it came to keeping our mouths shut and internalizing our fear and disgust. Complaining about how tough it is to be a female would prove that women didn't belong in the cockpit to many people eager to make that point. Any one of us would be used as the example of either how women lie or how we can't handle the job.

One male captain put together what was going on after flying with several female first officers who had been assaulted by Herb. He was incensed and voiced his anger to the chief pilot at IAD. The chief pilot didn't hesitate to act and quickly began questioning other male pilots, then the female pilots, to get to the bottom of these explicit stories. That's when the truth started to unravel. Plenty of pilots saw what was happening all along, they just needed to be prompted to speak up.

A few of the guys blamed us women for enticing this behavior from Herb, but most did not. When Herb took these privileges, like the other female pilots, I was not dressed sexy. I was in a shapeless unisex uniform. I was not drinking. I was not at a bar or a club. I did not say "yes," then confuse Herb by changing my mind. I had clearly and repeatedly told Herb "No" and "Stop." He did not have to figure out where I stood from my body language. He did not need to read my mind. Herb didn't even have these ridiculous excuses to fall back on. He had nothing to blame his behavior on, but himself.

It was the male pilots who spoke up and told the truth, whose voices finally stopped Herb. In the end, it was heartening to see just how many of my colleagues came forward to help us ladies. For a lot of them, they hadn't realized just how unwelcomed Herb's behavior was to us, and they regretted not getting involved sooner. We recognize and understand sexual harassment much better now. I must note — I believe absolutely nothing like this could or would occur today at United Airlines.

Before this all happened to me, if someone had asked me how I would handle being sexually assaulted, I certainly would have said, "No, that would never happen to me. I wouldn't let it happen. I'd kick some butt if anyone tried to touch me."

But then when it did happen to me, I didn't react like that at all. My own response to what Herb did was as much a surprise to me as his behavior was. I thought I knew how I would react, how I would handle things, but I was wrong.

I was scared. I felt alone. I felt dirty. I was embarrassed. I didn't kick any butt.

It took me years before I believed my voice alone had the power to change things. But I eventually got there. It takes one person at a time, for an entire society to get there.

UN-HAPPY HOUR
ladies welcome

My eye caught a brawny ramp worker aggressively striding towards me. I switched my attention from the landing gear brake wear pins, pausing my exterior aircraft inspection to turn and face this large man.

Perhaps he had just put live animals in our cargo hold, and was on his way over to hand me the paperwork? Perhaps we had delayed baggage coming, and he wanted to ask me if we would wait for it. I got through two 'perhaps' in my head, before he reached me.

Without any hesitation or even eye contact, he grabbed my hand, yanked it up to his mouth and pressed his lips over my knuckles with a loud, wet smack. My whole body stiffened, too startled to react.

"Sorry, but I just won a bet." He dropped my hand and laughed. Then he spun around to a pack of cheering ramp workers hooting and hollering at him.

"I kissed her, now pay up!" he shouted to the rowdy crowd.

"Naw, man, not her hand! You cheat!" They bellowed back, throwing their hands up in the air and playfully falling into each other.

He turned back around towards me. "Thanks for being such a good sport. I just won ten dollars." He beamed at his own audacity.

"You better split your winnings with me." I eyed him, swiping the back of my hand across my navy polyester slacks.

I knew what he did was inappropriate. But I had to admit, this whole scene was pretty funny. I was always that kid who took the dare. For these workers, this was just a fun break from their monotonous routine, and we would never see each other again. Through all of their laughing, I could see that I was more popular among the ramp workers than the average pilot. But I could also see that I wasn't given the respect or taken seriously the way the other pilots inherently were. I would gladly have given up some of that popularity for more respect.

Both inside and outside of the cockpit, I was often viewed differently.

"Laura, I understand how hard this is for you gals trying to be pilots." Marvin, an affable captain I was flying with, attempted to voice his support. "I was watching this documentary, and it explained how women's brains are different than men's."

"Our brains are different?" I didn't know where he was going with this, but I crossed my arms and settled in for a good story.

"Yes, you see..." Marvin paused, deliberating what words to use so that I would understand. "Female brains cannot understand mechanical concepts, like a man's brain naturally does. Men are able to block out unrelated stimuli when processing information, while women can't separate their emotions to focus logically on a task or concept."

Marvin hesitated, weighing how I was taking this revelation. "It's biological," he concluded by clasping his hands together. But I could tell he had more to say.

This was rich.

I sighed to myself and gave him the nod to go on.

"For example, a woman's brain simply cannot understand how a thermostat works." Marvin's sympathy and understanding of women continued. "I cannot get mad at my wife. No matter how many times I explain it to her, her brain is not capable of understanding mechanical concepts like that. It's not her fault." Marvin finished, waiting for a pat on the back for being so enlightened and tolerant of *my* biological handicaps in the cockpit.

"Actually, Marvin," I grinned at him, "I understand how a thermostat works."

"Okay, sure," he patronized me, quickly adding, "but my wife doesn't."

How do you burst someone's bubble when they think they are helping you? In some ways these nice captains were the most difficult to work with, because they viewed themselves as the good ones.

I couldn't get mad at them.

They were respectful and proud of themselves for accepting us women for the inferior creatures that we were. Just ask them. Though I appreciated that effort, the judgment that came with the label "female pilot" was hard to escape.

Before arriving at the aircraft at the start of a flight, the pilots usually meet for the first time in a Pilot Operations flight planning room. Each trip begins with an introduction of names, along with an exchange of handshakes as you meet who you will be working side-by-side with, for the next several days or more.

I concede that for most pilots there was a natural comfort; an assumption of competence that comes when the pilot you meet is a 6'2" man with neatly combed over hair and a baritone voice.

I have often felt the wave of doubt, discomfort and even irritation from a captain, when I walk up and stretch out my hand for that first introduction.

"I'm going to have to stay on my toes with this one," I overheard one of my captains groan to another, when he thought I was out of earshot.

This skepticism often carried through to flight training. One of my academic instructors had grown comfortable enough with me that he allowed his insights to roll into our conversations with unguarded ease. While droning through systems knowledge, he mistook me for just another one of the guys, and his thoughts casually went off topic.

"I had one of the 'female' pilots last month." He emphasized the word "female" so that the context of what he was about to say was immediately framed in an assumed understanding.

"Every question I asked her, she had the right answer." He gave me an annoyed, 'you know how it is' look, and continued, "But I knew she didn't understand what she was saying."

"You said she could answer every question." I was trying to get this straight, "so she got everything right?"

"Oh yeah, she could sure answer my questions, no matter how many ways I asked the same thing—she always came up with the right answer." He continued to complain. "Even when I had her explain the answer, her explanations were right on target."

"So, she knew her stuff?" I asked again, because his tone didn't match his words.

"Yeah, she really had it down," he continued on with a soured look, "but, I could just … tell … she didn't *understand* what she was saying."

I leaned back into my seat. "But she could explain everything—correctly?"

"Yeah, yeah—she could explain anything I threw at her. But I could tell that she didn't understand what she was saying."

There was that word "understand" again.

This instructor didn't see the need to offer more than, "You know—she was a female pilot," to justify his conviction. There were no more parts to his story.

He did know I was a female pilot, right?

Conversations like these created little daily insecurities that settled in my core. Did these absurd assumptions apply to me, behind my back?

A lot of the guys, albeit surprised to see me, were open to working with us women, and made a genuine effort to treat us with respect and objectivity. But, having us ladies beside them as flying partners, was often a challenge in unexpected ways. Buttoned into the cockpit together crossing the Atlantic Ocean on the Boeing 777, a warm-hearted captain lamented to me that he worried about his style of command when he was working with a female first officer.

"I flew with Megan," he confided in me, "and she was telling me how she had a really hard time on a recent trip." He continued, seeming eager for advice. "She told me how her captain on that flight had been rough on her." He paused to gauge my openness to what he had to say next, "and she said something to me that was so unexpected, I didn't know what to tell her."

"What did she say?" I looked up from my paperwork, now intrigued by the worry in his voice.

He hesitated, seemingly embarrassed to repeat her words out loud. He leaned towards me as an uneasy tension spread across his face, "She said the captain," he lowered his voice, finishing his sentence in an awkward hushed tone, "hurt her feelings."

He let out a long sigh, relieved to have someone to share this unsettling moment with. "My God, what was I supposed to say to that?" he sat up straight again, looking like a confused puppy, "I've NEVER had a pilot say *that*."

Yes, there was more to integrating women than just flight training. And yes, sometimes it was a challenge that went both ways.

Some men sincerely tried to do the right thing, and for that I was always grateful, albeit they kept me amused. However, some of these men who had no problem accepting us for the gals that we were, kept themselves amused by our presence.

"Guy talk" is a weird locker room to pass through. It seems almost all men are on the bro team, not just the Dicks, Herbs, and miscellaneous ramp workers. What counts as bragging can be a real head scratcher for me to understand.

On one Miami layover, I went for a walk on the South Beach boardwalk with my captain, and it happened again. He was a little round, a little soft, and no threat at all. He was another "nice guy." We stopped in and out of touristy souvenir shops and chatted about nothing. At one point I stepped into a dressing room to try on a beachy sundress. Note: I never came out of the dressing room wearing it.

The next night, we laid over in Chicago and ran into several other United pilots staying in the hotel. Sarah was one of those pilots. Yes, the same Sarah from Captain Herb's cookie crumb saga. We all went out to dinner together and before our water glasses were even filled, it started.

Sitting at one big round table that fit six, my captain began telling the guys how he went shopping with *his* first officer.

"Yup, my first officer here was trying on bikinis, and she kept popping out of the dressing room to show me," he said as he pointed to me with a nod and raised eyebrows.

Total complete lie.

His story kept growing and soon he was telling them how hot I was prancing around in a little string bikini for him on the sandy beach. Somehow, I got all wet in this scenario.

In his dreams.

My pleas that none of this was true only brought rowdy cheers from the guys to hear more.

Then another captain at the table started bragging about *his* first officer, Sarah. "She can hold her beer, that one. She drank us all under the table last night! My pockets weren't deep enough to keep up with her bar tab."

Cue the boyish laughter.

While I was embarrassed by everyone laughing at me, I felt angry when the lies started about Sarah. I watched her shift uncomfortably in her chair, and that made me uncomfortable.

All through dinner, Sarah and I looked across the table at each other with that familiar awkward smile, story after story. She knew I didn't model any bikinis. I knew she wasn't a beer-guzzling lush. After dinner, we both excused ourselves to the ladies' room together. For some reason the guys found this hysterical.

Finally, just the two of us, Sarah told me her captain bought her one single beer that she had nursed all night. He kept pushing her to drink more, but she declined his offers. I told her I hadn't tried on a bikini since my college days.

Just that little bit of shared understanding and unity that I felt with Sarah gave me a strength I hadn't experienced before. And watching *it* happen to Sarah, seeing her mortified, gave me a clarity that I could only get by seeing it happen to someone else.

This needed to stop.

It's a strange thing to explain. These men, our colleagues, thought they were complimenting us over dinner that night. It's puzzling that they would be so bold as to make up stories about us, right in front of us. But the really perplexing part was that they thought we liked it.

For these older guys, having a female co-pilot beside them in the cockpit was such an anomaly to all that they knew, we were their whopper fish story destined to get bigger and bigger. Everybody loves a good fish tale.

This got better as my seniority number rose and female pilots weren't such a novelty any longer. But it wasn't until years later, when I finally became the captain and my epaulets gained that fourth stripe, that all this horseplay ended for me. It was a long stretch until those captain bars were earned, though. Somewhere in the middle of that wait, I had enough, and my exasperation got the better of me.

Cruising one afternoon from Denver back home to Washington DC, my captain, Roger, left the flight deck to go use the blue room.

"Hey, Laura." Roger sounded overly cheerful when he returned. "This first class passenger back there was asking me about you." He grinned, with a definite snigger of satisfaction in his voice.

"Okay, and …?"

"He was a little worried seeing you up here. He wanted to know if … well, you know — what everyone wants to know." Roger was entirely too amused with himself.

"Okay Roger, you got me. What did this passenger want to know?"

"He wanted to know if you could actually fly the plane." Roger chuckled. "Or if you were up here for some *other* reason."

Roger was right. I heard this a lot.

"Okay, so what did you tell him?"

"Ahhh, you know," Roger just shrugged, "I told him, 'With a face like that, does she need to know how to fly the plane?'"

Roger played right into this man's fears because he thought this was funny.

This bothered me.

In house, I can take the ribbing and even the deprecation. But when a nervous passenger asks, and my captain decides he'd rather get a laugh and scare the passenger, than stick up for me — the joke is up.

"I need to go to the blue room," I stated as I unbuckled my seatbelt. "I'll be back in a few."

"Wait, are you serious?" Roger looked slightly indignant, or perhaps amused by me.

"I'm seriously going to the blue room." I stood up, "So, what was that passenger's seat number?"

Roger gave me his seat number, with a roll of his eyes and a smirk on his face.

Lounging in seat 2B was a well-dressed businessman. I swung the cockpit door open and walked right up to him, "Excuse me, sir, but did you have some questions about me? I would be happy to address them."

I started out assertive, but exceedingly polite. The truth is, though, I think I lectured him. I succinctly listed my qualifications, training record, and then gave him a brief summary of United Airlines competitive hiring process and continuing qualification requirements. I let him know that *all* pilots on our flight decks are qualified and competent. Just to be certain he got my point completely, I made it clear that I did not fall on the low end of those comprehensive requirements, either. I was in a mood, and this gentleman was on the receiving end of years of my pent-up irritation.

"I can assure you, sir," I took a breath and finished, "I was not hired for my pretty face." I tried to close with some humor, or maybe that was sarcasm.

With that I firmly shook his hand, turned around and returned to the cockpit.

After the moment passed and I had time to sit and think about it, I wasn't sure if I should start worrying about my big mouth or not. I was undeniably brazen and forthright with this passenger. But worse, I educated him in front of the entire first class cabin. It was packed full of Premier passengers, United's bread and butter.

He may not have appreciated that.

Maybe I should go back and apologize?

But then again, you want a self-assured pilot, right?

Anyhow, I stood up for myself, for my company, and for all women out there who have to deal with negative assumptions every day.

It turns out this wasn't the end to it. After the flight, that passenger wrote a letter to the president of United Airlines about me, about this incident.

Two weeks later I received an envelope from John Edwardson, the president of United Airlines. Inside this envelope was a copy of that passenger's letter, his response back to the passenger, and a personal note from Mr. Edwardson to me. The next day I received another letter from the Chief Pilot of the Washington domicile, with his comments to me regarding this passenger's letter.

February 1, 1995

Mr. John Edwardson, President
United Airlines
P.O. Box 66100
Chicago, IL 60666

Dear Mr. Edwardson,

I am a longtime UAL frequent traveler and an occasional correspondent. I travel 100 plus days a year and long ago chose to confine my travel where possible to an airline that kept its promises and could even find my luggage.

Last evening I flew UAL 1568 from Denver to DC. I boarded a little early and was somewhat concerned to see a young captain and a very youthful first officer board. With all the concern about safety in the media I hope you will forgive me for thinking that gray hair and older jet aircraft are my standards for longevity.

During the course of the flight I had the opportunity to chat with the captain, and I shared my view, plus one left handed comment that I hoped that diversity was not an issue in airline cockpits or brain surgery...as the first officer was both young and female.

As an enthusiastic employer of women, I assure you my comment was more political than social...I am concerned that everyone in a position such as pilot be unequivocally qualified, never mind gender, age or all the other societal issues.

The captain shared my conversation with First Officer Laura Savino ▓▓▓▓ who stopped by to reassure me about her qualifications and also about UAL's policies. I was amazed and impressed, taken back too! Ms. Savino's presentation was terrific and did all sides proud. My fellow travelers in first more or less gave her an ovation as she returned to the cockpit. Very impressive.

If you are ever in the position of advancing the cause of professional women and their opportunity at United, I would suggest Ms. Savino. She is a great spokesperson and would be a terrific role model for women all ages, youngsters included.

It's great for a customer to know your hiring system works so well.

Respectfully,

Bob Rief

Bob Rief
General Manager Outdoor Division
UAL # 00078 767596

Karhu U.S.A. Inc.
55 Green Mountain Drive, P.O. Box 4249
South Burlington, Vermont, U.S.A. 05406
Tel.: (802) 864-4519
Telex: 0062901490   Fax: (802) 864-6774

Passenger letter forwarded to me by the President of United Airlines, with his pen marks and notes on it.

Yes, it became clear how my brash initiative was perceived. It was not how I had expected.

The passenger stated he was "amazed and impressed" by me. Mr. Edwardson's personal note to me was very positive. It was the kind of letter any employee would love to get from the president of their company.

I was commended for standing up for myself. But more so, for standing up for all women and the unfair assumptions we face every day.

I can't say exactly where the turning point was for me, but somewhere along the way I developed the confidence to speak up, both for myself and for other minority pilots. And I spoke up with conviction.

By this point in my life I had put up with years of nasty Dicks and revolting Herbs. I also had enjoyed years of working with many secure, positive, and uplifting colleagues. I can't say which of these experiences impacted me the most. But after so many years of flying and of gaining the self-confidence that comes naturally with age, I developed a belief in myself and unapologetically recognized that I was a solid pilot with an excellent track record. I didn't deserve to be disparaged, disregarded, or laughed at. Nobody did.

I had arrived. I was here, a professional pilot for United Airlines. And I should be here. It was no mistake, no accident, and no gift. I earned my way.

No one else but me could decide how I saw myself, what I was capable of, and where I would end up in life.

THAT'S HOW I LEARNED
TO BE A GOOD CAPTAIN

30

"In one word, what would you use to describe the position of captain?" the captain representative for United Airlines asked me at my final interview.

My first thought was "leader."

"Guide," I stated.

"Guide?" the captain repeated back, with a doubtful look on his face.

Maybe I should have gone with "leader?"

"Yes." I spoke confidently. "The captain guides every person under them. Without words, the captain is the example, the *guidance* a young first officer needs to someday be a good captain herself."

"Ahhh, I see," and a smile came across his face.

I was subsequently told that "leader" was the number one answer given, but my answer scored more points for originality.

Lots of pilots have experience and are skilled with a stick and rudder, but it takes more than that to be a good captain. Those captains who exemplified the intangible traits of confidence, compassion and inspiration will forever be in my memory.

"Gear down, Final Descent Checklist," I called to my first officer. Smoothly in sync with each other, he reached up and moved the landing gear lever to the down position. The hydraulic actuators groaned into motion behind us, releasing the landing gear from the belly of our jet.

There is nothing aerodynamically efficient about the landing gear. Air does not slipstream quietly around this massive bulk of metal and rubber. Lowering the gear is like throwing the anchor out midstream on a sailing ship. It grabs the air and dramatically slows the jet down. This can be a useful tool to get down and slow down for landing, but the fuel burn spikes when that anchor goes out. Aside from the obvious need to lower the gear before touchdown, exactly when to drop them into place is a strategy each pilot plays a little differently. This is where the captain's personal style becomes apparent.

How talkative the pilot is with the passengers and how well she keeps the passengers informed during irregular operations is also a matter of personal style. Pilots are people, too. Some are gregarious, while others are more the silent type. A pilot with a quiet nature doesn't miraculously become talkative when a weather delay demands updates over the PA to the passengers.

There is a tight script pilots follow while operating their aircraft. However, a Captain's personality still plays a defining role in how things are done. The captain sets the tone, and their first officer must pick up on it and fall in line with their captain's habits and preferences. Some captains are easier to work with than others. Every first officer pines for the day they move up to the left seat and everyone bends to *their* idiosyncrasies.

Talented captains not only fly their aircraft well, but they also create an environment in which first officers and flight attendants want to work with them and with each other. These were the captains I watched—to learn what couldn't be taught at the training center.

I was privileged to fly with many remarkable captains over the years. Only once did my jaw drop when I realized *who* I was flying with, though. Early in my career, I flew with Robert Bragg on transpacific trips on the 747. Bob Bragg was the surviving first officer in the largest air disaster in history, when two Boeing 747s collided in Tenerife, of the Canary Islands.

Over six days, we flew JFK-NRT-HNL-NRT-JFK (New York— Tokyo—Honolulu—Tokyo—New York). These trips each had four pilots, twenty-four flight attendants and 380 passengers. Captain Bragg was the head of this massive operation and in charge of it all.

When Pan American World Airways sold their Pacific routes to United Airlines in 1986, the 747s and pilots who flew those airplanes came with the deal. In the midst of a successful career with Pan Am, Bob moved over to United Airlines to continue flying the same routes in the same airplanes he had been flying with Pan Am.

On March 27, 1977, PAA 1736 (Pan American Airways) and KLM 4805, (Koninklijke Luchtvaart Maatschappij, or Royal Dutch Airways; flagship of the Netherlands), both jumbo 747s, had each been diverted to Tenerife, along with multiple other airliners, due to a terrorist bomb explosion at their intended destination. Tenerife was a tiny island airport with a single runway. With so many unexpected commercial passenger aircraft arriving at this small airport, the tarmac filled up and numerous jets were parked on the taxiway. When it was time for them to depart, PAA and KLM had to back-taxi down the single runway to reach the end for takeoff, due to parked aircraft blocking the taxiway. When KLM reached the end, it spun around on the runway and positioned itself for takeoff. PAA continued to back-taxi down the runway, following KLM, with the plan to exit the runway onto a cleared taxiway short of reaching the end.

The two widebody jets were then facing nose-to-nose on the same runway, but half a mile apart. Obscured from each other in a dense fogbank, KLM attempted to take off without a clearance from the air traffic controller and crashed head-on into PAA. This collision between two fully loaded 747s remains the deadliest aviation accident, with 583 lives lost in the ensuing inferno of two fully-fueled widebody jets.

I glowed in the enormity of my situation, sitting beside this bigger-than-life legend in aviation, in a Pan Am 747 which had been sold to United — a virtually identical aircraft in which Bob was flying on that fateful day.

Bob used our long hours over the Pacific Ocean to draw out a map of the Tenerife airport and bring me through the accident step by step. He narrated the role of every person involved, while dragging his finger around his drawing to show me each aircraft's movement. Bob re-enacted his own actions for me, in our identical cockpit, just before KLM impacted his jet. I could hardly believe I was sitting beside this great man, the most famous pilot at

United Airlines, listening to his first-hand recounting of this aviation tragedy.

"I saw his lights down the runway and it looked so normal," he recounted, peering out our windshield to show me how he looked out on that tragic day. A chill quivered through me as Bob relived spotting the powerful nosewheel light of the KLM 747 shining directly at them from down the runway, through the fog.

"But then, I saw it was bouncing." Bob waved his flattened palm as he acted out the moment he spotted the rhythmic thump, thump, thump of the light on the nose gear strut, in motion. Every pilot knows that familiar pulse of light as the nosewheel skips over the runway centerline lights. That pattern meant the KLM aircraft wasn't stopped at the end of the runway, it was rolling down it.

I shuddered in my seat, feeling the intensity of Bob's realization in that moment.

"I yelled — Get off! Get off! Get off!" Bob winced. "The captain slammed the thrust levers and yanked full tiller for the grass." But their mammoth jumbo was heavy and slow to respond. "We just couldn't move out of the way fast enough," Bob sighed, still reliving the defeat.

When the KLM captain saw the Pan Am 747 ahead of them on the runway, he desperately attempted to pop his jet off the pavement and fly over them. The KLM 747 cockpit cleared the Pan Am 747, but the underside fuselage, gear and engines ripped into the topside fuselage of the partially turned Pan Am jet.

After reflexively ducking as KLM's massive belly filled Bob's windshield, he straightened back up to find he was now outside and perched thirty feet above the grass with the ceiling and walls around him peeled away like a tin can. Bob jumped to the ground, instinctively running from the crash until he came to his senses and stopped. He turned around to see what was behind him, and took in his burning aircraft with his passengers swarming out from the flames. On a badly injured ankle he darted back to the inferno to save passengers he spotted jumping from a wing into the fire. There were only 61 survivors, all from Bob's aircraft.

He continued his story, recounting small details of that horrific day. It was gut wrenching to feel his pain as he relived the ensuing minutes, yet awe inspiring to hear his survival story and relive these moments with him.

Pilots are intrigued by plane crashes, always eager to learn from the experiences of other pilots. Listening to first-hand details of this tragedy impacted me, but I was haunted by the part that broke Bob, in the end. Involved in the investigation which followed, a look of disgust washed over Bob's face as he told me he was sickened when he listened to the KLM cockpit voice recorder.

As the captain opened his throttles for takeoff, the second officer twice questioned him. "Is he not clear then," he challenged his captain. "Is he not clear that Pan American."

The second officer knew Pan Am was still on the runway.

The KLM captain rebuffed him, and proceeded with the takeoff roll. This is the part of the accident that Bob could never reconcile with.

The last sound on the KLM voice recording was the captain's scream at impact.

Bob returned to flying only months later. He may have been an icon in aviation history, but he was just an easy-going, ordinary man in person. On our layover in Honolulu, he took me and the other two pilots to his yacht club and bought me my first High Ball, and then laughed when I traded it for a glass of straight orange juice.

Honolulu Yacht Club. Captain Bob Bragg (on my left),
treating his crew to morning drinks. Dated 1990.

Bob was a talented pilot, and his flying skills kept everyone safe. But also critical to safety, he set a calm and comfortable tone on his aircraft. Bob had no ego, and everyone's voice was respected in his cockpit. I felt like I was part of a team. Not many people with his level of authority make everyone feel important and appreciated. Working under Bob, I wanted to do my best and I never hesitated to speak up. His uplifting demeanor, along with his unassuming determination to continue on as a professional airline pilot after unimaginable horror, made me believe I could do anything.

Robert Bragg passed away on February 9, 2017. I will be forever grateful to Bob for sharing his intimate thoughts about this deeply personal experience for him, and I appreciate the privilege of being taken behind the scenes by this remarkable man. Inspired by Bob's unbreakable spirit and harmonious leadership style, he was the first to show me how to be a great captain. I named my second son Robert.

A captain didn't need to be an icon in aviation history for him to have set an example I admired and wanted to copy. Until electronic signatures were accepted by the FAA, every flight plan was required to be signed in pen by the captain. At the completion of a flight, the first officer was then responsible for turning in this paperwork to the company for FAA-required record keeping. On my first day sitting in the co-pilot seat with United Airlines, I was a little distracted by pornographic scraps of paper everywhere. I forgot the flight plan, in the cockpit, at the end of the flight. Before reaching my next airplane on the other side of the airport, in a panic I realized that I had left these papers behind on the flight deck dashboard. I raced back to retrieve them.

I got back to the gate and squeezed through the line of boarding passengers already trudging down the jet bridge, until I reached the cockpit. My blood pressure jumped when I tumbled back through the open cockpit door and saw the dashboard was empty. Both pilots, fully enmeshed in prepping for their departure, turned their heads to look at me.

"Hi," I stuttered. "I'm sorry, I left my papers behind." I explained why I was standing there in their doorway. "Have you seen them?"

"I think I did," the first officer edged. He started digging through the garbage bag, until he fished out my lost flight plan. It was soaked in stale coffee.

I had the nerve to be indignant.

"Why would you throw flight papers in the garbage?" I questioned him. "Somebody obviously forgot them and would be back."

Both the first officer and the captain gave me an incredulous look. But I genuinely didn't understand why he would trash a found flight plan. If he didn't think the forgetful pilot would return, then he could have just turned the document in himself.

I took the wet papers and exited the cockpit, in a rush to get back to where I was supposed to be. I stepped out of their doorway and turned the corner hurrying back out of the aircraft when I overheard a snide remark from inside the cockpit.

"Was she blaming *me* for losing *her* papers?" the first officer griped to the captain.

I stopped cold in my tracks and listened.

"Yup, I think she was," the captain retorted.

It instantly hit me how I had come across, and I was embarrassed. At that moment, I wanted nothing more than to keep going with my rescued paperwork and disappear back up the jet bridge. After considering my choices for a moment, I spun around and walked back into the cockpit. Neither pilot looked happy to see me for a second time.

"I'm sorry." I grimaced, "That came out all wrong. Obviously, it was *my* fault for forgetting my papers." I looked directly at the first officer. "I didn't mean to imply you had done anything wrong. I apologize for my comment."

"That's right," the first officer jabbed me. "It was your fault."

But the captain graciously nodded at me. "That's alright," he said. "We all have our days. You're good. Don't worry about it."

The captain let me off the hook. Unlike the first officer, he accepted my apology and allowed me to step away with my dignity. I walked out thinking, *now that is the kind of captain I want to be someday.* He made me want to strive to make people feel good about themselves, even when they've made a mistake. Even when they were embarrassed because they had acted like an idiot.

The best captains continue to take care of their crews *after* they are not required to do so. One bitter February evening, after a painfully long day of deicing and snow delays, we went "missed approach" into Washington Dulles International Airport, IAD, and had to divert to Baltimore, Maryland, BWI. It was the last hour of a difficult four-day trip. I was exhausted and ready to go home, as were our flight attendants. The problem was, all of our cars were parked in the employee lot back at our starting point at IAD. We were all stranded at BWI, except for the captain, who lived in Florida. His plan was to hop onto the next flight to Miami, MIA, regardless of where we landed.

The flight attendants started pooling their money together to pay for a cab to get them back to their cars, sixty miles away.

"Don't you worry," the captain stepped in. "I've got you all covered." He walked with us to the front of the airport and paid two cabs to take us all back to IAD, refusing to accept any money from us. After he saw that we were safely off, he headed back into the terminal. By that time, he had missed the last flight back to MIA and was stuck in BWI until the next morning. He knew he would miss his last chance to get home that night, but he didn't hesitate to take care of his crew before considering his own situation.

United did hire busses to transport our passengers to IAD, our intended destination. But our captain felt it was *his* responsibility to get his crew home safely, and without the long wait our 150 passengers had to endure for those chartered busses to arrive. His generosity and selfless commitment to take care of his crew made an impact on me. Here was another captain I wanted to be like.

Years after this flight, my heart would jump when Emily Warner walked into my cockpit to introduce herself on a flight to Denver. Captain Warner was the very first female airline pilot in the United States. After years of flight instructing young men transitioning to careers at United Airlines, but not being permitted to take a pilot seat with United herself, she was hired by Frontier Airlines in 1973.

I have met some impressive people along the way, but I was the most grateful when Emily took the time to speak with me and share her story. Though I wish I had a female pilot ahead of me in the airline industry to talk with when I was young and starting out, Captain Warner gave me the perspective I needed at an important time in my career. I have nothing to complain about, compared to the walls she had to climb and the Dicks she had to get around to make it to the pilot's seat. Today, her uniform is on display in the Smithsonian Air & Space Museum, and I am a member of ISA+21, the International Society of Women Airline Pilots, of which Emily is a founding member.

The character and attitude of the captain influences the mindset of the entire crew on their aircraft. When I became the captain, I committed myself to bringing out the best of everyone working between our wings. Before every departure I would gather the flight attendants in the first class section of our aircraft and brief them on what to expect on the flight; time enroute, delays, weather, turbulence, cabin writeups, sky marshals, armed passengers, etc. If our passengers might spot something unusual during the flight, like an active volcano or wildfires, I'd mention that too. Regardless of the flight, I ended every briefing the same way.

"If you need anything, ask me, and I will get it for you. If you have any problems, come to me, and I will help you. You have my full support, and I will back you up. We are all on the same team. Let's have a good flight." And I meant it.

When I moved up to the captain's seat, everything got easier for me. As the old airline expression goes, I became the asshole in the cockpit. I wasn't really, but I could have been if I wanted to.

Many things taught me to be a good captain. When I flew with a captain, and a feeling came over me that I wanted to be more like him, I knew to pay attention.

ISA+21 conference, Sept. 2021. Photo taken by my friend, American Airlines Captain Morgen Reeb.

9/11
inside the quiet skies

31

September 11, 2001 changed the world, and we can never go back.

I was at work on 9/11. It was only my second day back to work from maternity leave, after giving birth to my second son. I wasn't in an airplane on this day, I was in Denver, taking a captain leadership course to begin my transition from First Officer to Captain at United Airlines. Just the day before, I introduced myself to this room full of male pilots by telling them that I had just given birth to my son at home, on the floor — not intentionally! So, I joked, how hard could this training be? That first day of class was full of laughter. Everybody was happy to be there, to finally be moving up to the captain's seat.

I woke up in my hotel room that morning, picked clothes out of my suitcase and got dressed, as I might do on any other day. Before heading out the door, I took a seat on the end of my bed. The stiff hotel comforter slid underneath me as I wiggled into my black flats, mindlessly staring ahead at a television resting on a bureau in front of me. A live aerial view of the World Trade Center glowed on the screen, as Katie Couric chatted via speakerphone with a woman in lower Manhattan. Thick black smoke billowed from the North Tower, dirtying the brilliantly clear morning sky.

Maybe I should go for the navy shoes instead, I debated as I watched the coverage.

214

Matt Lauer suggested that a small plane had flown into the tower. That speculation sounded unlikely to me.

I sat up and paid closer attention. I didn't want to be late for class, but I had friends and family in Manhattan, and I couldn't walk away from this unfolding story just yet.

I listened to Katie prattling away, but she wasn't going anywhere with the story. Just as I reached for the remote to click the television off, something appeared on the screen that grabbed my attention.

An aircraft was streaking across the sky headed *directly* towards the South Tower. This was no small airplane. This was a commercial jetliner.

What the hell?

Instantly, I was intensely engrossed. My back stiffened and my hands gripped the comforter beneath me. I shivered as if a cold hand had touched my shoulders and scraped down my spine as I watched a United Airlines Boeing 767 fly directly into the South Tower, exploding into a massive fireball on live TV.

I bolted to my feet, screaming, "Oh my God! Oh my God! Oh my God!"

I just watched hundreds … no, thousands of people die.

Someone had taken control of that jet and intentionally aimed it at the South Tower. If nothing else, I understood *that* immediately.

Katie said something like, "What in the world is going on?"

My shrieks echoed for no one to hear but me in that empty hotel room. My hand quivered, clasped over my mouth as I tried to hush myself. Piloting airplanes was my world. Suddenly, I did not understand my world. I was sick and utterly confused.

I don't remember how long I stood there, staring as that horrific scene replayed again and again. Eventually, I forced myself to walk away from the hypnotic loop of images. My legs were heavy and weak as I gathered my books and shuffled out my wooden hotel room door to the elevator. I had no idea what the reaction was going to be downstairs, where dozens of pilots would be gathering for class to begin.

The elevator door slid open, and I stepped out into the spacious lobby. Muted drapes hung lazily over large, picturesque windows, revealing a welcoming sunlit morning. A few guests sat dully on overstuffed furniture, quietly reading newspapers. Nothing had changed here.

I stepped across the lobby and down a tastefully decorated hallway until I reached our conference room. Most of the pilots in my group were already there, choosing between a bagel and muffin from the continental breakfast spread. The coffee smelled fresh and familiar ... and so normal.

I sliced into the center of the group, eavesdropping on conversations going on around me. Most of the guys had left their rooms before the first aircraft hit, while a few others had seen the initial report that a small plane had struck the North Tower. There was small talk about that initial news report, but nothing more.

"A second plane hit the other tower." I felt an urge to tell them what I had seen. "A widebody. Didn't any of you see that, too?"

I was met with blank faces and shoulder shrugs. Before I could make sense of my own words and explain what I was talking about, two hotel employees appeared, rolling a television on a wheeled cart down our hallway. They stopped outside our conference room and plugged it in. Class was delayed as everyone wandered over to the flickering screen to see what could be so important that hotel management decided our group of airline pilots needed to watch TV, *right now.*

We all squeezed tightly together around the screen. The evilness of the day began to unfold, and nobody moved. We remained huddled around that television for hours, anger and angst biting into each of us. The loss of two aircraft into the World Trade Center was only the beginning of our painful indoctrination into the depths of September 11, 2001. We couldn't yet fathom the lasting impact this day would have on all our lives, our country and every corner of the aviation industry.

Our instructors, privileged to insider information, were quick to pass along real time updates to us throughout the morning. The toll quickly rose to four aircraft, and before it was released to the media, we knew those doomed jets belonged to American and United Airlines. Although none of us could know the layers yet to unfold, each of us quickly understood that something sinister had snuck up on those pilots, our friends, as they worked. Someone took over their cockpits — our cockpits. That much was clear.

This was personal.

United Airlines garnered an extra conference room in the hotel to set up a private communications area for our group. If any of us had family we were worried about, we could go to this private room and United would take care of all phone expenses. I was the first to ease myself into this makeshift family resource center. The room was empty, but for four phones placed on four bare tables inside the four white walls.

I called my mother first, to reassure her that I was indeed in Denver and was not flying one of those planes. I was safe, but the edge did not come off her voice. She had news for me.

Wayne was missing. He worked for Cantor Fitzgerald on the top floors of the North Tower. His family could not reach him. Nobody could.

Wayne was our immediate neighbor growing up and my brother's best friend since childhood. Wayne ate and slept in our home throughout my youth, as though my parents were his own. Only two months apart in age, during our teen years Wayne and I had grown into dear friends and confidants. I had last hugged Wayne at my wedding.

Next, I called home. My husband's brother Cliff was a New York City police officer. My husband's best friend and the best man at our wedding, Mark, was a New York City firefighter. We lived in Virginia now, but had moved there from New York City, and that was where our friends and family still lived.

"Oh my God, do you see what's happening in Manhattan?" I blurted out when my husband answered the phone, my voice quick and short with rising panic. "Where are Cliff and Mark?"

Cliff was home. Mark was missing. His wife said that Mark had called her earlier that morning. "Honey, turn on the TV. I'm on my way to the World Trade Center."

Mark had been missing for hours by this point. He hadn't called his wife back to let her know he was okay like he always did when he got back to the station. We were all on hold, waiting.

Done with the phone, I shifted back into the hallway where my colleagues remained huddled, shoulder to shoulder around the television. A quiet rage and directionless energy saturated the air. But deep sadness and numbing helplessness is what felt the thickest, as more and more images of debris and death filled the screen.

Aside from the four known aircraft destroyed, there were still several of our aircraft in the air and unaccounted for. They weren't responding to their dispatcher's attempts to contact them, and had also gone silent to the air traffic controllers. As a group, we were lost among each other. No one knew what to think or how to feel. It was all so enormous.

One by one our cluster eventually broke up. Class was canceled, but we gathered together again for lunch that afternoon. The colorful spread of food across a buffet table and the smell of fresh baked rolls was a brief escape that invited each of us to sit and rest our thoughts for a moment.

But before we could fill our plates, a man I did not recognize entered our hotel dining room. He stopped and stood there, gazing at all of us with a stricken look across his face. He clutched a simple piece of notebook paper in his hand, torn and folded over to hide the words written on it.

"I have the names," he announced, in a soft voice. His intense expression grabbed our attention, though.

He had the names of our dead pilots.

The clanking of silverware ceased, and small talk fell silent.

We all stared at him and waited.

He began to read, failing to suppress the tremor in his voice as he stumbled through the list, pausing after each name for whispered gasps and angry protests to pass. That torn piece of note paper forced us to cross the line from hope to reality. Nobody was ready to do that, not yet. Everyone's reaction was different; some cried, some cursed, and some just blankly stared ahead.

The names were written down. It was true. It was final. These were the names of our brothers who had experienced something savage. Men who were unable to protect their passengers and their flight attendants this morning, just a few short hours ago.

This messenger was a pilot. He was one of us. He left, only to come right back with another list. A longer list.

The names of our lost flight attendants.

Everyone knew someone on those lists.

My lips quivered as tears rose up in my eyes. I removed myself from the dining room and quietly fled to the ladies' room. As the door swung shut behind me, the sudden privacy of the empty room crashed down on me. The Captain on UAL 93, Jason Dahl, had been an instructor at the training center.

The horror of watching my friend Jimmy perish in a fiery crash at an airshow when I was just a teenager rushed through me again.

Gutted, I slumped against the wall. Wrapping my arms around my chest I cradled myself and sobbed into the paisley wallpaper. It was a dark, overwhelming day.

Mark, our family friend and firefighter, was found in the hospital. He made it. Many of his colleagues did not.

Weeks after that, a random firefighter pulled my friend Wayne's business card out from charred debris that was the North Tower. Falling from his desk on the 105th floor, this tiny white card was clean and in perfect condition. So touched by this inexplicable miracle, this firefighter found Wayne's mother in New Jersey and handed it to her. None of us would ever be lifted by Wayne's sweet smile and boisterous laugh again.

Later too, I would get the tail numbers of our hijacked aircraft. With a cold chill, I found both of those United aircraft numbers written in my own logbook. I had sat in those exact seats, flying those planes on those exact routes.

There but for the Grace of God, go I.

Our cockpits lost their immunity that day, no longer a sanctuary isolated away from everything crazy in the world below. Our clean, private bubble of precision and solitude was invaded by ruthless outsiders, destroying our peace of mind with thoughts of blood on starched white shirts and sheepskin covered seats.

With all the lives stolen that day, the airline crews were the first to be killed. Their deaths were just the beginning, and freed the terrorists to take thousands more lives.

That our aircraft could be used as missiles was an unfathomable twist that no one foresaw. This was a new type of war.

I stayed in Denver for several more days as our instructors continued our training in captain leadership skills with feeble determination, before giving up. After a few days, the airlines started repositioning their out of place jets in the middle of the night. With only employees allowed onboard these flights,

I grabbed a seat on a 747 home to IAD. We departed at 1:00am from DEN, while the skies were still closed to the public and all the nation remained grounded.

"Mommy, mommy, mommy!" Nicholas, my three-year-old son squealed when I walked in the door that morning. He hugged my leg, ran in a circle with his arms out, then returned to feeding Cheerios to his stuffed animals while stacking blocks. I scooped up my sleeping infant son, Robert, from his bassinet. Cradling him, I settled on the floor beside Nicholas, taking in the joy and relief of having both my children close.

Nothing had changed here. Life goes on.

I my absence, our Nanny named Nan, who was more like a beloved grandmother to my children than hired help - had made sure my boys were safe and happy. Because of her, I could go to work with an easy heart knowing my children were not only cared for, but were loved.

"Whoosh!" Nicholas knocked over his building blocks with his flattened hand, while his favorite airplane noise whirled from his lips. "Boom!" he cheered, as his blocks crashed to the kitchen floor.

I looked at Nan with questioning eyebrows.

"Oh, he's been watching a lot of TV. The plane hitting the tower has been playing non-stop."

"What!" I barked at her. How could you put him in front of the TV to

Everyone loves reading in our house. My favorite part of the day was reading to Robert and Nicholas. With them in my arms, my heart was full.

watch that, while I was gone … flying planes? I knew Nan loved my boys, but these last several days had been so shocking and so horrific, there was no right way to handle it all.

I should have been home with my children.

I took a deep breath, trying to hold back the tears welling up in my eyes, but they fell down my cheeks as I pulled my boys in for a desperate, crushing hug.

I've always lived close to an airport. Since my earliest childhood memories, I've tuned in to the music of jets flying overhead. After 9/11, the skies went quiet.

The silence was peaceful, and thunderous.

The full effect of 9/11 wasn't instantaneous. At first it was hard to tell how things would shake out. The immensity of it all; profound outrage, layers of distress, grief and worry crept in over time. But to open the skies back up, the initial shock had to fade before calmer heads could get to work to conceive and then implement new security measures. Airports reorganized and reopened across the country, with Reagan Washington National Airport, DCA, the last to reopen on October 4, 2001.

With the re-openings, new security policies were put in place.

'Security Mania' had started. Let the show begin.

On one of my first trips back at work, a TSA agent confiscated my tweezers from my rollaboard in Chicago, ORD.

"This can be used as a weapon to hijack an aircraft," I was informed by the uniformed TSA employee — who, by the way, was fully aware that I was the captain flying this potentially hijacked aircraft.

"By that logic," I protested, "you should take away my car keys and my ball point pen."

He didn't think my suggestion was at all helpful.

The next week in San Francisco, SFO, my mini travel manicure kit was confiscated by another TSA employee. The same manicure kit that had passed through security dozens of times around the nation, since 9/11.

"Hey, if the pilot wants to take down their own aircraft," I smirked, "I'll bet they wouldn't need a nail file."

I was nearly arrested.

Days later, the TSA took away an adorable little Captain Hook pirate costume I had picked up for my son in Las Vegas, because in the package was a tiny hollow plastic hook, with a toddler sized handle for him to hold on the other end. (Labeled: safe for children under the age of 3).

"You are seriously taking away a toddler Halloween costume?" I was incredulous.

"This plastic handle can be used as a weapon to hijack the airplane," the TSA officer responded with a completely straight face.

"You do realize," I sighed, "I have an axe in the cockpit and a chemical fire extinguisher to hijack myself with."

I was quietly moved to a secure area for an invasive search after that comment. Every item of clothing on my body was unbuttoned or unbuckled, in search of hiding spots for a weapon, with the exception of my only actual hiding spot under my fitted uniform. My oversized captain's hat, where I kept my flight papers and a printout of door security codes, was completely ignored and remained on my head for the entire search. My flight was delayed forty minutes.

The flight attendants complained the sensors were turned up so high on the metal detectors, their underwire bras were setting them off. By this time, I had eight pieces of 22-gauge stainless steel wire *in* my neck from my reconstructive surgery. There was no amount of clothing I could take off to stop the alarms from going crazy each time I stepped through a metal detector. I might as well have been on the No Fly List, with the time and hassle it took for me to get through security every single time, multiple times a day.

We lost our minds after 9/11. A dog and pony show was put on display in the terminal, making security highly visible to give passengers a warm and fuzzy feeling that something was being done. This put me into a perpetual eye-roll.

Yes, security is important. Significant and effective changes have been made. It took a while, but real changes *behind the scenes* have happened, and we are all much safer.

Hijackings have been around as long as airplanes have been around.

Crew training to deal with hijackings has been around for nearly as long. Before 9/11, it was assumed that a hijacker wanted to go somewhere. He wanted to 'arrive' at a destination. This was a trainable event for us pilots. We were taught various ways to cooperate, appease and keep a hijacker calm until trained personnel could *take care* of the situation. That whole concept no longer applies.

We still train for hijackings, but the idea that a hijacker just wants a ride somewhere is complete tomfoolery now. There is no longer a plan to cooperate or appease anybody. Forgive me for going no further, but rest assured our training has been updated for the times in which we now live.

Another keen enhancement to safety, at least in my mind, is that our passengers feel empowered now. Look at UAL 93, which perished into a field in Pennsylvania. With just the slightest knowledge of what had happened to other commercial aircraft that morning, those passengers knew this was not your ordinary hijacking. There was an uprising.

No training required.

For this reason, 9/11 could not happen again. At least not like before.

On September 11, 2001, we were all robbed of our naiveté, and in part, of the joy of aviation. My father once told me, "Once you have children you will never again know peace of mind. Some level of worry will always be with you." Peace of mind, the cornerstone of my private cocoon in the sky, was lost on that day.

The very root of who I thought I was as a pilot had been irreconcilably altered. Being competent, skilled, and dedicated to the safe operation of my aircraft is no longer enough. More is expected. Something different is needed. There is not one pilot or any airline employee who is not passionate about their passengers' safety and the sacred duty entrusted to each of us to ensure that.

On 9/11 our country was attacked. Our friends, families, and colleagues were brutally taken. The horrific loss of these dear people must never be forgotten.

On that day also, the entire world came together. Airliners landed into airports they didn't operate out of, and had no company employees to help their passengers, or even gates to park their jets at. That didn't matter. We all belonged to the same family that day and the airlines took care of each other, grateful for every safe landing and happy to help every passenger and crewmember regardless of which company they were with.

Pilots and flight attendants were stuck at foreign locations around the world, where hotel employees and random citizens in the street comforted stranded crewmembers, and embraced them with compassion and generous offers to help in any way they could.

We saw the best of and worst of humanity on 9/11. None of it should be forgotten.

It took time, but life fell back into sync after 9/11. Deep, underlying differences in the aviation industry and how I did my job, became permanent — and normal. Much was lost on that day, but our joys and our dreams could not be stolen, and our all-American passion for freedom grew stronger and more powerful across our nation.

This is the United States of America, where every person can live whatever life they choose. Where a woman can speed above the earth, in full control and with the command authority of a jet boss, and be a friend, daughter, sister, and mother to her babies.

We win.

ARCTIC SKIES
Texas style

A pilot's words and actions are all recorded. Unlike other occupations, a pilot's last words and actions become a theatrical performance, played as entertainment by the media, critiqued and analyzed by cable news "experts," who have little idea what they are talking about.

But other pilots throughout the world will relive those words and actions, when that doomed flight becomes a simulator lesson to be re-enacted again and again. We get the do-over that our hearts wished those pilots could have gotten.

I sat alone in the cockpit of my empty A320. The heat from the instruments warmed me in the dark winter air. My foot tapped to the soft clicking of the onboard computers and instruments coming to life as I brought power to them. I gazed over the nose of my parked aircraft and peered into the bright lights of the terminal building shining starkly in front of me. From the outside, I mindlessly watched our passengers churn about behind the large panes of luminous glass enclosing them. The flowing colors of so many people moving past each other reminded me of fish trapped in a gigantic aquarium.

I turned my focus back to my flight papers. I tugged on my tie, loosening it slightly as I felt the starch in my collar scratching against the back of my neck. Taking it all in, the uncertainties of the next leg began to weigh on me.

Only an hour ago, I had put my signature on a flight plan and fuel load with little concern. Now, as updated data spewed across my cockpit printer, the picture was rapidly changing. Soon, I would be leaving my safe parking spot in Denver, DEN, to fly into developing ice storms shaking the skies above Texas. We were headed down to San Antonio, SAT, a destination that was usually a warm corner and grateful relief for me in the winter. I had my aircraft fueled to not only reach SAT, but added enough reserve fuel to confidently continue on to two alternate airports after that. This glut of fuel was to cover all my bases *just in case* the weather really turned sour. I had not one, but two back up plans.

Fuel is expensive, but more significantly—it's heavy. It costs fuel to carry fuel and there is a high price tag that comes along with taking on this much extra fuel. It was my call. I didn't care about costs.

This was my first day flying the line (scheduled passenger flight) as a captain for United Airlines, after weeks of training in this seat and years spent as a first and second officer. Having just returned from maternity leave, I had not flown or even thought about airplanes for the previous months before the start of training on September 10. The Airbus fleet was also entirely new to me, as I had flown all Boeing aircraft with United Airlines up until then.

My time at the training center, followed by flying revenue flights in the aircraft with a check airman, was successfully behind me. I was set free on this day to command this aircraft with the stand-alone responsibility to safely get my passengers to their destinations. This was a trust I deeply appreciated and took to heart.

Our company dispatcher, the licensed professional who built our flight plan and then follows our flight from beginning to end, pinpointed Austin, AUS and Dallas Fort Worth, DFW, as my best alternates. But these backups were no longer giving me comfort, as ice storms were now moving towards those airports as well.

Time came to register my first complaint as the captain of a flight. I dialed up our dispatch department in Chicago and carefully selected the correct sector, grateful for the privacy as our flight attendants arrived and walked right past me into the cabin to prepare for passenger boarding.

"Dispatch, Sector 31, Steve Richards." Yes, this was the dispatcher name on my paperwork answering the phone.

"Hi, this is Captain Savino. Flight 706. Denver to San Antonio."

"Yes, Captain, what can I do for you tonight?"

"Well, I'm looking at the data for SAT, and also for DFW and AUS. It's looking doubtful we will beat the weather and make it into SAT tonight. Our alternates aren't looking great now either. Do you have anything better for us?"

"Yup, sure is looking ugly down there, Captain."

I waited through his pause, listening to the rhythm of his fingers clacking on a keyboard.

"That whole sector of Texas is in a low pressure area with high winds, low ceilings and reports of moderate icing at the lower altitudes."

I knew we were legal to depart Denver and make a go of it. The visibility was forecast to be just at the authorized minimums to shoot an approach at our planned destination, and that was the bottom line. But poor weather is like a crowbar to the knee of the air traffic control system.

I expected airborne delays on our arrival, meaning a controller would have us descend into the bad weather, but then make us wallow around in the heart of it while we waited for a landing clearance. Ice can accumulate quickly on an airframe, and the thought of lingering at low altitudes left me with a hollow feeling.

"You see I am High Minimums?" I pointed out to the dispatcher my status as an inexperienced captain; not yet legally allowed to fly the aircraft to the lowest published weather minimums.

"Yes, I am just looking at that now."

My status did pop up on his computer screen. Good to know.

"This is my first day in this seat. I really don't need a christening by fire," I joked, being sure to get my point across.

"Sorry, Captain," he responded with a solid laugh, "AUS and DFW are as good as it's going to get down there tonight."

This phone call put an end to my scant hope of improving my options, and we politely hung up.

I sat back and let out a breath as I peered outside through my grimy side window. I spied Cory, my first officer, stomping ankle deep in pink deicing fluid doing the exterior inspection of our aircraft as feathery snowflakes floated down onto the tarmac.

I grinned at my new privilege of rank that kept my feet dry and mused at how it could be that a miserable, raw night in Denver would be more appealing than a landing in Texas. My gaze slipped back inside, relaxing in the warm glow of the cockpit instruments. I was oddly pleased with my circumstances.

Birds generally avoid flying in bad weather. They keep clear of ice, fog and heavy rain, while a plane is designed to operate in this environment. A lightning strike can destroy an entire flock of geese, but merely cause a burnt smudge on an aircraft. Birds stick to only the lowest levels of the troposphere, where jets reach far into the stratosphere. On the ground an aircraft is cold, heavy, and awkward, making the transition to flight remarkable. Birds are still birds on the ground. It's all so intriguing to me.

Although I understood that when it came to weather, I needed to curb my optimistic predisposition, I was ready for the challenge in front of me. I was well trained and well prepared. I was confident to launch.

This was going to be an interesting night.

Our passengers boarded, shaking the cold from their hands as they packed carry-on items into the overhead bins. Our ground crew, a hearty labor force perpetually outside in unbearable weather, buttoned up our doors and sealed us inside our metal tube. We kept still for deicing trucks to shower us until our wings lost their shine under a gummy blanket of propylene glycol. Then we hustled off to the runway. On takeoff, a sweep of blowing snow curled under our wings and scooped us into the night air as we left the frozen asphalt behind.

United 706 was underway.

The flight started off with such normalcy that I felt alert and energized, but also half-lulled into a complacent calm.

We peacefully streamed through still, lonely air seven miles above the earth's surface, occasionally flashing our landing light at passing aircraft and receiving a friendly flash back. This social "hello" carries the same familiar feel of comradery as when I give a slight wave to other bikers on the road, as I cruise by on my motorcycle.

Heading south in bright moonlight, I watched as storm cells rose up from the ground and took shape off in the distance at head-spinning rates. This time lapse view was as real as it gets.

We crisscrossed the skies from Colorado to Texas, using our radar to avoid isolated pockets of rain and turbulence in our way. Inflight, I see geography in my mind as vertical and always shifting. The sky is alive and unpredictable, and I look to the shape and movement of the clouds with a seriousness that only a pilot understands.

This weather front ahead of us with its mountainous build-ups, was a growing obstacle which we had managed to avoid, so far.

As we headed farther south, I felt like I had entered a high-stakes game of dodgeball. We ducked left and right, managing to stay clear of all but the occasional billow. One hundred miles out from our destination, we began our descent for the airport. I knew we wouldn't be able to keep in the clear for much longer as we flew into the building weather system and the bright lights of cities passing underneath us faded to just soft glimmers through the haze.

White puffy masses rushing past our windshield gave us a dizzying reference in the moonlight, and a sudden head rush as our speed forward became apparent. Some pilots keep their eyes inside when they streak through cloud decks, but I take it all in: the sensation is like nothing else.

We worked harder as the gaps of clear air narrowed until eventually the wet clouds came together and closed off any hope of skirting them.

We arrived over SAT shortly before midnight to find the air traffic control system was "down the tubes," as they like to say. We wanted to land, but the controllers had other plans for us, as I expected they would. A slew of other airliners who had arrived before us were already spinning in layers of a holding pattern, in a clear pocket of airspace, awaiting their turn to the runway. Moving to the end of the line, we took our place in queue at the top of the stack and began the tedious ritual of flying in circles in an imaginary race track in the sky, while gazing down upon our fellow inmates trapped in the same endless loop.

Bad weather slows everything down, much like how lane closures for construction can bring speeding traffic to a crawl. In this case, SAT only had one runway that was plowed, so every aircraft had to get in line for this single runway. Flying in pointless circles to kill time and wait our turn to land was a standard government delay tactic. But this burned—or, more significantly, wasted — a tremendous amount of fuel.

My mind paced in the cockpit as the weather continued to deteriorate below us and the runway conditions worsened with each mind-numbing circle that we flew. A continuous stream of data flowed out of our printer from our dependable dispatcher. Adding commentary to his weather reports, he pointed out that the visibility and runway conditions at our backup airport of AUS were now more hazardous than at SAT, our destination down below us. I appreciated his diligence, but he couldn't hold my hand up here. I could see what was happening and I can promise you, Cory and I were on top of the deteriorating weather conditions and what that meant for us. Our minds were nowhere else.

With plan B out the window, I had to ensure that I saved enough fuel to reach plan C. DFW was our only remaining backup airport. I popped some numbers into my calculator and the results came up shorter than I had hoped.

"Cory, we can burn 2,000 more pounds, and then time's up and we're heading to DFW." I'm guessing he had already been doing the math in his own head, as he quickly agreed and waved his typing finger for me, ready for action with our navigation system. Cory had the big picture.

We continued to spin in circles with the precision of a Swiss watch, impatiently waiting for the occasional clearance to tick down to the next lower altitude. The controller peeled aircraft off the bottom track and cleared them into the airport with the reliability of a sun dial at midnight. When it would be our turn was anybody's guess. I briefed our flight attendants with all that I knew, which was not much. It was a waiting game for us as well as for our passengers, as they glared at their watches, and I watched the numbers tick down on my fuel synoptic page.

Cory and I scrutinized the vivid primary-colored images moving across our radar screen for a hint of what was developing around us. We continued to circle, vulnerable and impatient, and completely at the mercy of our air traffic control prison guards.

At long last we were the bottom aircraft in the stack and finally cleared towards the airport. But 'towards' the airport was all that we got. The controller assigned us various heading and altitude changes, resulting in the most indirect and time-consuming path to the runway imaginable. He needed to delay us even further because we were catching up to an American Airlines jet ahead of us for the runway.

With each step down in altitude, we came closer to the overcast thickening below us, until we finally dipped down into it. We lost the moonlight as we sank into thick wet clouds and were blindsided with turbulence that rattled glasses in the galley and splashed my diet coke onto my knee. I heard a baby crying in the back, and my heart momentarily ached for my sleeping infant at home. I increased the flow of cold air into the passenger cabin, as I always do in turbulence. It is harder to vomit when you are cold.

Air may not be visible, but turbulence is as real as an ocean wave knocking you over. Air is a fluid; we measure it, calculate it, read it on our instruments, and we depend on it to hold our wings up and feed our engines. But as uncomfortable as turbulence can be for passengers, aircraft are designed to slice right through it. Rough air is the normal and expected operating environment for a jet.

At last we lined up with the runway. Locked onto the invisible tractor beam to the pavement in a steady descent, we broke out underneath the dense cloud cover.

I smiled as the yellow beams of my landing lights shooting into the fog were instantly replaced by a spectacular view.

Vibrant runway lights cut through the black midnight air, brilliantly outlining two miles of perfect straight pavement directly ahead of us. Strobe lights flashed in a rolling sequence along the ground, leading my eyes directly to the runway. This welcome might as well have been the red carpet at the Oscars rolled out just for us.

A million falling white flecks danced in our intensely bright landing lights, creating a sparkling blanket of white crystals cascading past our windshield and blowing down to earth. This soft flowing blanket of snow and ice was the only weather between us and the runway now.

Breaking free from the clouds would have been an undeniable relief, except ...

Something felt wrong.

I grappled with an unfamiliar sense of confinement, like I was trapped in a hole and peering through a tunnel. My momentary confusion dissipated with a shake of my head. It took me but a second to understand.

I realized that I could only see out the windshield directly in front of me. All the remaining cockpit windows, and there are several, were coated with a thick layer of solid ice. Even Cory's half of the front windshield was completely opaque, no longer a pane of glass to look through, but a glacial wall to look at. My panoramic view of the world was shrunken down to one single pane of glass.

I had never before encountered an ice accumulation rate that exceeded the abilities of my aircraft anti-icing system to dispel. Not on any aircraft. Not at any airline.

If this ice was able to accumulate on our powerfully heated windshields, then was ice also plastered to other parts of our aircraft? Like putty in warm hands, ice can remold the shape of the wings and mess with the perfect mathematical formula that allows an airplane to fly. Ice is more threatening than bricks falling from the sky. It's quiet. It's patient. Ice is insidious.

Instinctively pushing the thrust levers forward, I increased my airspeed. Even though I was hand flying, I was suspicious of the computerized fly-by-wire flight control system and the artificial feel I was receiving through my sidestick.

How much ice can this aircraft handle before my wings lose lift and my flight controls are compromised, and how much warning will I get? This disquieting question slid into my thoughts. I really wished I had more time and experience on *this* aircraft.

This was a hell of a first day.

My heart settled into a more consistent rhythm as the runway grew closer and safely reaching it became more assured. Gear down, spoilers armed, flaps extended and yet another checklist completed by Cory, as I flew the plane. I had already shifted my thoughts to our touchdown when the American Airlines flight immediately ahead of us declared an emergency.

The pilot's voice boomed over our shared frequency to our shared air traffic controller. "San Antonio tower, American 423. On the Go. Our windshields are iced over. Unable to see the runway. Declaring an emergency."

Those guys were flying *completely* blind! At least I had one windshield that held up against the ice. Contrary to urban legend, planes do not just land themselves and the pilot being able to see outside is a critical requirement.

For just a few seconds I felt lucky that *we* didn't have it worse. But I did not see what was coming next. The controllers closed the runway for an aircraft in distress.

"United 706, go around." We were told to abandon our landing.

I was stunned just for a moment. Then I was furious. We had made it and now this controller was denying us *our* landing slot and sending us climbing back up into the frozen surf we had just escaped.

"What did he just say?" I looked over at Cory. I could tell by his equally dumbfounded expression that I heard the controller right. It was true.

"Climb and maintain 3,000," the controller continued, "maintain runway heading." He wasn't messing around.

Those words felt like shards of glass.

"Oh crap," I involuntarily shared my concern with Cory. His chosen words of agreement were a little harsher than mine. Just what sort of amateur was this controller? Fine for him to send us back into it. What was the worst thing that could happen to him? He might fall off his stool? I wasn't afraid. I was mad.

I felt betrayed.

No matter how meticulously you dot your *i*'s and cross your *t*'s, there is always an unpredictability to flying that you just can't get around. The jet in front of us declaring an emergency was my flying monkeys suddenly swooping down on Dorothy.

I didn't see that coming.

The domino effect began. The plane behind us, and the one behind him, were also sent around. I jammed the thrust levers full forward to max thrust. Our aircraft bucked under the power surge, pushing passengers rudely down into their seats as we shot back upwards. Bullied again by turbulence, I gripped my sidestick to control the aircraft. I didn't want to overstress the airframe by fighting back too vigorously, though, and allowed our heading and altitude to bounce along with the currents, taking us and our passengers for a queasy ride.

The baby continued crying in the back, his sobs piercing my heart as I pictured my own infant at home crying in someone else's arms. My passengers' anxiety scuttled through my mind, but that thought didn't remain there long enough for me to make any Captain speech of calm reassurance to them, or to my flight attendants.

A sickening ache whispered through me as we punched back into the black confinement of the wet clouds. I knew these clouds had already coated my aircraft in ice.

We shouldn't be here. I know better.

I keyed my mic, "San Antonio, United 706, low fuel." I moved onto plan D.

I was improvising.

"Roger, United 706. State fuel remaining." Our controller didn't miss a beat.

I shot back my answer, but I held back the entire truth.

"Laura, we have forty more minutes than that!" Cory sounded alarmed, like he just realized his captain was losing her mind and actually didn't know how much fuel was in her tanks.

"I know." I gave him a determined smirk. "But *that* fuel is in my back pocket."

Yes, I am that captain who lied, because I am that captain who didn't want one more minute of ice accumulation on my aircraft.

Plan D worked like a charm. We were promptly vectored back to the airport. We climbed, then descended and quickly ended up right back at the exact spot we had started from. It was ten minutes later and my hair had grown an inch. I prayed there would be no more surprises between us and the runway. I had nothing left in my back pocket.

As we sank closer to the runway for the second go at it, the controller reported a strong crosswind with even higher gusts, and standing snow and slush on the runway.

"Oh great, my first day as captain and I am going to slide off the runway," I sarcastically quipped to Cory. Glancing over to make quick eye contact with him, Cory's ambiguous facial expression of kindred support could have meant, "We've got this and I love your calm wit," just as well as he could have been thinking, "I hope the black box didn't record me saying anything dumb on this trip."

Perhaps I needed to check my humor.

I didn't actually think I would slide off the runway, but it was a risk I knew to take seriously. The runway was covered in still accumulating wet snow mixed with freezing rain. The crosswind was at the maximum demonstrated ability of our aircraft, so I would be approaching with my nose pointed into the wind and not down the runway, with the plan to straighten out just at touchdown—a standard technique made tricky by my lack of side window visibility. Once on the runway, using my brakes could cause the aircraft to slide, so I would be counting on my spoilers and engine reversers to work properly to bring us to an aerodynamic stop on the rollout. With all of that on my mind, I was still vying just to reach the runway without accumulating any more ice.

We did make it all the way to the runway this time. The tires hit the concrete, splashing into moving slush. I immediately pushed the nose down to gain directional control, and then smoothly eased both engines symmetrically into reverse to keep the aircraft rolling in a straight line as it slowed. The powerful reversers scooped up wet snow and ice, blowing it wildly into the air. A blinding white wave crashed over my windshield. The screams from my engines suffering from full reverse thrust mercifully washed the baby's crying from my ears and filled my head with thoughts of machines and madness. I held onto the centerline with my feet working the rudder pedals, until I purposefully turned off the runway and settled onto a taxiway.

"That was great flying." Cory's furrowed forehead relaxed, as he took a deep breath and the tension eased across his face.

"Thanks."

I surveyed our new surroundings. We could have been adrift on an iceberg, it was so barren and bright-white clean around us. Any hint of taxiway markings or signage was completely missing, hidden beneath glossy layers of snow and ice.

I turned to Cory. "Where is our gate?"

This was surprisingly my biggest concern now. It was so trifling, it was almost funny to me. Cory stepped right up to the plate. He was familiar with SAT.

I crept along to the terminal building, as my pulse quieted to a normal beat and my tongue itched with a bitter taste. Safely at the gate, I reached up to shut the engines down and saw my hand tremble as a massive adrenalin dump worked overdrive on my system — my body utterly depleted.

No one would ever know how bad that was.

"Holy shit!" the mechanic greeted us as he stuck his head into the cockpit. "You have a foot of ice accumulated on your nose!" He looked absolutely blown away.

Curiosity overtook my exhaustion. I needed to see for myself. After the last passenger disappeared, I climbed down the jet bridge stairs welcoming the chilled air as it filtered through my damp shirt, and I sucked it into my lungs. The wing anti-icing system had worked beautifully, holding those airfoils to their true shape. But the rest of my aircraft was not recognizable, loosely resembling an Arctic exhibit that might be found in the Smithsonian.

Warmly ensconced in my hotel room that night, I wrapped myself tightly in the blankets and gazed at the ceiling. A sense of pride for the beauty and power of my machine flowed through me. And more so, I felt honored for the trust that my passengers had given me.

As the last of my energy drained away, I hugged my pillow and rolled over into a deep, long sleep.

WHAT IF THE PILOT GETS SICK?

I hear that pilots are thought to be cocky.

Yes, it's true a pilot is confident. We are not just secure in our abilities; a pilot is confident in other pilots' abilities as well. We work as a team. The workload is divided, and we always back each other up. Redundancy boosts safety. If one of us makes a mistake, we both made a mistake. Aside from enhancing safety, this makes for the absolute best office environment because there is no competition. You want your colleagues to excel. This may sound like a small thing, but believe me, it's nice.

Without instinctive self-confidence for quick and accurate decision making, a pilot would not make it very far in this occupation. Flight training and checkrides weed those without this fortitude out of our group. Sure, we practice all the routine parts of flying a jet, but it's the twists from the normal–from the expected — that decides who stays and who goes.

On any typical simulator training session, an approach and landing may start off as humdrum as tying your shoes, but then it begins to sleet outside, so it gets just a tiny bit more interesting, and then *shazam* — we have a hydraulic pump failure, so no speed brakes for that slippery runway now. And oh my, the left engine is on fire as well. Oh wait, the "flight attendant," and by that I mean our sadistic simulator instructor talking over our shoulders in a peculiar high-pitched voice, tells us that the cabin is filling with smoke and our passengers are choking.

I know this sounds like a good time. But it's not.

Boeing 777 flight simulator — crossing over Pearl Harbor on approach into HNL, Honolulu, Hawaii.

These twists and turns are the heart of our training, though. Because some day there will be a surprise twist that will be very real. No matter how far-fetched a scenario might be that the instructor dumps on us in the simulator, we have to get it right. There is no fudging the final outcome.

Although we depend on each other, each pilot is capable of the full operation of their aircraft solo—completely on their own, with no help from anybody. It can be done, but operating a large commercial aircraft all alone is exhausting and an immense workload. Just one time at United Airlines, I got to find that out firsthand.

I was in the middle of a line check as a captain on the A320 when it happened to me, adding both a twist and a turn to my normal routine. What is a line check? A pilot's proficiency must be periodically observed and evaluated during a typical route segment by a qualified check airman.

This could be scheduled or a complete surprise to the pilot being observed. Much like random drug and alcohol testing which pilots regularly submit to, you just never know when a line check is going to happen.

The check captain evaluating me that day was named George. He was actually a pretty cool guy and impressively relaxed for a check airman. We departed for Washington, DC, DCA, on a regularly scheduled passenger flight. We had a full load of both passengers and cargo. George took the first officer's seat in the cockpit, and he was a very efficient co-pilot for me. But the fact was, he was a senior captain bestowed with the power to decide whether I was competent or not, and he was not there to help me. He was there to observe my skills and make a report. Having someone watching your every move while jotting down concealed notes about you, never feels good.

To make this flight just a little more interesting, and by that I mean more stressful, it was also a Lifeguard Flight. Commercial airliners regularly transport donor organs for immediate transplant. When we have this special container onboard, we add the word 'Lifeguard' to our regular call sign and receive priority handling by Air Traffic Control.

Looking back to the first time a courier made this special delivery to my cockpit, I was a little confused. A man in a uniform I did not recognize entered the cockpit and placed a generic Igloo cooler on the floor just behind my seat. It was so plain, it could have easily held a six pack of beer.

"What's this?" I turned to question this stranger.

"Eyeballs."

It actually was eyeballs.

Although I knew what that red and white cooler was all about this time around, it was always a surprise to suddenly become a Lifeguard Flight. It's not the sort of thing that allowed advance notice.

Some days are just really good flying days. A day when the sun is shining bright and you just can't help but smile and plod along forward because everything is going so smoothly. Regardless of the particular pressures on this upcoming flight, this was one of those days for me, so far.

We crossed over the country not only uneventfully, but in record time on our way to DCA. As an airborne ambulance, we cut to the head of every Air Traffic Control line throughout the system. All that was left was the approach and landing into DCA, then I would get to go home to my waiting children. I already anticipated a tricky approach ahead of me into our nation's capital. The runways are short and surrounded by filthy green water at Reagan Washington National Airport. Other airports in the system had this same challenging design, but unique to this airport, pilots have to dodge a minefield of Prohibited Areas while landing their jets. Just to pile a little more on, this happened to be a bitter winter day, the winds were howling, and the airport surfaces were coated in a thin film of ice.

I expected to have my work cut out for me on this landing, but I didn't expect the twists that were coming.

Ever since we ate our crew meals, George had been grumbling that he did not feel well. His face grew progressively paler as the ride grew bumpier on our descent into DCA. But it was time to land the plane, and George's full focus was required for the task at hand. He would just have to wait until later to feel nauseous.

"Flaps one," I called to George as we slipped into line behind another aircraft, also following the Potomac River south towards Reagan National Airport.

"I really don't feel well." George sounded weak and his words rushed, like he just had one short breath to get them out.

Sorry to hear that George, but I still need my flaps … now.

Then I heard the electric hum of his seat traveling in its tracks … backwards.

Um, George, we're landing right now. Kind of need your help up front.

"Lifeguard United 614, cleared for the River Visual Runway 19." The air traffic controller needed a response from George, who was working the radios, but rolling *away* from his headset. He continued traveling backwards away from his duties, until the flaps lever was out of his reach and his seat bumped the rear stop. That's where you roll back to after the plane is parked safely at the gate and you are ready to climb out of your seat and leave.

Time always grows compressed on arrival, but as a Lifeguard Flight we were zipping in on fast-forward.

"Hey George, you okay?"

He wasn't answering me, and he wasn't answering the air traffic controller either. We both needed his attention. However, George was busy wheezing like a cat trying desperately to get out that big, wet hair ball. The only sounds coming from his mouth were spastic, gagging noises gurgling up from his gullet.

Then George flung himself out of his seat, and in one swift move yanked his hat from its hook and retched chunky orange liquid into it. Stomach bile continued spurting out of his mouth, spraying over his fingers as he clutched his hat by the brim.

I couldn't handle more than a glance at what was going on behind me before quickly turning back to my instruments. George's tie was hanging down, dipping into the syrupy fluid that filled his hat. His mouth was lathered in orange foam and tiny bubbles oozed down his chin. *Was that the salmon tacos he had for lunch?*

The foul stench of puke instantly filled my nose and went right to my full stomach. I could feel acidic bile rising in my throat and I started to gag. I tried to sound routine as I stepped in for George and answered the controller, but my voice was broken up into weird short gasps as I tasted the smell of George's vomit each time I opened my mouth to speak.

I was ready to start heaving myself, but *holy geez* I was busy! Sure, I had thought about the "one pilot incapacitated" scenario. But train, train, train and never had I practiced anything like this. I imagined pilot incapacitation happening somewhere during cruise, where I would have had plenty of time to prepare to be this one-armed paper hanger for landing. Or perhaps, the incapacitated pilot would be sitting quietly in his seat and the only clue something was wrong, would be his awkward silence caused by coronary failure. I never imagined I would be choking down chewy spittles of cheesy, fish taco vomit in my mouth as I landed solo.

I heard a pause and I thought George had finally finished puking behind me. I listened to him panting now, his breathing short and shallow. But no, George was just taking a moment before he advanced to projectile vomiting, sending spurts of regurgitated fish, spinach, and stomach acid shooting across the flight deck. A warm orange chunk landed on my forearm, while other wet bits splattered across the throttles. I had to wrap my fingers over it all with a squish and keep flying.

Damn I was busy and grossed out. I ran all the checklists alone, playing both pilot roles. I charmed the controller with all the expected responses and made the required "prepare for landing" announcement over the passenger address system for our flight attendants, all while hand-flying the airplane in ridiculously gusty, turbulent conditions on a complex visual approach into DCA. And all while swallowing back little bits of vomit in my mouth. Not a soul outside of our rancid, rotting-fish cocoon had any idea of the nightmare I was living.

I'm guessing George was trying his best not to distract me, as he got low onto the floor and tried to contain himself. His knees rubbed vomit into the carpet, and he desperately cupped his hands over his mouth as warm liquid oozed though his fingers with each gut-wrenched gag and cough. And the smell. It was too awful for words. I cannot even begin to describe how thick the air was with that rotted stench.

George crawled back into his seat just before I reached the runway. As much as he wanted to get back to work, occupying his seat was about all that he could pull off.

My seat settled with a thump as the landing gear found the concrete, compressing the struts as the full weight of the aircraft dumped on them. In an instant the wings stopped producing lift and became nothing more than dead weight for the tires to take on.

The ground spoilers deployed automatically as advertised, throwing up ten little flaps on top of the wings, 'spoiling' our lift as the air banged into them. I flipped the thrust reverse levers up over the throttles and yanked hard and fast, throwing our engines into reverse thrust, aggressively halting our forward momentum on this short, slippery runway.

In agonizing, disgusted misery, I taxied to the gate and parked. It was the longest taxi of my life. We kept the flight deck door locked after landing until every last passenger and flight attendant had left the aircraft.

Needless to say, the mechanics weren't too happy when they boarded and walked in on us. I believe the cleaning crew was even less thrilled. Thankfully, our eyeball filled Igloo was spared any flying vomit and was ready for pick-up.

George did thank me, and he apologized more than I can remember someone ever apologizing to me before. Of course, he didn't need to apologize at all. But what else do you say when you vomit all over somebody while they are flying a plane? And this even became a funny story — much, much, much later.

George was too sick to debrief me, or to even complete the paperwork evaluating my performance. He told me to just go home and he would get to the paperwork on another day.

Sometimes unexpected things have happened which I simply could have done without, regardless of how good the story was later. But I always got through it.

My evaluation arrived several days later. I passed my line check. In fact, George gave my flying skills such glowing praise, in a document that would go into my permanent record, it was almost worth it all.

Almost.

THE PUPPY SNUFFER

34

What is that tired old cliché? "Flying is 99% boredom and 1% terror."
I don't know about the boredom part, but the 1% terror is something I can
vouch for. Don't assume that terror is about self-preservation, though, or just
about my passengers' safety. That feeling of immense responsibly extends to
everything between my wings, including all precious cargo.

"Flight attendants, please be seated for departure" My first officer, Jay's
voice, boomed over the cabin speakers — his ordinary voice right there
beside me, competing with his much louder voice echoing through our
cockpit door.

This simple line is code, from the pilots to the flight attendants. *You
have two minutes to get into your seats.* With over two hundred sophisticated
computers onboard our Airbus 320 aircraft, we rely on our best guess
to pinpoint when our takeoff clearance will come. We then give this
information to the flight attendants, by forcing every person in the aircraft
cabin to listen to it.

We were departing Portland, Oregon, PDX, that morning, for Chicago,
ORD. Only seconds after giving the two-minute warning to our flight
attendants, the voice of the controller rasped into our ears. "United 490, fly
heading 095, runway 10R, cleared for takeoff."

From behind tinted glass over a mile away, a man watched over us from a tall tower across the airfield. He could see us, but we could not see him.

Oops, that wait was a lot shorter than two minutes.

The flight attendants are skilled at finding their seats quickly when they hear the engines spooling up, although they don't always appreciate having to scramble, and this miscalculation could slow down my desired flow of hot tea to the flight deck.

Jay clicked through the final items on the checklist, each item vanishing off of his monitor as our artificial intelligence acknowledged the task had been accomplished. My thoughts jumped through a quick review of the engine failure procedures for this runway, like when I was a gymnast taking that deep solitary breath, all alone within myself before the start of my vault.

Got it.

I rolled my aircraft forward until I was looking straight down the runway. White centerline stripes marred by burnt rubber, flowed down the pavement until they vanished into the distance. I curled my fingers over the smooth round knobs of the thrust levers. Feeling the building power humming inside the palm of my hand, I eased them forward until the turbine blades reached just the metrical shriek I was listening for. Steadfast in front of me, my aircraft nose developed a rhythmic spring as our forward pace down the runway picked up speed.

Runway stripes streamed underneath me, and steel rudder pedals quivered against the soles of my shoes as I made imperceptible steering corrections with my feet. The deaf airport rabbits ignored us screaming past them as they nibbled on freshly cut grass along the pavement edges.

"80 knots. Thrust set," Jay called out.

"80 knots. Cross checked," I confirmed, with a brief glance inside to the instruments.

"V1 ... Vr ... " Jay announced as we reached each of our calculated velocities.

I squeezed the control stick back towards me and felt myself lifted into the air. The runway, followed by the buildings and treetops, vanished beneath me. My stalwart view of the aircraft nose did not change, though.

It stayed quiet and still in the exact same position in front of me, while the background dropped away.

Once free from the ground, my flight controls responded to the lightest touch, and I felt content and safe. I always waited for a disagreement with Mother Nature when I entered her territory, but today the air was calm and cooperative.

I lowered my guard just a bit and enjoyed the smooth climb out.

Radio chatter scratched in my ear as scores of other jets droned around us, each doing their own thing in this tightly controlled airspace. I could see nothing but my own aircraft's nose, though, and the clear sky straight above me.

We squirreled our way up and away from the airport. Eventually leaving the high workload of congested airspace behind, we entered the freedom of upper jet route airspace. Once we leveled at our final cruise altitude of 35,000 feet, I checked the aircraft systems, scanning my screens like skimming over a text book with illustrations. All was well. With a series of taps into my autopilot system, I sat back for the ride.

I didn't know a thing about Jay, my first officer, yet. So here began the "getting to know you" stage of our trip. Working with a new colleague at the start of every month, if not more often, pilots have perfected their introductory routine and never have to worry about coming up with new material. The audience perpetually changes. We may start the morning as complete strangers, but by the time we get to a restaurant for dinner after that first day is over, we are laughing and comfortable in a way that most servers find it hard to believe we only met that morning. By the end of the week we are old friends and there is surprisingly little we don't know about each other.

"So, Jay, I take it you're married?" I noted his wedding band and the ziplock baggie of home-baked cookies in his flight bag.

"Well, I am right now," Jay sighed. "I think Beth, that's my wife, is pretty upset with me. She called me when I was in the middle of my walk-around, crying that the basement was underwater, but I couldn't talk. I actually hung up on her." Jay rolled his eyes. "Really, a burst pipe? Why do these crises always happen when I'm away?"

"Because you're always away, Jay." I gave him a smart-ass wink at the obvious. This is an understood drawback of our occupation. Being a pilot would be absolutely perfect, if we just didn't have to travel so much.

"So … kids?" I edged forward.

"Oh yeah, we just had a baby," Jay boasted with a hint of pride lightening his mood.

"That's great. Congratulations. Boy? Girl?"

"I said we just had a baby, not we just had a boy," Jay jokingly chastised me. "Obviously, it was a girl."

I guessed there was going to be more of this kind of humor ahead of me on this trip, the kind I wasn't sure if I should retort, or not.

"How about you? Family?" Jay moved on.

"Married, with two boys at home … and a nanny to take care of the house and two boys at home," I shrugged with a grin. This quip was as vulnerable as I could muster on this subject.

Married life had taken me by surprise. As much as I diligently planned out and studied in my professional life to ensure I was prepared for anything, my personal life was a chaotic mess. Not until after having my babies did discussions come up about how I would continue to work and what role their father would play in raising them. Dom was an exciting boyfriend, but being a husband and father were dynamically different roles. I loved being a mother and enthusiastically adapted to changes parenthood brought, but I had assumed these changes would fit in naturally to our marriage. In this case, my fierce self-reliant nature allowed me to overlook missed conversations that should have taken place before marriage.

Jay and I continued with small talk, comparing notes about the hotel we would be laying over at that night and debating which was better, a yoke or sidestick. I showed him the red penguins sewn on the ankles of my socks, because there is something about the isolation of the cockpit and being locked away from the rest of the world, that lends itself to revealing personal details that you might not even share with your best friend.

"I get so bored with this stiff uniform; my socks are my hidden self-expression." I poked fun at myself. But this was absolutely true about me. "Just wait until you see my socks tomorrow," I laughed.

Jay picked up our shared one-liter water bottle and carefully filled his cup. "Ha, I can top that. You couldn't guess *my* hidden self-expression." Jay mocked me, as if he actually had some cagey secret that could top my penguin sock reveal.

All at once, our cockpit flipped into a tumult of alarms and flashing lights. The color red blinked in front of us. A monitoring computer sensed an emergency and was screaming for our attention. A continuous chime banged out of our speakers, too loud to talk over, as if the Master Warning Lights fiercely flashing red into our faces weren't enough to ensure our full attention.

I reached up and instinctively punched a warning light, silencing the alarm and changing the flashing red lights into a stream of steady red lights. An attention demanding digital message glowed across our center monitor.

SMOKE: AFT CARGO SMOKE

This was bad.

"You can guess later," Jay quipped as he dropped the water bottle behind him, instantly freeing his hands. The nearly-full bottle rolled until it banged into the locked cockpit door on the floor behind us.

The ECAM (Electronic Central Aircraft Monitoring System), a clever computerized brain that knows all things at all times, had already assessed the situation and digitally supplied us with the appropriate checklist to battle this emergency.

"Smoke in the aft cargo compartment. You've got the airplane. I'll do the ECAM," I announced out loud. Yes, we have a verbatim script memorized for just this situation.

I turned all my attention to the emergency checklist that had popped up on my screen, forcing priority over what *I* had previously selected to view. In turn, Jay concentrated completely on flying the aircraft, navigating and communicating with air traffic control and our company. Only during irregular operations such as this, do task assignments need to be called out loud by the captain. And just like everything else, even the most unexpected situation has a rehearsed protocol.

Before I had a chance to take any action, the warning message and digital checklist blinked out, disappearing off the screen and leaving it oddly blank. Simultaneously, the frenetic warning lights went dark, leaving the cockpit abruptly peaceful now.

The sun shone a shade brighter outside our windows as the cockpit lights returned to black and white dullness. My sense of alarm did not just go away, though.

I mulled over our rapidly changing situation, ripping through systems knowledge in my head to put this puzzle together. There was no fire indicated … now. So, smoke was no longer sensed in the cargo bay. Perhaps it was only a passing glitch in the system?

Perhaps.

"Gremlins?" Jay threw out, mirroring my optimism.

With so many complex computers and electric signals, random glitches are not uncommon, and "gremlins" is often the best explanation we can come up with.

Our fire detection system works by detecting smoke particles in the air. Years back, an aircraft made an emergency landing due to a smoke warning in the cargo bay. The pilots thought their aircraft was on fire. But in the end, it was just their load of flatulent pigs setting the smoke detectors off. Airlines carry all sorts of crazy things in their cargo bays, besides luggage.

At this moment, I wished we had pigs in our hold to explain everything. But then that thought triggered something inside me. An overwhelming, anxious feeling flashed through me, like that panic you feel in the dark in that second you realized you missed the bottom step.

"Jay, don't we have animals in the hold today?" My mouth went dry as I started digging through our paperwork to find our weight manifest.

"Oh God, two dogs!" Jay understood where I was going with this and returned the sickened expression on my face.

Sensing even a momentary fire in the aft cargo compartment would have triggered an automated defensive mode, isolating that compartment from the rest of the aircraft by closing ventilation valves and shutting off oxygen to it.

"The warning is out. No fire, then." I didn't waste a second. "I'm going to work on getting those valves back open and try to get the ventilation system back up to the cargo hold."

I didn't want to say it out loud, but I'd hoped it was not already too late for those poor dogs. Not only was the fresh air supply cut off to the now sealed compartment, but that warmed, pressurized air was also a source of heat for those dogs. As breathtaking as the view may be out the window from 35,000 feet, the reality is it's a harsh environment up there. Our current outside air temperature was 60 degrees below zero, and the wind was blowing at 230 miles per hour.

Killing man's best friend is not a problem in modern jetliners, save an anomaly like what was happening to us today. Systems and technology have come a long way over the years. But animals still come last when the passenger cabin is in any sort of jeopardy. On the classic Boeing 727, which had been the most common passenger aircraft in the airline industry for decades, pets were sporadically sacrificed for the safety of the passenger cabin. The flight engineer had a switch on his panel, which every pilot woefully knew as "the puppy snuffer," and which every pilot hated to use, but occasionally had to. I believe Boeing innocuously labeled it the "aft cargo heat valve."

Air Traffic Control commonly assigned rapid descents when funneling airliners from the big open blue sky to the narrow runway. In order to go down and slow down concurrently, a pilot must reduce thrust as much as possible by bringing the throttles back for a flight idle descent.

The engines on the 727 weren't as powerful as later model engines, and the pressurization system was equally antiquated. Thrust at idle simply could not pump enough air into the air conditioning system to supply the passenger cabin *and* the cargo compartments. So, the pilot would have no choice but to divert warmed pressurized air heading for the cargo compartment, to the passenger cabin … snuffing out Spot and Fido.

We didn't have a puppy snuffer on our A320, but our dogs were not in a good position.

"United 490, descend and maintain flight level 240." Oblivious to our situation completely, the Chicago controller threw a wrench into my work to save the dogs.

Time grows compressed when you enter Chicago airspace. We were going to get very busy, very quickly. Jay continued to monitor ATC and take on all of the flying pilot and non-flying pilot duties combined, freeing me up completely to concentrate on the cargo hold and getting air to the dogs. But, I had little time left before Jay would need me back in the loop with him.

I paged through my flight manual for the Cargo Smoke procedure.

"Here it is," I announced out loud, and started reading the procedure methodically from the top. Pilots do everything methodically from the top.

"All right, we've determined the warning was temporary. Smoke is no longer being detected. We can reset the system and get those valves back open with circuit breaker C7."

After moving my seat to the back stop, I unbuckled and got up. Reaching above my head, I ran my finger over the C line of circuit breakers on the ceiling and counted over seven. I snapped it out, then reset it.

Holding my breath, I waited to see if that fresh flow of oxygen into the cargo hold triggered the smoke alarm back to life. Nothing is more serious than a fire in flight. An aircraft burns quickly and there is no escape. The alarms and red strobes on my panel remained quiet.

I hopped back into my seat and relieved Jay of the flying duties. Everything fell back to normal, for all appearances. An unsettled feeling hung in the air, though. But it was all about the landing now. No distractions allowed.

I had to force the dogs to the back of my mind. They were alive or they were not — and I couldn't do anything about it.

Soon, we were part of the daisy chain of airliners lined up in the sky to land in ORD. Whether arriving or departing, there is nothing Midwest about the pace at which things move at ORD. Only the most talented air traffic controllers make it at O'Hare, and they "pilot push" because they can get away with it. The airport is exclusively open to professional pilots. This is why ORD is safe. It is so complex, and so congested, no amateurs are allowed in the game.

Trying not to interrupt my own focus in this complex airspace, my thoughts kept sneaking back to the aft cargo compartment. I kept a keen eye on the indicators that monitored the cargo holds, looking for any irregularities. Nothing stood out as unusual and I was feeling somewhat relieved as more time safely passed. It certainly appeared to be a gremlin in our detection system, but I couldn't be sure.

Did I do the right thing, opening the cargo hold up to the rest of the aircraft ... to save a couple of dogs?

Soon a clear view of ORD with tiny airplanes streaming down onto its runways lay in front of us like a child's play set with the bottle green waters of Lake Michigan resting beside it. Did the controller allow us to keep flying straight ahead for the runway right in front of us? No, the controller turned us out over the white capped waters of Lake Michigan, vectoring us away from the airport. The whole city of Chicago disappeared behind us, and soon all we could see was choppy open water in all directions as we flew east on an extended tour of the massive lake. There was a razor-sharp line of aircraft stretched out clear across Lake Michigan, passing us flying the opposite direction, all riding on the same invisible track towards a runway.

"So, do you think he forgot about us?" I rolled my eyes at Jay as we continued to drone out over the water for what seemed an absurd duration flying in the wrong direction. Sometimes, I think those controllers are down there just knee slapping at how much fuel they can make us waste flying the wrong way. But today, wasted fuel was not what had me anxious to get on the ground.

At last, we reached the end of the long line and turned back towards the airport, taking our place behind the last aircraft headed for the runway. I pushed up on my sunglasses, grateful our U-turn had shifted the intense morning sun behind us now, and I could focus on the runway ahead without tears in my squinting eyes.

We sunk towards the ground at a precise three-degree angle. Leaving the cool water behind, grey buildings passed underneath us until our tires hung over a seamless strip of pavement.

"Twenty ... Ten" The steadfast mechanical voice of our radio altimeter counted down our height above the runway, until we settled onto the pavement. Instantly we transitioned from a flying machine to a land vehicle. I nimbly swapped control from my hands to my feet; steering with the rudder pedals as the ailerons became useless on the ground. With the touchdown behind us, I was eager to get the aircraft parked and the engines shut down.

I was done waiting.

Were the dogs okay?

We crept safely into our parking spot and began the shutdown process. Once the engines were powerless and still, we continued working together to put the remaining systems to rest as Jay ticked through the parking checklist. Interrupting our flow, our eyes connected as the hydraulic moans of the cargo doors cycling open grabbed our attention. The ramp workers were already at work on the right side of the aircraft, emptying the cargo bays. Live animals were always pulled off first.

Jay ripped through the last items on the checklist and hastily swung around to look out his window. He craned his neck, angling for a view of the aft cargo as it was removed from the holds on his side of the aircraft.

"Geez Jay, don't leave me hanging here." We hadn't spoken, but we both knew what Jay was searching for on the ramp.

"I can't see," he moaned. A traffic jam of ground personnel and their trucks had already swarmed our aircraft. Frustrated and knowing the baggage cart would drive away just as soon as the dogs were off loaded, Jay impulsively slid his window open and pushed his head and shoulder outside for a better angle to look back towards our tail.

He burst back in, with tousled hair and a grin.

"They're shivering … and barking!" he exclaimed and burst into an ear-to-ear smile.

Yes!

My heart skipped to a joyful bounce as a warm wave of relief rushed through me.

Now I felt ready to leave and head over to our next aircraft. I packed up my things, feeling carefree to move on and do this all over again. I popped out of my seat and felt my shoe squish into wet carpet. The water bottle Jay had tossed when our smoke alarms sounded, lay innocently against the closed cockpit door, empty.

"Oh, guess I didn't get the cap back on." Jay grimaced.

I had a gnawing feeling as I realized the water had disappeared under the carpet. I squatted down and yanked a corner of carpet up at the Velcro seam, looking to see where all the water had gone. Two worn metal-toed boots shuffled through the doorway and I turned my eyes up to see a gruff mechanic staring down at me.

"You are directly above the E&E Bay[1]. You had better hope that water is not coming through the ceiling down there." He paused and glared straight down at me, "Captain."

The dogs are okay, I consoled myself.

Jay and I were lucky we had an excuse not to stick around and see what the mechanics discovered. We had a tight connection and needed to hurry off to our next aircraft. Nobody could argue with that. We got away with merely completing some extra paperwork in the aircraft log before heading out the door.

We found out later that the bottle of water had showered into the E&E bay and damage had been done. Enough damage to ground the aircraft, cancelling the outbound flight that afternoon. This costly event generated a letter to every pilot in the company, warning of the damage associated with spilled liquids on the flight deck. We weren't the only ones to have a spill in the cockpit, but ours was by far the biggest.

In hindsight, I had made the right decision to save the dogs. I used my best judgement and knowledge, and I was lucky too. The dogs were cold, I'm sure. But thankfully they were just fine and were blissfully picked up by their owners. It couldn't have been a happier outcome. Unlike the water spill, no one would be the wiser that Rover and Spot had a rough go of it on that flight.

Not too many things about my occupation have a grey area. In fact, my job is probably as black-and-white an occupation as it gets. But on this day, that elusive 1% popped up and I had to make a call. There may have been a checklist for everything on my jet, but sometimes I had to fill in the blanks. This is how life goes sometimes, and one can only do their best. I think women, especially, tend to look at things from all angles, weighing this and that and then reconsidering this and that, again and again.

Sometimes I just need to feel good that I had used my heart and my intellect the best that I knew how, and let it go — whether the outcome was all that I'd hoped for, or not.

---

1   Electronics and Electrical Equipment Bay

HOPPING MAD

The nickname "Baby Einstein" followed me long after I could be looked upon as the baby in the group. I'd like to think this moniker stuck with me because I was a solid pilot. Perhaps, but Einstein I was not, and sometimes it really showed.

After a brutally long day of flying, followed by a restless night of sleep, I scurried down to the hotel lobby far too early for breakfast. I'm sure it was a lovely hotel, but I never saw it in the daylight and I really don't remember much about it. I know I was hungry when we started out that morning, and still exhausted from the night before. With my eyes half-closed in the back of the hotel courtesy van, I watched the blackness of night disappear into a clear sunlit morning on the drive back to the airport. This layover in Tucson, Arizona, TUS, was as ordinary as it got.

The jet that we had flown in the night before was gone when we arrived back at the airport. Another crew had taken it because their aircraft had maintenance problems, leaving us stuck with their lemon that was left behind for repairs. The midnight maintenance crew had been working on this aircraft through the night, but repairs came slow in TUS. United Airlines owned nothing at this airport in Arizona. We had no spare parts of our own and even the mechanics working on our jet were rented from another company.

The lead mechanic finally delivered the updated maintenance logbook to me in the cockpit, squeezing past the gate agent who was standing arms crossed in our doorway, palpably stressed to fall behind schedule this early in the morning. Partnered with my first officer, Ted, we taxied out, departed and landed just forty minutes later into another desert airport, Phoenix, Arizona, PHX. Short hops can be draining, transitioning immediately from the intensity of departure to the high workload of arrival, with no time in between to eat or take a break

Our brake temperatures shot up at touchdown, the quick hop and building heat of the desert already taking a toll on our machine. I tip-toed my jet to the terminal, caressing my toes on the brakes to tamp down the rising brake temperatures. Just as soon as we shut the engines down and completed the Parking Checklist, Ted hopped out of his seat to do the aircraft exterior preflight inspection. With only thirty minutes at the gate for our brakes to cool, we were already at risk for another delayed departure, and it was only 7:30 in the morning. I needed to make the most of our short ground time, and waved to the guideman outside to come plug in and speak to me. Pulling his earphones from his neck and placing them over his ears, he plugged his cord into the jack on our nosegear assembly.

"Yes, Captain?" His voice shot into my ear.

"I need to release the brakes at the gate here, to let them cool," I informed him.

"Chocks in. Cleared to release brakes," he answered in a curt voice. This was a quick turnaround, and he understood with no further questions. He did not want my jet delayed at his gate.

My empty stomach gnawed at me as I hurried to turn the cockpit around for our next departure, and I looked up performance data I needed to consider for hot brakes. Ted returned and climbed back into his seat. Before he even had a chance to complete his flows, the guideman's hurried voice boomed into my ear, "Standing by for pushback clearance." Sitting in the pushback tug now, his returned eye-contact made it clear he was ready to move us immediately, for an on-time departure.

My whole mind settled into the zone, efficiently stepping through coordinated procedures to begin aircraft pushback and start the engines in synchronized teamwork with Ted and the guideman.

"I left my purse on the catering truck!" Becky, one of the aft flight attendants exploded into the cockpit. She slammed our door open in complete alarm, as if the cabin were on fire and she was alerting us to burning passengers jumping for their lives from the emergency exits. My train of thought scattered in every direction.

"Please, please, please, everything is in my purse," she cried, without hesitating for a window to interrupt us. "I don't even have my car keys. I'm done in Chicago and go home. We can't leave my purse behind!"

I had to make a call. If I chose to keep moving forward with the departure sequence, Becky would be out of luck in Chicago without her keys, or even her phone or wallet to find another way home. If it were my purse there would be no decision to make. It would be illegal for us to depart without my wallet, containing my pilot and medical certificates. With Becky, there was a choice.

As a woman, I felt for her.

As the captain, I did not feel for her.

"Okay, we'll call the caterers and see if they have it." I folded. Sisterhood won out.

I instructed the guideman to hold everything while Ted radioed the catering company.

"Yes indeed," they answered. "We found a purse left on a cart. A driver will be right over to drop it off."

"How long will that take?" I mouthed for Ted to ask them.

"Give the driver three minutes. He's heading right over to you now," the caterer shot right back.

Great, that isn't so bad.

With clear skies above us, I was already calculating how I could make up for those lost minutes inflight.

We waited for *fifteen* minutes, with the catering company schmoozing us over the radio the entire time. A garbled voice kept us hanging with constant assurances. "The truck is on its way," was followed by, "he's right around the corner." Several times we were told, "the driver is just crossing the ramp towards you now." We spent every one of those fifteen minutes expecting a truck to pull up beside us. I impatiently stared across the ramp searching for that truck, until I had memorized every blackened tire streak and grease stain across the pavement.

"He's coming around the corner right … now … " I was told. One. More. Time.

"Noooooo, you can't leave my purse behind. He's coming around the corner right now!" Becky pleaded, her eyes watering, because she knew I was about to pull the plug on this purse rescue debacle.

Eyeing the aircraft parked at the gate beside us, I could see their workers closing up their cargo doors.

"If Southwest pushes, they might block us in," I lamented to Ted.

"We can't catch a break," he groaned.

Our guideman spotted the same thing. "Southwest is buttoning up over there." He nodded to his right. Even through blackened sunglasses, his irritated expression was clear.

When the catering truck finally arrived, our aircraft was sealed up tight. Our door was closed and the jet bridge pulled. Even though we had not moved, we were no longer connected to the terminal building and the gate agent had recorded us as departed 'on time' to benefit their station stats.

Two men dressed completely in white, hopped out of the catering truck. A stout, mustached guy stood clutching a black purse, while the other one sprinted across the ramp and commandeered a luggage conveyor belt on wheels.

They raised the conveyor belt up to Ted's side window, the only opening in the airplane they could pass something through. Still hugging the purse, the stout fellow climbed onto the rolling belt. Standing up, he rode it up to the opened cockpit window, like he was an overstuffed piece of luggage. Just as he reached the top, his partner on the ground punched the red stop button, jerking the conveyor belt to an abrupt halt—throwing the purse hugging caterer toppling forward.

I reflexively grabbed my armrest, certain he was going to topple off the side of the conveyor belt and plummet fifteen feet down to the concrete below. But he tumbled forward and smacked hard into the side of our aircraft. Flailing out in panic, he grabbed at the open window frame with his free hand and just narrowly caught himself from falling off the side of the belt. He hung on tight, and *now* I worried that his forceful grip had damaged our window track.

I hated this entire day so far.

Ted grabbed the purse from his hand, and before he could even pass it off to Becky, the guideman standing at the nose of the aircraft resumed barking in my ear.

"You have the purse now, don't you?"

That question did not need an answer.

So here we were, back on the fast track and completely out of sync, with our rigid routine in shambles. Mood and circumstance aside, everything is a procedure. Our verbal ballet resumed, and every performer read from the same script:

Ground: (guideman): "Standing by for pushback clearance."

Captain: "Nosewheel steering disconnect message is displayed. Cleared to push, brakes set."

Ground: "Roger, cleared to push. Release brakes."

Captain: "Brakes released."

Ground: "Cleared to start engines."

Captain: "Roger, cleared to start engines."

Ground: "Set brakes.[1]"

Captain: "Brakes set. Pressure normal."

Ground: "Tow bar disconnected."

Captain: "Disconnect headset."

But the mechanic missed a beat in this dance. He was supposed to say these lines next …

Ground: "Disconnecting, watch for salute."

This line would be followed by the guideman telling the captain where to look for him to get this salute.

"On your left," or "On your right." But, the connection between us went dead. The guideman had disconnected his headset, without saying his last two lines.

---

1   (at completion of pushback)

After the guideman disconnects his headset, the captain is to sit tight and wait for the guideman to move clear of the aircraft, come to attention and salute, signaling the captain that all ground personnel are clear of the aircraft. The captain acknowledges the guideman's salute by flashing the aircraft nose gear light. Only then the captain is free to push up the thrust levers and roll away, and the guideman is free to leave, too. Generally, this is followed by the guideman riding away on the tug and we never see each other again.

We lingered there waiting for the guideman's salute.

"He's pushing," I sighed to Ted, as Southwest began to move backwards from the gate on our left. We started to discuss options to get around him, when Becky jumped back through our closed cockpit door again, bubbling, "Thank you, thank you, thank you." I appreciated that she was grateful, but I just needed Becky and her purse out of the way at this point. I really wanted our predictable cockpit rhythm to stop being interrupted.

Mixed in all this disorder, I saw our guideman driving away on his pushback tug. I reasoned that I had been distracted and I must have missed his salute. Or maybe he drove away and never saluted at all, in line with his missed phraseology. Either way, he was gone and I continued on.

Captain: "Taxi clearance."

Our pre-set script resumed and I requested Ted radio for our taxi clearance, which he did without question.

Relieved to finally be on our way and to have all of this chaos behind us, my focus flipped to getting around Southwest and to our upcoming taxi route. I contently pushed the thrust levers forward. My engines obediently responded with an increasing high-pitched scream as the turbine blades sliced through clean air with growing speed and force. I felt a little jerk in my seat as tires became unstuck from the weight of the aircraft. The struts bounced just a bit as the wheels began to roll and the whole machine stiffly released and began to lumber forward.

I caught a puzzled look on Ted's face. He was straining to look straight down below his side window, a blind spot for me. He mumbled something, but I couldn't hear him.

Then I saw what he saw.

A guideman was staggering back away from our rolling nose gear. His headset was around his neck, but the cord was hanging loose and dragging along the pavement at his feet. He stumbled backwards — right towards our engine inlet.

The turbine blades were powerfully vacuuming him in.

The cord tangled around his legs and he tumbled onto the pavement like a clumsy toddler. On his hands and knees, he launched into a frantic crawl across the ground, his arms and legs flailing on the concrete as he desperately scrambled away from the howling engine and massive landing gear rolling towards him. I felt the enormity of my ship as I looked at that man helplessly splayed on the ground before it. My feet flew onto my brakes like I have never slammed those brakes before. The entire powerful machine jerked to a violent halt, just short of reaching him. He sprang back up onto his feet and instinctively sprinted away. At a safe distance, he stopped and spun back around. He gave me direct eye contact with a mixed look of inconsolable fear and seething anger. That glare seared a snapshot picture in my head, and my heart.

Then, he lost it.

He twisted and stomped and swung his fists into the air towards the aircraft — towards me. His white teeth flashed as he screamed and bellowed, cursing while swinging his head in wild shakes of fury. He hopped up and down, swooping his arms towards the sky and kicking the air with his boots. He released his emotions with his entire body. I had never seen anything like this before. I just sat there, my feet clamped down on the brakes, and I watched as it occurred to me that this must be where the expression "hopping mad" came from.

But, but, but… I had seen our guideman drive away on the tug.

Wait a second. Were there *two* guidemen?

Did I know there were two men down there, with one outside of my sightline from the flight deck? No, and here was another missed beat. The guideman had also skipped the line:

Ground: "One man push," or "Two man push."

Since he didn't tell me there were two of them, I thought he was working alone down there. I was wrong. I was floored.

I'm guessing this poor fellow had just come as close to death as he ever had. I'm certain I had just come as close to killing a man as I ever had.

Was he removing the tow pin from the nose gear when I started rolling forward? He must have heard the engines powering up? Did he try to complete the job and save the aircraft from damage, rather than run when he first had the chance?

I felt horrible.

I continued watching him curse me out as these questions flooded my head, frozen in my seat with my feet still crushing down the brake pedals. He finally turned away from my blank stare and headed back towards the terminal building. But he didn't walk away quietly. He continued his wrath, stomping in long strides and punching at nothing with closed fists, purposefully yelling into the air as he made his way across the ramp and away from me. *Probably a good thing that I couldn't hear him.*

Once he reached his door into the building, he quieted down and turned around for one last look at me. A cold silent glare. I got the message.

He left me with one last kick in the air with his black steel-toed boot, then disappeared into the terminal building, slamming the metal door shut behind him.

I'm sure at least some of my passengers sitting on the right side of the aircraft were a witness to it all. How could they miss it?

Well now, where do I go from here?

I would have liked to have gone back to bed and started my day over again. My stomach ached for the staggering terror I had caused this man.

I tried to set my emotions aside and compartmentalize what had just happened, as we got back to business and began our taxi out. But the scene kept replaying in my thoughts. I couldn't let it go and halfway to the runway I babbled to Ted. "Geez, that was awful."

He laughed at me. "He's not dead, Laura."

"But I can't believe I did that," I protested. "I'm not used to being stupid."

Ted gave me a wry, brotherly eye-roll.

Then a thumbnail memory flashed into my head, from an earlier time in my career. I tried to shake this recollection away from the checklists and performance numbers properly on my mind, but it kept replaying like a song lyric that gets stuck in your head.

While taxiing at JFK International airport a few years back, I listened as the air traffic controller fervently tried to contact an unresponsive British Airways jumbo jet on the tarmac apron. After several New Yorker styled admonishments from the irritated controller, "Get movin' Speedbird, you're blockin' the ramp," the pilot finally responded with a thick British, "Hold on there, mate. Cock up, I think we just squashed a chap." Sure enough, a ground worker was crushed and dead under their massive widebody tires.

Thinking back to that early morning departure in PHX, I am so grateful our guideman had been able to get out of the way. I never got to tell that man I was sorry. I wish I had, but we have never met.

I didn't even consider brushing this incident under the rug, and I filed an FSAR, a Flight Safety Awareness Report. The company received my report, and I assume the guideman's also. I expected to receive a phone call, but I never did. These reports are used in a database to pro-actively enhance safety procedures. Ultimately, it was a learning experience.

Sadly, ground workers are often injured or even killed on airport tarmacs around the world. These individuals labor right at the feet of behemoth aircraft, often while guiding moving jets or loading baggage and freight in blistering heat or bitter cold, while dodging speeding airport vehicles, breathing in deicing fluid and jet fumes, and enduring constant ear-splitting noise from thunderous turbine engines. These people are invisible to the public, but their back-breaking labor is what keeps our jets moving.

This may have been just another day at the airport, but for me this was *my* mistake and it deeply affected me.

My mind should have been exactly where my aircraft was at that moment, and on the people working around it. But my thoughts were hurrying forward because we were late. I allowed distractions to pull me out of focus and off routine, making it easy for me to rationalize that I must have missed the guideman's salute.

This experience grounded me. It slowed me down. I didn't allow myself to feel pushed any longer, either by myself or external influences. And I never allowed myself to assume something again, because it was convenient to do so and moved things along.

I almost killed somebody that morning and that dark feeling has never completely left me. But that experience developed me into a better pilot, and I daresay, a more patient person. All hard lessons leave me with something constructive, when I let them.

UNDER THE BIG BLUE TOP
flight attendants and passengers and birds, oh my!

An airline is a busy circus with a mixture of performers under the overarching tent of the blue sky. But unlike a circus, the paying audience is part of the act. So, *nobody* better fall from the trapeze. Aside from passengers, the flight attendants are the only other group pilots share a workspace with. Yes, we are all in the aircraft, but that is about the only thing our jobs have in common. The pilots are separated and secluded away during the flight, while the flight attendants are packed in the cabin with the passengers. They may visit the pilots in the cockpit inflight, but no different from passengers, the flight attendants are locked out of the flight deck at low altitudes, for takeoff and landing, and any other time the captain feels a sterile cockpit is needed for safety and removal of distractions.

Equally, pilots are generally out of the loop regarding life in the cabin, while the flight attendants are tuned in to our passengers and put their skills to work directly with the people in our care. Regardless, a rundown of most issues and dramas happening in the back of the plane eventually make their way to the pilots in the front of the plane. There is just something about the seclusion of a cocoon seven miles above the earth and a captive audience who you likely will never see again, but have sincerely bonded with, that allows for the most unguarded thoughts to spill out among virtual strangers.

On international flights we easily had twenty or more flight attendants in the aircraft cabin, many of whom would cycle though the flight deck on their breaks. Joan and Calvin might pop in under the guise of delivering some leftover caviar and water crackers, then casually settle into the jumpseats and prop their feet up on the cockpit sidewall. Before you knew it, they were unbuttoning their cuffs, rolling up their sleeves and filling us in on the bohemian couple taking unusually long trips to the blue room. Or perhaps we might get an earful of the squabble one flight attendant had with her spouse before leaving the house that morning, or a clash between the flight attendants working in the tail of the aircraft versus the more senior flight attendants serving first class passengers.

While the cockpit is generally a comfortable place to gather, the relationship between flight attendants and pilots can be an ambiguous one. This often became more apparent on long haul flights.

"Thanks for the coffee, Joan." The captain gratefully received the steaming paper cup on a flight to Taipei, Taiwan, TPE.

"My God, these stockings are cutting off my circulation. Look at the pockets on my uniform, they are all fake. I don't even have a shirt pocket to put my pen in." Joan scowled, standing up to reach under her skirt and adjust her stockings.

"Any chance for a first class omelette?" the captain optimistically queried, glossing over Joan's gripes.

"No," Joan retorted. "No leftovers."

"None at all?" He tried a different entrée. "How about some waffles?"

"No Captain, none at all." Joan was talkative, but not on this topic. "I'll bring your crew meal if you're hungry."

While Joan went back and forth with the captain, Calvin rested his elbows on the back of my seat and leaned in towards me. "You know, you could be pretty if you put some make-up on," he casually declared, and then waited for me to say thank you for his cosmetology insight. How do you respond to something like that? I was flying him around the earth, but it wasn't my competency shining, it was my nose.

I had nothing.

A short time later, I left the flight deck for my break, and stopped into the forward galley to make myself a cup of tea.

"Hey, Laura," Joan greeted me, just as chatty in her own workspace as she was in mine. "Would you like a first class omelette? We have plenty of leftovers."

"What?" I failed to hide my confusion. "Didn't you tell the captain there were no leftovers?"

"There are no leftovers for him," she scowled. "But there are plenty of leftovers for you," she added with a chortle.

"Ahhh, no thanks." I hesitated. "I'm good."

"Here, I'm getting you an omelette," she insisted, snapping open the warming-oven door. "The leftovers are just going in the trash. You might as well have one." She pushed me, almost too eager for me to enjoy her prize. Clearly, she was making some point that was beyond me. I was reaping the benefits of it, though, so I felt obligated to be thankful. *First class omelettes are pretty good.*

I had no idea what the captain had done to lose the good food or what I had done to earn it. But I could see the power struggle. That's the way it was. Sometimes I was on the right side of this game, and sometimes I was not, although I likely didn't know it at the time. Flight attendants control the food. Starvation is the greatest peril a pilot faces, and on a thirteen-hour flight, that is a lot of power.

Flight attendants are a mixed lot. We have everything from the career senior mamas to the cool Gen Z's who have a full life outside of this job, but just want to have some fun and enjoy the travel perks. Some loved me — girl power! Some appeared bitter towards me. Some just felt comfortable around me in a way which they weren't with the male pilots. No matter their background, I will say this: all flight attendants work hard. But it is a different kind of work than that of a pilot. They are valued by the company in a completely different way than a pilot, too. This disparity was well understood, bringing subtle conflicts between our two groups.

"Look down there, that's the Aleutian Islands," I pointed out to Phyllis, a flight attendant who had just stepped into the cockpit. "And that frozen tundra is Russia. Isn't it breathtaking?"

"You have a first class amenities kit in your bag," she snapped, noticing it as she leaned over my shoulder to look out the window.

"I do?" Then I realized she was talking about the leather, zippered pouch a check airman had given me on an initial-operating-experience flight, years back when I was just a probationary pilot. He handed it to me on that first day, with the instructions to empty it out and use it to hold my Leatherman tool, pen light, calculator, cockpit key and other miscellaneous items floating around my flight bag.

"I'd be fired if I stole from the company." She appeared personally offended by my thievish ways.

"Look, I have a pillow from first class behind my back, too." I offered.

"That's just ridiculous." She glared at me. "I could report you for stealing."

"Okay," I shrugged my shoulders. I really didn't care.

This is the thing, there was so much I could get in real trouble for as a pilot, the thought that the company would care what I used to keep my flight bag organized never crossed my mind. There is such a marked difference in expectations between our employee groups, it's like we work for different companies. I even have pockets in my uniform shirt that are not sewn closed, because not one person cares if I have a smooth, streamlined look. They care that I have someplace to put my maglite, or pen, or whatever I need quick access to. But then again, nobody cares about my people skills, or if I could read a drunk person's body language, handle endless "Mile High Club" jokes from strangers or keep passengers calm while preparing them for a water landing.

Regardless of our differences, the flight deck was a guaranteed escape for the flight attendants. It was their break room in the sky and the doors were always open.

Welcome to the Sky Lounge and Smoker's Club.

Before smoking was banned on flights and even long afterwards, many of the pilots relaxed at cruise altitude with a lit cigarette between their lips, puffing away until the entire cockpit was a gray billow of exhaled tar and nicotine. Throughout any trip, the flight attendants would come up to the flight deck if they needed to light up, also. The eventual 'Smoking Ban' meant nothing to these nicotine addicts. They rationalized this trifling rule did not apply to the tiny room up front, the cockpit. For a long time, the company and FAA turned a blind eye to this exception. The smoke would grow so heavy and stagnant in our crowded little bubble, on long flights the captain directed the junior man (a.k.a., me) to execute the 'Cockpit Smoke Evacuation' procedure to clear it out. I'm talking the actual procedure used to combat smoke in the cockpit due to fire.

This procedure was no joke.

Standing on my seat, I reached up to open a port beside the crew escape hatch in the ceiling of our cockpit. A shiver raced down my arm, as I stretched up to *intentionally* open a hole in the only metal layer separating us from the deadly stratosphere.

"Are you sure about this?" I winced, hesitating to take the next step.

"Just open it." The captain waved his hand at me while he lit another cigarette, then passed the Marlboro pack to a flight attendant lounging on the seat behind him. Clenching my shoulders and ducking my head, I opened the small door then jumped back down to the floor, with everyone laughing at me. A powerful, sucking phenomena right out of a Stephen King thriller, shook the cockpit as the pressurized air surrounding us whistled out the hole with an ear-splitting shriek.

The smoke magically disappeared, like a genie streaming out of a bottle. Just as soon as I could breathe again and relax, certain that I had not been shot out into the wild blue yonder, out would come a fresh pack of cigarettes and the cycle would start all over again. This would go on non-stop, the entire way around the globe. The whole insane sequence was unsettling, and fascinating at the same time.

Occasionally, the atmosphere on the flight deck was the opposite of a relaxing spot to sit back and take a break. Some years later and now a captain myself, I saw it coming just as we lifted into the warm air, pulling away from the runway in Vancouver, Canada. It was aimed straight at us. A large singular bird, its wings fully fanned out with long, wide feathers.

I tensed for impact, while also holding out hope it would swoop over the top of us, caught in the air currents flowing around our massive airframe. It grew larger, shooting like a cannonball directly at my wide eyes, until its enormous wings covered my windshield completely. My view was only blocked for a flash of a second, then it was over.

Thwack! A vulture shattered across my windshield with a hollow, chilling thud that only something dead can make.

Direct hit. Dead bird.

Chunks of yellow gore and thick red syrup manically streaked across the glass in every direction, until my entire windshield was smeared with this puréed paste. I enjoyed just about everything aviation. There are some exceptions to that, and this would be one of them. I hated killing anything, and this liquified Canadian raptor was definitely dead.

The view out my window was not pretty, but that was not the worst of it. The windshield was intact, but the bird had shattered my windshield wiper. The broken remains of the metal wiper arm, now caught in the wind, was doing a mad dance on the glass, violently slapping the pulpy remains of the poor bird. Tiny remnants of feathers fluttered in the slime, and our windshield heat kept it all moist and sticky for the entire flight.

Enter Susan, the first flight attendant to visit us for her break.

"My God, what is that?" she exclaimed, gawking at our windshield.

"Dead bird."

"Oh, that's disgusting. And that banging is giving me a headache."

Exit Susan, never to return for the remainder of the flight.

Bird strikes are fairly common and rarely dangerous, except for the poor bird. Often, we don't even know we got a bird, until someone notices the sticky sludge on an aircraft wing or tail. When an airport is built, it's like setting out the welcome mat for birds and wildlife of all kinds. With miles of barbed wire security fencing protecting pools of standing water, open fields and forests, an airport might as well be an animal refuge. The more protected an airport is, the more wildlife flocks to it, and the more money is spent trying to shoo away Canada geese, deer, foxes, and an entire assortment of vermin from the runways.

When dealing with the hazards of their natural environment, birds are quite clever with self-preservation and adaption. However, from *my* observation, birds have developed absolutely no ability to sense the unnatural danger of a jet aircraft in their path and seem to head right towards us at every chance.

Birds are the only unwilling participants in our aerial circus. I wish I could save them all.

The pilot is fully invested in the safe control of every flight, and they can't walk away from the cockpit no matter how unpleasant things may get up there. Likewise, a flight attendant is responsible for the safety of their passengers inside the cabin, and that is where they must stick it out until every passenger has arrived at their destination and left the aircraft. Pilots and flight attendants may have enigmatic relationships at times, but we trust and depend on each other. I know my flight attendants have our passengers' backs, and that is all that really matters.

WINDSHEAR! WINDSHEAR! WINDSHEAR!

No matter how a flight begins or ends, in between the view from my office is always incredible and stirring. The most fundamental truths of nature are sublimely revealed from 39,000 feet, like how the horizon isn't a straight line, but naturally follows the curvature of the earth in a smooth, great arc—completely unblocked by jagged mountain ranges or cityscapes from high altitudes.

When great swatches of earth are viewed in one glimpse, the organization that humans have brought to the surface is obvious. After passing over hundreds of miles of barren Arizona desert or untouched grasslands across the Midwest, perfect irrigation circles or precisely squared roads will pop up, looking fake in an otherwise random landscape, as if someone had thrown down their math homework on scraps of graph paper.

We alter the earth for many reasons. What is striking from a distance, is the vast effort to join things together. A deliberate connection between people can always be found. Whether by one gravel road stretched between isolated cabins, or a highway unnaturally cut through rocky terrain between massive cities, ultimately everybody is tied together.

Only an aircraft is tied to nothing. There is a complete sense of detachment and isolation in the sky.

There is rarely any weather at high altitudes, and the ride is clear above the clouds. But as serene and beautiful as my workspace is, we always have to return to earth and face the weather and terrain that had been so gracefully passing beneath us. Often, this descent and landing are not quite so peaceful as the flight was getting there.

I could have been looking at a Bob Ross painting on this flight from San Francisco, SFO, to Denver, DEN, the Rocky Mountains were that colorful and flawless. Glistening snowcaps resting on crooked peaks flowed by beneath my window.

"United 223, descend and maintain 16,000," the controller's voice streamed into my ear. We entered Denver airspace and streaked downward, maneuvering gently around isolated pockets of building afternoon storms. Wistfully leaving the smooth air behind, we lowered ourselves into the currents and eddies flowing off the irregular mountainous terrain.

I spotted a narrow smoke stream weaving through pine trees and quietly rising into the air. Curious, my eyes followed it down to a single chimney atop a tiny speck of a house, nestled together with a handful of other equally tiny wooden houses in the foothill of one mountain crest. I am often amazed at my privileged view of our country, and the world, spotting anomalies like this and invading the privacy of people hidden away.

"Look at that tiny little community down there," I wondered out loud to my first officer, Jeremy, as the details sharpened of the rocky landscape and timbers underneath us in our descent. "Talk about remote living, who are those people living in such seclusion?" I searched for a road or anything to connect this cluster of people to the rest of civilization, but my naked eye could find nothing yet through the thick pines.

Jeremy chuckled. "That's my hometown, Laura." He remained lounged deep in his seat, without bothering to search the ground for answers like I was.

"Stop making fun of me," I cautioned him with a sideways look.

Jeremy started narrating stories of his childhood to convince me. It turned out he wasn't joking at all. "I only realized I was living in the middle of nowhere myself," he reminisced, "when I started high school and finally traveled a bit, and realized that other schools had things like sports teams, marching bands, and real proms."

"Real proms?" I questioned.

"There was a total of four kids in my senior class. Our prom was lacking a certain something with three guys and just one girl there."

And here I had envisioned Grizzly Adams sitting by that fireplace, sharpening his axe on a grindstone. For some reason that I couldn't quite put my finger on, I looked at Jeremy with a whole new kind of respect. I was intrigued. Finally traveled a bit? *I would say you checked that box, Jeremy.*

I wanted to hear more, but our arrival into Denver had begun and very quickly we were too busy for small talk.

"United 223, reduce speed 250 knots," the controller added a few minutes later.

I eased the power levers back, chagrined that our airspeed was already being restricted. We didn't want to slow down yet, but the air traffic controller needed our speed back to fit us in line, much like cars funneling through a toll plaza on the highway. We continued towards the airport, extending leading edge slats and lowering trailing edge flaps, changing the shape and size of our wings as we progressively slowed to lower and lower speeds. Much like a bird fans out feathers, a pilot makes their wings larger and more arched to fly at slower speeds to land.

"United 223, report company traffic 767, one o'clock and three miles." The controller pointed out another United jet making its way for the same runway ahead of us.

"In sight," Jeremy responded. After glancing over to me for my nod of agreement he added, "and Runway 16R in sight."

"Follow your company 767, cleared for the visual Runway 16R."

Since we could see everything for ourselves on this clear day, the controller stepped out of the picture, freeing us to set our own pace to the runway and keep a safe distance from the aircraft ahead of us.

Even though we were on a visual approach, I still kept the ILS (Instrument Landing System) on my primary flight display, with altitudes and lateral guidance plainly in front of me. I felt a ping of satisfaction as the course needle came alive and floated to the center of our indicator, and our alignment with the runway flowed into place both through my windshield and on my instrument display.

"Gear Down, final descent checklist," I called to Jeremy.

With the repositioning of just the tiniest lever, the sleek doors underneath us swung open, allowing massive wheels to drop down. With three solid mechanical thuds the gear locked into position.

Everything was falling into place smoothly, although our descent to the runway was like driving over a gravel road. An afternoon thunderstorm was moving toward the airport, and we jerked along in choppy air making me work a little harder to pin down the target airspeed.

Suddenly our airspeed erupted into a steady climb. I knew to be alarmed. Jeremy saw it too.

"Up 15 knots, Laura."

"I see it." I said nothing else. We both knew what was happening.

In one sweeping motion I slammed the thrust levers to the forward stops while yanking the nose upward with my other hand.

"WINDSHEAR! WINDSHEAR! WINDSHEAR!"

Our aircraft warning system boomed over our loudspeakers in a deep synthesized voice, with the complete calm that comes with a cool British accent. Yet, the urgency of our situation was perfectly captured with this loud, unambiguous warning.

Riding the edge of a stall, I fought back as the winds swung around our ship on its way towards a tailwind. In seconds, that tailwind would steal away the lift beneath my wings as the forward flow of air over them dwindled.

"United 223, Microburst Alert, Runway 16R, Winds ..." The controller's urgent voice reverberated over our radio.

No shit.

I tuned out the rest of the controller's words pouring into my ear. He was seconds behind us, and *his* indicators had nothing but old news.

There was no discussion with Jeremy and no eye contact needed. Jeremy answered the controller with only a double click on his mic, which meant "I heard you, now don't bother us again." I'm certain the controller was watching our aircraft struggle to pull up. He could see us tussling against the winds as our silhouette plunged below the invisible glidepath that he was accustomed to viewing planes follow to the runway like perfect tin soldiers. He knew not to distract us from flying our aircraft. He kept silent and waited for us to get back to him.

I imagine the sudden and aggressive change in power and pitch may have caused more than one passenger to cinch their seatbelt in surprise, and perhaps some fear. The intimidation of the engine's full roar was in such contrast to their tranquil window view of the Rockies in the distance, and the low flat plains bending in graceful brown waves below. Only minutes earlier, they were bored by the announcement, "Thank you for flying the Friendly Skies today, we'll be on the ground shortly," with generic instructions to stow their laptops and adjust their seatbacks to the full upright position.

This unexpected excitement and intense workload were not entirely unpleasant for Jeremy and me, though. A pilot is gratified by a demand for their skills, when all of their tough training pays off. The absolute requirement to succeed is a perk of the job, and the pilot personality rises to the challenge of these unforgiving expectations.

I have died many deaths in simulator flight training, most often during windshear scenarios much like this. Crashing may sound counterintuitive, but that taste of failure is *effective* training. Fighting for your life is a dark struggle, even when it's fake. I flashed back to that sickening feeling of hitting the ground. Except this time there would be no 'clink' where I'm magically poofed back five miles with the chance to try it again. Until there is a hole in the ground, a pilot will not admit defeat or quit trying. We are the first ones at the scene of the accident and we are fully vested. Jeremy and I were going to succeed.

"900 down, 800 down," Jeremy barked out our vertical speed, our rigorous training in full effect. I willed our turbines to spool up to full power more quickly, as the grassy plains rose up just outside my side window.

C'mon! C'mon! C'mon!

My shoulder harnesses dug into my collarbone as I leaned into the thrust levers. With a building surge, the engine power kicked back in and the downward sink mercifully reversed into a strong, unyielding climb, weighing down my outstretched arm.

Once sufficiently safe from the ground, Jeremy moved on to other things.

"Denver, United 223. On the go. Windshear." Jeremy invited the controller back into our lives.

All in one breath, the control assigned us an altitude and heading, then cleared us for the visual for runway 7. He gave us initial instructions to start us off in the right direction, and he said good-bye to us, washing his hands of giving us any more instruction.

This was strictly business for the controller, whose job was to send us off to another runway, one preferably without a microburst waiting on the edge of it. A microburst is an isolated phenomenon which occurs in one pocket of space for a short burst of time. Then it's gone.

Jeremy ducked his head down to type, attempting to update our computers with the new runway so that I might have at least a minimum pool of information about this completely unexpected approach ahead. I love having guidance and the comfort that it holds, but there just wasn't time to do this.

"Forget about it, Jeremy. I've got the runway." Our screens were useless for navigation or vertical guidance, now. Looking out my window and using my eyes was all I had, and all I needed.

I loved it.

Let loose from any guidance, I was totally free. No assigned headings or altitudes to comply with. No needles or printed profiles to follow. We were out of danger and now I was having fun. I made up my own pattern for Runway 7. I climbed and circled around to where I wanted to be with nobody's voice in the game but mine.

My unhappy aircraft, however, still had our old runway programmed in. I was headed the wrong direction, at the wrong altitude, for the wrong runway. As I arced around to Runway 7, bells, chimes and an irritating mechanical voice wailed out in loud protests at each of my navigational crimes as I committed them. I ignored them all.

Evoking the high I felt on my first solo flight as a young girl, a stirring feeling of independence and autonomy surged through me as this huge machine mirrored the precise movements of my hands and feet. I was in complete control and put my aircraft exactly where I wanted it.

I lowered my jet back down to the ground, coasting onto the smooth pavement.

My landing was perfect. I glided onto the pavement so softly, I swear the passengers didn't know we had touched down. Looking back, I still can't believe how amazing this touchdown was. It made me think of the old adage, "It ain't bragging if it's true."

Let me be clear, not all of my landings are wonderful. They are all safe and stay in the envelope, but they aren't all a dream come true. But on this day the flight ended elegantly, so all was forgiven. This is the way that it is. No matter the challenges of a flight, a pilot is judged by how smooth the landing was for their passengers.

With the hard work behind us now, an explanation was owed to the passengers and flight attendants for the schizophrenic maneuvering over the airport, as if we just couldn't decide which runway to land on. So, it was not quite over.

"Ladies and Gentlemen, you may have noticed we changed landing runways rather late in the game," I heard my voice crackling over the speakers. "We flew into some … disagreeable winds for our planned runway, so decided it best to change over to a different runway. Thank you again for flying the Friendly Skies today."

Not great, but at least I caught myself before saying the forbidden word, "windshear." That word seems to invoke images of planes crashing to the flying public.

Then I remembered Channel 9! If a passenger was interested in listening in to our radio communications with ATC, then they got the whole truth. So be it. There would be a handful of passengers who had the big picture.

God help them.

When things get precarious and my day goes in an unexpected direction, I enjoy my job even more. Having an unshakeable joy for my work and the challenges that come with it, is the litmus test that verifies I have made the right career choices. To quote Muhammad Ali, "Grass grows, birds fly, waves pound the sand. I beat people up."

Everyone has their own thing, and it doesn't matter who else understands it.

STEP UP

When the circus tent is huge, one single person's importance can be overlooked. But there is power in stepping outside your box and doing unexpected things.

One clear autumn day, I landed in IAD for my final leg of a four-day trip. Absolutely nothing had gone wrong on the flight. I had no extra paperwork or industrious mechanic holding me in the cockpit after parking. As eager as I was to head home, I lingered in the cockpit doorway to nod bye-bye to our passengers before I headed out the door myself. One stern looking man locked his eyes on mine as he steamed down the aisle. Looking right past the flight attendant, he focused on me. His classic suit and laptop case marked him as a businessman. With only a glance at my uniform, I braced for him to demand his coat from the first class closet as soon as he reached me.

"Are you the captain?" He started speaking, still several feet away and charging towards me.

"Yes, sir." Slightly startled at being addressed by my correct title, my perception of him radically shifted.

"I was sitting in seat 10F." He didn't stop walking. "It looks like something has popped up on the wing. You know, like a bolt or something like that. Maybe you might want to take a look at it." He barely slowed his pace as he passed this observation on to me in his rush out the door.

It seemed a plain remark made by a hurried man. It was a remark that got my attention, though. After the last passenger exited past me, I walked down the empty aisle until I reached row 10, and I took a seat in 10F. I peered out the window to see his view of the wing. Just like he said, on the other side of this gentleman's window a raised bolt balanced precariously higher than the others on the smooth wing top. Returning to the cockpit, I interrupted my first officer as he packed up his flight bag.

"Hey Ryan, come take a look at this."

Dodging the cleaning crew now vacuuming the airplane, I retraced my steps back down the aisle with Ryan in tow and had him take a seat in 10F.

"Take a look out that window. See anything unusual?" I asked him, not putting any specific ideas in his head.

The curved window captured his reflection as he pressed his forehead to the oval frame and peered out. I caught his expression before he said a word to me.

"Hell, yeah," Ryan spit out.

This bolt had no business standing out like that.

Next, I shared our nameless passenger's discovery with a mechanic. Having him also take a seat in 10F, he appeared far more interested than I had expected. Rarely does a mechanic look surprised, and his concerned gaze at the wing unsettled me.

Ryan and I left the aircraft, clearing the path for the incoming pilots to take our seats. Before abandoning this ship, I scrawled out a note to the outbound crew and clipped it onto the captain's side chart holder:

> Capt.—
> Raised bolt on right wing. Observable from seat 10F.
> Maintenance is aware. Safe flight. Capt. Savino

The next week, one of my friends approached me in our Pilot Operations room underneath IAD.

"Hey Laura, I'm the captain who got your note about that raised bolt last week. That bolt had somehow failed and all hell broke loose after you left. Our flight was canceled that afternoon, and that aircraft is still grounded."

I had no idea.

Occasionally, a passenger takes up the role of participant, and moves past being just an audience ticket holder. Even though that passenger, that hurried businessman, was getting *off* the plane, he still took the time to speak up. He would never know how important he was.

Still today, I wish that I could thank him.

I can fly a jet, but I don't have eyes in the back of the airplane, and I sure can't see the innards of my complex machine. If my aircraft suffers a mechanical anomaly, it doesn't take much before I shrug my shoulders and call in an expert. Mechanics are the overlooked brains to an airline and the cornerstone to everyone's safety.

Not only is their knowledge and skill-set way beyond my bag of tricks, but they perform their duties every day under the most brutally physical outdoor conditions. On days when I shuddered to leave my cozy cockpit, and my exterior aircraft inspection walkaround became my aircraft run around, I would invariably pass mechanics staged around my jet for the long haul as I breezed past them. Whether holding metal tools in bare hands outside during frigid Chicago winters, or standing unsheltered on scorched metal wings in Arizona desert heat, these professionals care for our great flying machines without complaint.

Airline mechanics are licensed by the FAA (Federal Aviation Administration), holding an A&P Certificate (Airframe and Powerplant) with mandatory rules and regulations to comply with, just like pilots. Mechanics certainly did not name themselves, because a more apt title would be something like 'Computer Geek Aerospace Tech Engineering Wizard.' Planes have gotten far more sophisticated, and so too have the people responsible for maintaining them, but they just humbly stick to title 'Mechanic.'

You just never know when you are suddenly going to need else's expertise at an airline, and more often than not — it's a I sat comfortably in my seat, running through my preflight che preparing my aircraft for our departure from Dallas Fort Worth, DFW,

Laura Savino

Los Angeles, LAX. Outside my windows, the backdrop of baggage carts, fuel trucks, and ground workers swirled by, when that very ordinary airport scenery started to appear different, somehow. I sat upright, pulled off my sunglasses and paid closer attention through squinted eyes.

"Hey Mike, look up for a second." I nudged my first officer. Mike took a moment away from his programming and intuitively followed my gaze. He knew from my tone he was looking for a problem. His face immediately met mine with the same perplexed expression.

"What's going on with the windshield?" he asked, echoing my thoughts.

Our solid, perfectly arched windshield appeared soft and sloppy. Smooth ripples rolled down the glass in tiny waves, like the ocean tide rippling onto the shore in lopsided breakers.

Mike reached up and poked the windshield with his finger. "That's hot!" he yelped in pain as he snapped his whole arm back.

Our windshield was melting? My only logical thought was to remove heat from it. I reached up and flipped the window heat switches off, and waited to see what happened next. The glass stopped moving. Freezing up solid, the windshield held its last bizarre, warbled shape. We now had a funhouse mirror for a windshield. We would have laughed, if we had any idea what was going on.

"Well, this doesn't look good," I sighed, turning to Mike. "Let's get a mechanic up here before the agent starts boarding the passengers. If you would please do the honors."

Mike radioed for a mechanic, and then we both sat back to stare at our funhouse mirror and wait. Of course, the window had cooled and settled back to its original form, looking quite ordinary again by time the mechanic stepped through our door. It's bad enough when I bring my car into the shop for a problem that disappears when the mechanic takes a

en the mechanic arrived, I fed him the details of what I had seen,
or a look of exasperation, combined with an annoyed eye roll
of my story.

nod his head as I spoke. "Hmm, I see," he said, with
nt of disbelief. I was pretty sure there was no sarcasm in his voice

282

either. This seemed like such a strange reaction to me, or non-reaction. I did just tell him our windshield looked like it was melting. But, he was unflappable.

He reached up and flipped the window heat back on. In seconds, the carnival was back in town, only this time tiny bubbles began to form in-between the glass layers. Come on, this was just not believable. I started looking around for a hidden camera.

While this completely bizarre magic trick made no obvious impression on the mechanic at all, Mike and I sat there flummoxed.

"Sorry boss, you're not going anywhere," he stated matter-of-factly, flipping the window heat back off. "This windshield needs to be replaced. That should take a few days," he continued as casually as one might say, "Do you want fries with that?"

I cocked my head and looked at him. "And does this happen to you often?"

"Oh yeah, it happens. Delaminated windshields seem to be a quirk."

"This is a 'quirk?'" I think I meant that as a rhetorical question, but our mechanic did not take it as one. I had opened the door and school was in. I will spare you his very long, very technical explanation. *You are welcome.*

The bottom line was that the windshield anti-ice system had gone mad.

The mechanic walked away, presumably to locate a new windshield. It didn't matter, the plane was grounded. End of story. Mike and I packed up our flight bags, put our blazers and hats on, straightened our ties and walked back up the jetway bridge. We were done with this aircraft.

I was grateful to find our gate agent standing alone behind the podium and our passengers lounging in the seating area waiting for boarding. That I had delayed the flight to have a mechanic 'take a look' at something, was all that our gate agent knew. So, that's all that our passengers knew.

I introduced myself to the agent, "Hi, I'm Captain Savino," and I gave him a quick rundown of our situation.

Giving me only a nod of the head, he responded by picking up his microphone and making an announcement. His voice boomed through the cavernous boarding area, causing me to slowly shrink away from his side as every head turned in our direction. He made our mechanical delay sound more dramatic than even I thought it was, describing a Funhouse of Horrors to our passengers, as if there was boiling glass flowing right over the pilot seats. The passengers expectedly turned their frustration and their questions to the gate agent, the apparent voice of authority echoing through the terminal. However, it just took one observant passenger to identify my uniform. Word was out, and I was quickly surrounded by anxious passengers shooting questions at me. Most wanted to know the *time*; time to fix the airplane, time to get a new airplane in that case, time of our departure and time of our arrival. Then their grilling evolved to how much time I had as a captain. How much time I had flying airplanes at all, etc. *You see the direction this was going.*

One passenger told me straight out, that she felt more comfortable seeing a male pilot, than a woman in the cockpit. I asked her "Why?" and her response was, "I don't know" with a shrug of her shoulders. I continued to talk to different passengers gathered around me, and this evolved into something I didn't expect, as I listened to each person's story.

One disheveled man was on his way to his mother's funeral; she had just passed from cancer. A large group was traveling to a family wedding. An exceptionally young woman was headed to Los Angeles to audition for a musical, while another equally young woman in a wheelchair was continuing on to Seoul for an experimental medical treatment. Many passengers were concerned about missing their connecting flight in LAX. I jotted down a list of airlines to contact, to check on their departure status and see if they could hold their flights for our late passengers, or 'runners' as they're called.

"Captain, we're taking a flight to China once we get to LA. We're going there to adopt a baby." A middle-aged man waited for the crowd around me to dwindle before he approached me.

"We can't miss that flight," the woman clutching his arm sniffled. "Please, they have to hold the flight for us," she implored me.

I added their flight to my list and headed through an unmarked door and down the steps to the heart of the airport in the underground beneath us. My best captain authority voice and inside phone line scored me some good information from the US carriers, but got me nowhere with China

Southern Airlines.

Once in the air and finally on our way to LAX in a replacement aircraft a couple of hours later, I continued my efforts to ensure that the worried couple made it to China that day. I continued to press China Southern to wait, using a United operations employee as the middleman, through our cockpit printer. He relayed messages to me, which I relayed to a flight attendant speaking to the couple sitting in economy. It felt like a high-end version of the game telephone.

Geoff, in operations, asked me some basic questions about the passengers and what luggage they might have to slow them down.

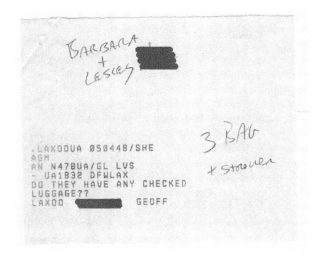

After collecting information regarding the passengers, I passed on our updated arrival time. Geoff replied:

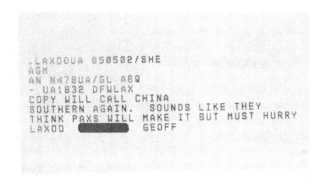

"But will they hold the flight, if they are a few minutes late?" I typed back. A few minutes later Geoff answered.

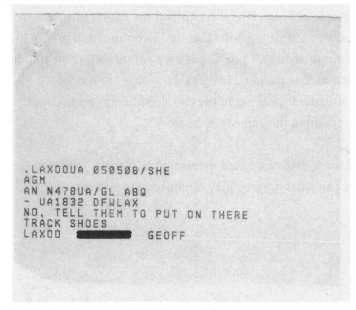

```
.LAXOOUA 050508/SHE
AGM
AN N478UA/GL ABQ
- UA1832 DFWLAX
NO, TELL THEM TO PUT ON THERE
TRACK SHOES
LAXOO ██████████    GEOFF
```

Two minutes later, Geoff followed up with:

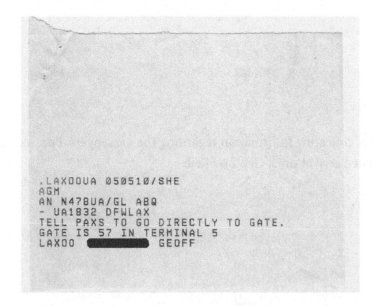

```
.LAXOOUA 050510/SHE
AGM
AN N478UA/GL ABQ
- UA1832 DFWLAX
TELL PAXS TO GO DIRECTLY TO GATE.
GATE IS 57 IN TERMINAL 5
LAXOO ██████████    GEOFF
```

I later found out, the couple breathlessly made it to their departing aircraft before they closed the jetway door. The China Southern agents knew they were coming and did hold out a few extra minutes to get them on.

Reaching LAX, there was one flight I didn't have to ask about, because I knew it would wait. A handful of our passengers were on my next flight to Seattle, SEA, which wasn't going anywhere until we arrived. We landed so late into Seattle that night, the Crew Desk asked me to waive our contractual rest period, so as to not delay our departure early the next morning.

"How do you feel about that, Mike?" I asked my first officer before answering the crew scheduler.

"I'll do it," he grimaced. "And thanks for asking me first," he added. It didn't hurt that it was the end of our four-day trip, and we were both highly motivated to get home ourselves.

I never forgot that collection of people in DFW that day, or how that one delayed flight impacted each of them. This is the other component, of course, of our collection of interesting people in the sky. The passengers. They aren't here for the entertainment of it all. They paid for admission to this flying circus because they needed to get somewhere, and it was my job to get them there. I was connecting people, bringing families together and helping folks achieve important things in their own lives. That palpable realization helped me feel a little better about being apart from my own family. Whether noticing something important like an out of place bolt or having inside connections to hold a flight, sometimes no one else is in the position to do right, save you. Even if there is nothing to gain personally, stepping up always feels good in the end.

MOTHERHOOD BLEW AWAY MY FAIRY DUST

"Twinkle, twinkle little star. How I wonder what you are." I leaned against the phonebank wall, singing softly into the handset of a payphone in the middle of Terminal C at Chicago O'Hare, ORD.

"Keep singing, Mommy," Nicholas' little voice reached out to me from 517 nautical miles away. It was bedtime, but he wasn't sleepy yet.

"Up above the world so high. Like a diamond in the sky." My voice wavered in the bittersweet sadness of my life.

"Come home, Mommy." Now his voice turned sad, too, knowing I was almost done with his bedtime song and about to hang up. That was our routine, and the third night in a row this week.

"Twinkle, twinkle little star. How I wonder what you are." Tears streamed down my cheeks as I finished. "Night, night Nicholas. Give Robert a big hug from me. Mommy loves you both."

I turned slightly to avoid the stare coming from the man talking on the phone beside me. We had just stepped off the same flight and we both rushed over to the nearest payphones. I was the pilot who just flew him here, now slumped against the wall, cradling a public phone while singing a toddler tune and crying. I'm sure he was relieved he was witnessing this *after* our flight.

Becoming an airline pilot was the fulfillment of my dreams, and an aspiration with limitless new goals to go after throughout my career. I started off as a flight engineer at United Airlines and kept climbing the ladder until the captain's seat was mine, working my way through every fleet, carrying my passengers to hundreds of destinations worldwide over the years. I was privileged to be a pilot on the Boeing 737, 747, 757, 767, and I was in the first wave of pilots to fly the incredible new 777 when it launched at United Airlines. Coming back from maternity leave, I returned to work as a captain on the A320.

I was a young, respected captain who had picked up the nickname *The Teenage Captain,* which one fun-loving mechanic in DCA labeled me and everyone joined in. Finally, I could wear my hair however I liked. My idiosyncrasies ruled the cockpit. I set the mood on the airplane. Nobody questioned my experience or competence.

By all appearances, life couldn't have been better.

They say be careful what you wish for. I'll add, be careful even if you worked really hard and sacrificed a lot to make that wish come true.

Every takeoff was still exhilarating and every landing a personal challenge I looked forward to. I loved the way flying pulled together the coordination of my hands and feet, and stretched my mind with endless calculations and problems to solve. I thrived on the heavy responsibility that came with my position and enjoyed the camaraderie of working closely together with other professionals.

But after I had my two beautiful boys, the sparkle of the job faded. Constant travel and being away from home weighed on me. I was chronically homesick for my children in a way I never imagined was possible. I was in pain.

Aside from missing them, leaving my children meant constant worry — and agonizingly, reliance on others. Although I had a couple wonderful nannies over the years, I was also plagued with other nannies lying to me. Or worse in another way, nannies bonding with *my* children.

"Who are you?" a mother standing beside me in the pickup line outside my four-year old son's classroom questioned me.

"Nicholas' mom," I answered, as if that should be perfectly obvious as I gently rolled Nicholas' little brother back and forth in his stroller. My younger son, Robert, spit his blankie out of his mouth and squealed, "Ni ko wis!" when he heard big brother's name.

But the mom looked at me as if I had two heads.

"I know Nicholas' mom," she retorted, correcting me.

"I *am* Nicholas' mom," I actually corrected her.

"Sorry, but we all know Nicholas' mom, and it's not you," another mother jumped in from behind me in line. She appeared alarmed, as if some strange woman was about to abduct my son.

It was then I realized our nanny had been accepted as one of the moms, and she never bothered to correct this misunderstanding. She had taken my place.

"That would be his nannie," I countered, glancing away to hide the look of hurt and embarrassment across my face.

"Well, here then," the second mom handed me a flyer after some hesitation. "We're all signing up for this. Maybe you'd like to join and get to know some other moms." Her subtle smile didn't reveal if she was being helpful or making a snide point. I glanced over the sheet of paper and smiled back. It was a flyer for weekend 'Mommy and Me' classes at a local children's gym.

I had no consistent schedule to allow me to sign up for something like this. I nodded and thanked her, as I swallowed down the tight feeling in my throat.

We all entered the classroom, and Nicholas' little blue eyes lit up as he ran over to me for a hug, reassuring the concerned mothers, and by that I mean busybodies, that I was no stranger to *my* little boy.

I helped my son gather his backpack and craft for the day, when another little boy began to wail from across the classroom. His mother and the teacher squatted down, trying to console him.

Several other mothers joined in to try and comfort the little guy, and the story came out. His mother was going to visit relatives for a night, and she was telling the teacher that someone else would be picking up her son the next afternoon. This news put the boy into uncontrollable sobs, which five mommies, a lollipop, and the classroom guinea pig couldn't comfort.

"Oh, he'll be okay." I joined into the mom pack. "I'm gone half of Nicholas' life. He's just fine." I tried to reassure the guilt-ridden mother.

"Really, he's going to be fine. It's just one night." *All of this drama for one single night away from* home? *Seriously?*

"For *him* it's not normal to be separated from his mother." The teacher cut me down. Just as the other mothers started mommy shaming me in the hallway, the teacher stepped in and finished the job. *Why didn't she just stab me in the heart with an icepick?*

I was an outcast.

Worse, I felt like my son was an outcast. We weren't in the clique of cookie baking mommies and playdate exchanges. Nicholas was missing out on things that his classmates weren't. Was living *my* dream hurting *him*? The guilt was overwhelming.

I didn't see this pain coming, but others did.

"What, you're pregnant!" my Captain loudly exclaimed, as I finally gave him a reason why I kept refusing lager with my Wiener Schnitzel at our favorite restaurant in Frankfurt, Germany.

"Yes," I shushed him. "That's what I said." I didn't tell him this was my second baby.

"That's the thing with you female pilots, you have babies and then that's all you ever think about in the cockpit," he stated, apparently feeling completely free to offer me his observations. "And that's how it should be," he continued. "A young mother should be thinking about her baby around the clock. That's how it works." He was speaking from his heart, oblivious to how hurtful this was for me to hear. Hurtful, because there was a lot of truth to it.

Pregnancy was another brick in the wall between me and my fellow pilots. But unexpectedly, it broke down other walls. On rare occasion I would use the flight attendant employee restroom at various airports, rather than hunt for that elusive ladies' room on the pilot side of our vast employee underground. Instead of finding the usual pragmatic, single stall facility and total privacy, walking into a flight attendant lounge was like stepping backstage to a Broadway show. Many of these flight attendant powder rooms were lined with vast rows of vanities, fully loaded with a dizzying array of hair products and huge mirrors illuminated by a perimeter of bright bulbs against pink walls. Finely coifed heads would turn when I entered this enclave. A unicorn horn growing out from my forehead would not have called more attention to me than the pilot bars on my shoulders and hat on my head. I did not belong here. I felt like I was invading their privacy. I wasn't a member of *this* club.

But all of that changed once I became pregnant and waddled through those same doors wearing my hideous maternity uniform, which closely resembled a navy-blue snow cone, inverted with armholes. Suddenly, I was one of the girls and a part of their traveling mommy club. I connected with these women in a way that I never could with the male flight attendants or pilots. This unspoken bond of motherhood I shared with the flight attendants was more powerful than any of our professional differences.

Cindy was the third flight attendant to come visit us on the flight deck. She was working in the tail of the aircraft and she didn't even pretend to bring us coffee, or to find any reason at all to come take a break on the flight deck. She just made herself comfortable in the jumpseat, leaned back, kicked off her shoes, and crossed her legs.

"There's a sad little girl back there, just eight years old and traveling all alone," she sighed. "Poor thing is bored out of her mind."

It was a five-hour flight from New Orleans, MSY, to San Francisco, SFO. "Didn't her mother pack her a backpack of crayons and coloring books?" I asked.

"That's just it, she's going home to her mother. Her father put her on the airplane."

"Well, there you go." We eyed each other and both broke out laughing. That was all Cindy and I needed to say about that, and we were synced together in maternal understanding. On the other hand, my first officer, Peter, had no idea what was going on or what was so funny. But he was smart enough to know not to even go there.

Don't get two mothers started.

I folded a paper airplane, wrote some silly flight facts on it with smiley faces, and signed it in my best fancy captain scroll. Then I took out a Red Robin's five-pack of crayons from my purse and tucked it inside the paper plane. I unwound some blank paper from our cockpit printer and handed it all to Cindy to bring back to the little girl. It may not have qualified as an iPad, but at least it was something. I make a sharp paper airplane.

After she left, Peter just had to say it. "You carry a pack of crayons in your purse?"

"I have two boys, Peter. It's my emergency supply." Funny, but Cindy didn't question a thing.

There were days I missed my children so badly, my heart ached every moment I was at work. No matter how breathtaking the view or how luxurious the hotel, guilt wore me to my core. Like never before, I caught myself second guessing my life in a way I imagined only happened to other people.

Then I would get a reminder to be grateful for all that I had.

"I'm forty years old," Katie, another pilot, confided in me. "I just can't believe I will never be a mother." The two of us were alone in the 777 cockpit, cruising at 38,000 feet over the Atlantic Ocean, on our way to an early morning arrival in Paris. We would sleep when we got to our five-star hotel, then meet in the lobby and take a walk to the Eiffel Tower, stopping somewhere along the way for crepes and cappuccinos. But for me, at seven months pregnant, it would be a caffeine-free cappuccino this time.

Katie took this picture of me in Paris, seven months pregnant.

Katie and I, relaxed by the yellow moon light shimmering over the black ocean below and by the intrinsic trust shared between two women, confided our deepest joys and regrets to each other. Melancholy that I was here at work, nibbling on Saltines with a barf bag by my side, I listened with a tender open heart.

"My husband was volatile." She quietly told me her story. "I had to leave before we had children." Her voice wavered. "My chance to have a child is over now. I just never imagined marriage would be like that."

I comforted her, and I understood. I too was in an explosive marriage that needed to end.

I would become a single mom before my youngest was out of Pullups, left to raise my two boys on my own. I only felt relief when Dom left. You really never know what goes on behind closed doors, no matter how idyllic someone's life may appear. Katie and I discovered we were two perfect examples of this.

As much as I could, I made up for my absence at home by taking care of the children I was surrounded by while at work. On one night flight to Denver on Christmas Eve, a flight attendant stopped into the cockpit and lamented that we had crying children in the cabin who were convinced Santa was going to skip their house tonight, because they weren't home in their beds.

This was weighing on my heart, when the air traffic controller called out passing traffic to us. Spotting this aircraft, his bright red beacon light was impossible to miss in the dark night sky. I had an idea.

"Oh my goodness boys and girls, this is your captain speaking and I see Santa, with Rudolph leading the way! Everybody look out your left window," I announced over the PA to the entire passenger cabin. This passing jet sure did look like Rudolph zipping by us.

"Santa told me he is on his way to Denver right now," I cheerily continued my story. "But he told me he has lots of rooftops to land on along the way. Our plane will definitely get to Denver first. You will all be home in your beds long before Santa arrives."

Just as soon as I ended my PA, my flight attendant interphone started to chime.

"Hello," I answered the phone.

"That was amazing!" the flight attendant gushed. "All of the kids rushed

Christmas is always fun at home. I caught this picture of Nicholas, Robert and our kitty Huey playing in front of the tree.

over to the left side of the plane. The whole cabin went along with it for the kids. Everyone is laughing and smiling."

I felt my eyes well up as I thought of my own boys at home in their beds waiting for Santa ... and for me to come home.

After landing, parent after parent thanked me. I even got a few hugs from grateful mothers. "My daughter wouldn't stop crying, until she saw us *passing* Santa in the sky. She will never forget what an exciting Christmas Eve this was. Thank you."

Her little girl gave me a hug. "I love Rudolph," she whispered in my ear.

There were many days when I couldn't be with my own children, but I took every chance to do what I could for the children I was with in the sky. One privilege of being the captain was that I could pick up my mic and make any PA I wanted. I could delay a flight to accommodate a family, or I could arrive late for a flight if I came across a lost child in the terminal who needed my help. I didn't have to get permission from anybody to do the right thing. For that short period of time that my passengers were dependent on me, trusting me, they were my family, too.

After my babies came along, the sun shone brighter on my life, but the fairy dust faded on my amazing aviation career. I wasn't as sure as I had been about where I belonged and about the choices I had made. Often, I felt like an outsider looking in on my own life, perpetually out of place and not where I should have been. But as it turns out, my boys were perfectly happy with their lives. I was the only one who felt slighted.

In the end, I didn't regret my choices. People often put aside their passions and aspirations for noble reasons when they have children. Someday, when my boys become parents themselves and they have big dreams for their children, I want them to remember that their own dreams still count.

As full and successful as my life has been, there was much that I missed out on—but I would have missed out on even more had I given up on my dreams. I truly loved putting on my uniform and going to work. If I hadn't made it, if I hadn't become an airline pilot, I would have lived a life of regrets and what ifs. I would have missed out on the incredible feeling of joy and accomplishment that rests deep inside me and is a fundamental part of who I am.

Every choice in life means foregoing something else. What ultimately matters is finding peace with the choices you've made, and believing they were worth it. For me, my place in the world of aviation and my place at home with my children both give my life meaning.

When I'm at work and the glow of my instruments soothe me on a dark night, with hundreds of passengers seated behind me depending on my skills, I don't feel the immensity of it all. The big picture seems remote, lost to me when I'm a part of it.

When I'm raking leaves in my yard and a thunderous rumble grows above me, rattling the wooden handle into my palms, it is then I feel the wonder of my ordinary life. I gaze upwards at the passing jet and analyze the configuration, while the child in me remains awed at the monumental scale and the cold curves of a mysterious machine slicing effortlessly through the air above.

All of my questions have been answered.

I marvel at the straight line of passenger windows streaming by and I feel a maudlin connection to each of those people sitting in their seats, trusting that they will be safely delivered to some far away part of our planet.

I squint to see which airline it is, and I vaguely wonder which of my friends are at work today?

Enjoying a fun day walking around Washington, DC with Nicholas and Robert. Photo taken by my cousin Danny Flack.

A WORD AFTER

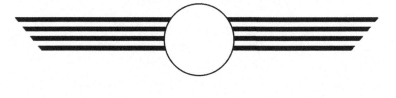

I didn't set out to be a ground breaker or to buck conventional wisdom, I only wanted to be a pilot. I hope you found yourself in my story and feel emboldened to go after whatever makes *you* feel alive and strong too, with confidence and no apologies.

I've learned over the years that I could not demand respect. I could only earn it. I could not tell a person how to think or feel about me; they had to form their own opinions and come to their own conclusions from their experiences with me. The same holds true for how I saw myself.

For me, self-confidence came from one small triumph at a time. I had to step forward and take risks to show myself what I was capable of. This is what experience truly brings.

I fell in love with my day-to-day life, instead of focusing on some far-off accomplishment yet to happen.

And no matter what, I kept moving forward.

I am no longer flying as an airline pilot. When I broke my neck early in my career with United Airlines, I lost everything in an instant. Though chided by my neurosurgeons to be grateful to be alive—and to get married and have babies and forget my "silly career," the total and complete loss of my own potential devastated me. I fought my way back to the cockpit and went on to fly every aircraft in the United Airlines fleet and moved up to the captain's seat.

Many years later, I suffered a second devastating neck injury after a fall in a flight training simulator. Faced again with the sudden end to a career I loved, surprisingly didn't destroy me this time. Having achieved all I had dreamed of, my mind opened up to what else I could do with my life. Today only 5.5% of pilots are female, roughly the same number as during Amelia Earhart's era. Having never had a female boss, or women ahead of me to ask for advice, I'm excited to now be that person I wish I had known when I was a young woman needing support.

Not everyone gets to live out two passions in their life. After a long career in the cockpit, I am now determined to use my experiences to encourage others to take risks and go after their own impossible dreams and find their full potential at any age.

I also hope my voice helps young people discover that STEM (Science, Technology, Engineering and Mathematics) is a tangible part of everyday life, and each person is a master of it, but in different ways. Helping young people connect with something they didn't yet know existed, much less thought they would be interested in, is my most fulfilling accomplishment.

Shortly after I was hired by United Airlines, when I was trying to fit into the crowd of starched uniforms and broad shoulders, I drifted over to another female pilot in Flight Operations one afternoon. Michelle and I hardly knew each other, but we naturally gravitated towards each other as the only two women in a room of a hundred colleagues, deep in the underground of Chicago O'Hare International Airport.

Michelle and I shot each other understanding glances, both knowing what it felt like to be on the wrong end of office jokes. Even though we were each a member of this group, we still felt like flies on the wall to the chatter which filled this testosterone-charged room.

"Look at these guys," Michelle said, leaning in close to my ear, sure that no one else could hear. "How many of them assume we shouldn't be here? My dad is a pilot, and he had me in the cockpit of our family plane since I was in diapers. Flying is in my blood. I've been a pilot longer than any of these flyboys."

I nodded with a fixed smile on my face. But I did not counter with my own story. I couldn't. I couldn't even be candid with Michelle, someone very much in my shoes.

Or was she?

Somehow, admitting that I never knew an airline pilot until I was an airline pilot, felt like a confession. I found myself hanging onto every one of Michelle's words. As she revealed more of her background to me, I couldn't help but to fall in love with Michelle's airplane themed childhood and marvel at her entire family's enthusiasm for aviation. The only family passion handed down in my family was our mutual love for pasta and my grandmother's fresh gravy from her garden.

But now Michelle and I were in the exact same professional position. Although I started out as that little girl on the curb marveling at the thought of ever meeting a pilot and Michelle was born an insider to this world, as time passed my comfort level and confidence caught up to hers. We both grew into equally competent and respected captains for United Airlines.

I will never underestimate the advantages of having a family leg up or having the world just presume you have "the right stuff" because of your physical stature or background. But none of that matters as much as optimism, a feeling of self-purpose and just wanting something so bad, you won't give up until you have it.

If I could whisper into the ear of that bored little girl I once was, I'd tell her that something may feel impossible when you are the outsider looking in, but once you are there, it's never as scary as you imagined.

Whether your dream feels too far off to reach, or you just can't pinpoint that ultimate passion to pursue, sometimes you just have to pay attention to what gives you joy and head in that direction. And then when one thing leads to the next, go for that next thing every time. I definitely didn't have it all worked out at first, but I didn't need to.

Henry Ford once said, "If you think you can do a thing or think you can't do a thing, you're right."

"I am the luckiest person I know!" I bubbled one day to my Captain, while gazing out of the cockpit window, taking in the spectacular view from 40,000 feet of icebergs breaking off of Greenland and floating out to the open sea.

"No, no you are not." He shook his head at me. "You are not lucky, you are fortunate. We make our own fortunes, Laura."

He was right.

Go make your own fortune.

SUPPLEMENT
9/11 COCKPIT TIMELINE

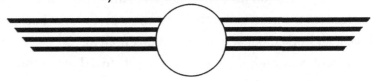

I was with my colleagues on 9/11, but I was not in the air. What was it like for the pilots airborne at the time?

For them, it was barefaced reality. They couldn't turn off the TV and walk away when it got too painful. They knew what was happening. They knew what was at stake while they were still in the air piloting their aircraft and trusted with hundreds of lives seated behind them. For them, it was too real to feel surreal. They had to act.

Timeline:

7:59 am—AA 11, a Boeing 767, departs Boston Logan International (BOS) for Los Angeles (LAX).

8:13 am—AA 11 pilot responds to air traffic controller instruction to change heading, but only seconds later does not respond to the next instruction to change altitude. The air traffic controller tries contacting AA 11 repeatedly, but never receives a response.

8:14 am—UA 175, another Boeing 767, also departs BOS for LAX.

8:19 am—Flight attendants onboard AA 11 phone company ground personnel from the tail of their aircraft and report that two flight attendants had been stabbed, a passenger had his throat cut and hijackers were in the cockpit. American Airlines immediately notifies the FAA and FBI.

8:20 am—AA 11 transponder is turned off, the device which transmits flight data and makes their altitude, speed and location concisely known to air traffic controllers on the ground and to other airborne aircraft.

8:20 am—AA 77, a Boeing 757, departs Washington Dulles International Airport (IAD) for Los Angeles (LAX).

8:24 am—Hijacker Mohammed Atta accidentally transmits to Air Traffic Control from the cockpit of AA 11, an announcement intended for the passenger cabin. "We have some planes. Just stay quiet and we'll be okay. We are returning to the airport."

Receiving the confusing message, the controller transmits back,

"Who's trying to call me, here? American 11 are you trying to call?"

Still believing he is making a PA to the passenger cabin of his aircraft, Atta continues, "Nobody move, everything will be okay. If you try to make any moves, you will injure yourself and the airplane. Just stay quiet."

AA 11 executes a U-turn and heads directly toward New York City, and toward UA 175, who is following AA 11 on the same route to LAX. Given the sudden loss of the transponder signal, erratic turn off-course, lack of communication from the pilots and the nefarious radio transmissions from their cockpit, it is now apparent to the FAA that the pilots are no longer in control of their aircraft and AA 11 has been hijacked.

8:37 am—ATC calls UA 175, "Do you have traffic at your twelve o'clock, at ten miles south bound. See if you can see an American seventy sixty seven out there please."

UA 175—"Affirmative, we have him. He looks about twenty … yeah about twenty nine, twenty eight thousand." (AA 11 had been assigned thirty-five thousand feet.)

ATC—"United one seventy five, turn thirty degrees to the right. I want to keep you away from this traffic." (UA 175 is vectored around the oncoming, hijacked jet AA 11)

8:40 am—Twenty-seven minutes after losing contact with the pilots of AA 11, the FAA *finally* reports the known hijacking of AA 11 to NORAD (North American Aerospace Defense). Three minutes later, they also report the hijacking of UA 175 to NORAD.

NORAD waits six minutes before ordering the 102nd Fighter Wing of Otis Air National Guard Base, in Falmouth, Massachusetts to scramble two F-15 fighter jets. By this time, AA 11 has already crashed. Otis is 153 miles from Manhattan.

8:41 am—UA 93, a Boeing 757, departs Newark (EWR) for San Francisco (SFO).

8:42 am—UA 175 pilots make their last radio transmission, before their controller loses contact with them and their jet also erratically turns around and head towards New York City.

8:46 am—AA 11 continues flying east until finding the Hudson River, then turns south and follows the river until it crashes into the North Tower.

8:50 am—United Airlines maintenance center in San Francisco receives a phone call from a flight attendant on UA 175, through a direct line available to flight attendants to report broken items in the passenger cabin while airborne, that her plane had been hijacked, the pilots were dead and another flight attendant had been stabbed.

8:56 am—AA 77 transponder is shut off and the pilots stop responding to transmissions from air traffic control.

9:03 am—UA 175 crashes into the South Tower. The fighter jets from OTIS were still twenty minutes away.

9:06 am—The FAA replays the audio tape from AA 11 and confirms the hijacker said they have "some planes," plural. The FAA is now certain multiple hijackings were taking place, with an unknown number.

After two aircraft crash into the World Trade Center, airlines go into crisis mode. Messages tick out over every aircraft cockpit printer, as dispatchers uniformly send warnings to each of the aircraft they are tracking.

9:23 am—UA 93 receives the printed message:
BEWARE ANY COCKPIT INTROUSION. TWO AIRCRAFT IN NY, HIT TRADE CNTER BUILDS

Warned and aware of possible danger to their own flight, airline pilots took aggressive precautions to prepare for the possibility of a hijacker attempting a takeover on *their* aircraft. Inside cockpits, crash axes were taken out of storage holders and placed across pilot laps, chemical fire extinguishers were moved to within easy reach, and blades were opened up on Leatherman tools.

9:24 am—Twenty-eight minutes later, the FAA finally reports the hijacking of AA 77 to NORAD and their direct heading towards Washington, DC. Jets are immediately scrambled from the 1st Fighter Wing from Langley Air Force Base in Hampton, Virginia, 130 miles south of Washington, DC.

9:28 am—Sounds of a struggle and screaming is transmitted to ATC from UA 93. The pilots have the presence of mind to transmit "Mayday, Mayday, Mayday," while fighting for their lives against terrorists who apparently were able to unlock their cockpit door and walk right in. Strapped into their seats and savagely attacked from behind, the pilots fiercely fight back, but are overcome by the crazed hijackers armed with box cutter knives.

UA 93 becomes the fourth aircraft violently taken over by terrorists.

9:32 am—Making the same mistake as Atta Mohamad on AA 11, the hijacker on UA 93 also transmits his message intended for the passengers, to ATC; "Keep remaining seating. We have a bomb onboard."

9:37 am—AA 77 crashes into the Pentagon.

10:03 am—UA 93 crashes into a field in Pennsylvania, never making it to their intended target, presumably Washington, DC. Flying low enough for cell tower coverage, passengers call loved ones and tell them their pilots are dead and hijackers are in the cockpit. Multiple passengers are informed of the crashes of previously hijacked aircraft. With the cockpit door locked, a loud passenger uprising in the cabin prompts the hijackers in the cockpit to give up on reaching their target, and they dive the aircraft into the ground in Shanksville, Pennsylvania.

Dispatchers from every airline contacted their pilots in the sky and worked with air traffic controllers to safely get every aircraft on the ground. At the time, there were 4,452 airplanes in the skies over the Continental United States.

The air traffic controllers across the country watched as a locust storm of jetliners swarmed downward, dropping into whatever suitable airport they happened to be over. Although there was an unprecedented number of pilots bringing their aircraft in for landings, the United States has 503 commercial airline airports and the blitz was spread out across the country.

ABOUT THE AUTHOR

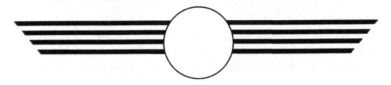

Captain Laura Savino piloted the B777, B767, B757, B747, B737, A319 and A320 as an international airline pilot for United Airlines.

Laura flew for Eastern and Pan Am regionals before that. On her way to becoming a commercial airline pilot, she worked as a flight instructor, charter pilot, freight pilot, aerial sightseeing tour pilot and aircraft repossessor. She has flown planes as tiny as a car and widebody aircraft larger than a football field.

Learning to fly as a teenager at Morristown Municipal Airport in New Jersey, Laura continued her aviation education at Purdue University, graduating with an AS in Applied Science and a BS in Aviation Technology.

Bringing her love of flying and family to the pages, Laura is an award winning author, taking first place in the 2020 Pennwriters competition. Her inspirational stories can be found in three editions of the Chicken Soup for the Soul series, published by Simon & Schuster – *Be You: 101 Stories of Affirmation, Determination and Female Empowerment, The Magic of Cats: 101 Tales of Family, Friendship & Fun,* and *Attitude of Gratitude: 101 Stories About Counting Your Blessings & The Power of Thankfulness.*

Medically retired from United Airlines, Laura is now in the position to be the mentor she wished she knew as a young pilot entering the aviation industry. Enthusiastic to help others find their place in STEM fields, Laura is a motivational speaker and is available to participate in events at schools, businesses, clubs and associations.

Laura is proud to be a member of the Ninety-Nines International Organization of Women Pilots, the International Society of Women Airline Pilots (ISA+21), Women in Aviation International (WAI), the Experimental Aircraft Association (EAA), and Smokehouse Pilots Club, where she lives in Virginia with her two sons, two cats and a lizard.

Please find more information on her website: https://laurasavino747.com
Email: LauraSavino747@gmail.com
Twitter: @LauraSavino747
Instagram: @LauraSavino747

FREEDOM FORGE PRESS

ABOUT US

Freedom Forge Press, LLC, was founded to celebrate freedom and the spirit of the individual. The founders of the press believe that when people are given freedom—of expression, of speech, of thought, of action—creativity and achievement will flourish.

Freedom Forge Press publishes general fiction, historical fiction, nonfiction, and genres like science fiction and fantasy. Freedom Forge Press's two imprints, Bellows Books and Apprentice Books, publish works for younger readers.

Find out more at www.FreedomForgePress.com.